Tolley's
Managing a Diverse
Workforce

T0330509

Routledge
Taylor & Francis Group
New York London

First Published by LexisNexis
This edition published 2011 by Routledge
2 Park Square, Milton Park, Abingdon, Oxon OX14 4RN
711 Third Avenue, New York, NY 10017, USA
Routledge is an imprint of the Taylor & Francis Group, an Informa business

© Taylor & Francis 2004

A CIP Catalogue record for this book is available from the British Library.
ISBN: 978-0-406-97149-4

Contributors

Authors

Nikki Booth

Nikki graduated from the University of Westminster with a BA Hons in Social Science, majoring in Criminology and Law. She went on to complete her conversion at the University of East Anglia and her Legal Practice Course at De Montfort University. Nikki trained as a solicitor in Norwich and worked closely with a part time Chairman of the Employment Tribunals before moving to Fosters. She has been heading up the Employment Unit since 2001 and has seen it more than double in size since taking over this role. Nikki is currently on a career break, travelling, but intends to return to legal practice in early 2005.

Nikki acts for both employers and employees across the complete spectrum of employment law. Such issues have included claims for race discrimination against the MOD, which are currently at Court of Appeal, in regard to establishing the jurisdiction of the tribunal for the armed forces based outside the UK, as well as bringing and defending claims relating to sex, references, unfair and constructive dismissal, redundancy and maternity rights. Nikki has also been successful in claiming costs against applicants in a number of cases, particularly where the applicant or their representative had insisted on continuing with claims which were misconceived or without merit.

Fosters

Fosters Solicitors of Norwich has been established since 1761 and has offices in Norwich, Wymondham and North Suffolk. Fosters is a high street practice undertaking a cross section of work from commercial to family, mental health and crime. Fosters have doubled in size over the last 10 years and are proud to offer such specialisms as mediation, employment, insolvency, professional negligence and company law, as well as the wider remit of conveyancing, wills, commercial property, family law and crime and defence.

Clare Robson

Clare's background is in retail management for Safeway, where she has worked for the last eight years. She has specialised in Human Resource management for the last four years, focusing on recruitment practices, absence management, disciplinary and grievance procedures, and health and safety, in which she holds a certificate from the HSE for the supervision of health and safety in the workplace

She has a honours degree in Sociology from the university of Sunderland where she studied for four years including a secondment spent at the Universite d'Angers in France.

In the last year Clare has faced the challenge of successfully managing Safeways through the inevitable period of uncertainty surrounding the potential takeover bid by Morrisons and more recently since the bid was approved and the takeover has been successful, the harmonisation programme between the two companies. The priorities have been to ensure effective communication to all colleagues of developments as they were taking place, to manage any redundancies and job transfers appropriately and to introduce new terms and conditions, initially to new employees and then existing staff. With the emphasis moving towards vocational training, Clare has recently qualified as an NVQ assessor and hopes to have the opportunity to provide more staff with the chance to train in-house towards the nationally recognised retail standards qualifications.

Jacqui Welham FIOSH RSP FIIRSM

Jacqui holds a Diploma from Loughborough University in Occupational Health & Safety Management. A fellow of both the Institution of Occupational Safety & Health (IOSH) and the International Institute of Risk and Safety Management (IIRSM). Jacqui is also a member of the Board of Governors of the IIRSM.

Jacqui is Managing Director of Total Control (Anglia) Limited, providing a health and safety consultancy and training service to clients in a wide variety of organisations, including retail, manufacturing, service and local authorities. Risk assessments are undertaken for clients on a regular basis, although the company philosophy is to train employees to undertake risk assessments in their own workplace, where they will have an intimate knowledge of the day-to-day activities of their own organisation. Total Control is a City and Guilds registered NVQ centre for Occupational Health & Safety Practice, as well as providing IOSH and CIEH training courses.

Jacqui's previous books include: *Tolley's Risk Assessment Workbook Series – Retail, Tolley's Risk Assessment Workbook Series – Stress, Recreational Diving Health & Safety Handbook, Frogman Spy* and *Successful Holidays – and What to do if They Are Not.*

Contents

Table of Cases

Table of Statutes

Table of Statutory Instruments

1
Introduction

What is diverse/diversity? 1.1

The *Collins English Dictionary & Thesaurus* (21st Century Edition) defines diverse as:

> 'Having variety; distinct in kind, with "of every description" being an alternative phrase. Diversity being: the state or quality of being different or varied.'

Paramount to diversity is the organisational culture and the working environment. Managing people's diversity effectively can add value to the organisation. Very often companies will limit their actions to compliance with race, sex and disability legislation. As there is no definitive legislation on managing diversity, employers may not even realise that there is a need to promote a culture where differences and diversity are valued. If a workplace is to be free from discrimination and be a place where everyone is treated fairly and equally, diversity has to be managed as part of the safety management system and a positive culture towards diversity promoted.

Who are diverse employees? 1.2

Diverse employees are those employees who do not fit within the stereotype of 'normal'. They are those people who receive additional protection under employment and health and safety laws. They are perceived as being at 'risk' of harm from poor or less favourable treatment.

Diversity includes almost all ways in which people differ, such as education and sexual orientation, as well as the more obvious ones of gender, ethnicity and disability. The difference may also be considered in the role people play within the organisation, for example homeworkers or loneworkers.

The following groups have been identified, for the purpose of this book, as being diverse within the wider group of workers/employees. Some of the groups may only be diverse on either health and safety or employment law grounds, while others are defined as diverse by both.

Women 1.3

This extremely large group of employees are diverse on a number of levels. One of the main reasons is discrimination. Women can be discriminated against in a number of ways. For example, a high percentage of women are still paid less than men in similar roles. They can also be, and are, treated less favourably on the grounds of their sex. Discrimination can effect a number of issues, such as:

- chances of promotion;
- selection for roles and employment; and
- harassment.

This is not to say that men are not discriminated against on the grounds of their sex, merely that it is more likely that a woman will be discriminated against.

Women of childbearing age fall into the realms of diversity by nature of the fact they could become pregnant and the work they are undertaking could harm them or the unborn foetus. More importantly is where a woman is pregnant and subsequently when she becomes a mother (particularly new mothers). There are a number of additional rights afforded to pregnant women, including the right to attend antenatal classes, to receive maternity leave and, if eligible, maternity pay. New mothers (and existing ones who qualify) have the right to request a change in their hours and have time off to look after their child or any other dependants. The latter points do apply to men also and should be borne in mind as society moves towards a more even match of men and women who look after children.

Religious groups 1.4

Employees within this group have been diverse for some time due to the fact that they have additional needs, which are attributed to their religion or belief. For example, when Sunday trading regulations came into force, they had a large impact on Christian workers, as they did not wish to work on a Sunday in accordance with the rules of their faith. However, their rights and those of other religious bodies have now been protected against discrimination following the implementation of the *Employment Equality (Religion or Belief) Regulations 2003 (SI 2003/1660)* relating to discrimination on the grounds of religion, which came into effect on 2 December 2003.

Religious groups are also diverse on a number of levels. Their religious needs and duties must be considered in respect of their need for prayer time (with regard to Muslims) and their general working week in regard to religious days, for example Sunday/Sabbath working and religious festivals. Companies should also ensure that their policy takes into account religious needs in relation to dress codes. However, it is important to remember that health and safety regulations will be deemed to be a justifiable reason for not allowing a form of religious dress.

These employees are also at risk of discrimination, and not merely due to the additional consideration they require, as mentioned earlier in this section. They can be discriminated against in much the same way as women in relation to selection, promotion and harassment.

Lone workers   1.5

There are some employees who work on their own as part of their normal day to day work. However, working alone can sometimes put people in a vulnerable position because it may be more difficult for them to summon help if things go wrong or if their health and safety is at risk. People who work alone face the same hazards in their daily work as other workers, however the degree of risk of harm is often greater for them than for other workers.

Who is a lone worker?   1.6

There is no literary definition of a lone worker, but the range of employees working alone is diverse and extensive. In general terms, lone workers are people who work on their own with little or no supervision, in the event of an emergency there is no one to give them assistance or summon help. There is no time limit attached to working alone and so someone could be a lone worker the whole work period or only for a limited time.

The work can be undertaken in a number of situations, for example:

- people who work by themselves in retail premises, eg:
  - in a garage;
  - in a small shop; or
  - in a kiosk;
- home workers;
- people who work separately from others;
- people working outside normal hours such as:
  - cleaners;
  - maintenance; and
  - repair staff.
- mobile workers who work away from their base; such as:
  - health visitors;
  - Environmental Health Officers;
  - HSE Inspectors;
  - postal staff;

- ○   social workers;
- ○   home help;
- ○   drivers;
- ○   architects;
- ○   painters and decorators;
- ○   milkmen;
- ○   estate agents;
- ○   doctors;
- ○   district nurses;
- ○   midwives;
- ○   sales staff;
- ○   police officers;
- ○   meter readers;
- ○   window cleaners;
- ○   lorry drivers;
- ○   cleaners; and
- ○   home visitors;
- ●   staff, whom although they are on the company's premises, are working apart from colleagues:
  - ○   hospital staff;
  - ○   security staff;
  - ○   maintenance staff on large industrial sites;
  - ○   teachers; and
  - ○   prison officers.

This list is not definitive, employees may be lone workers for a number of reasons.

Home workers   1.7

There is a growing tendency for more companies to have their employees working from home. From the employer's point of view, there is a saving in working space and overheads. The employee also gains by having to avoid spending time and money travelling, and they can enjoy any relevant home comforts. The use of computers and other modern communication aids means that there can be an immediate exchange of information so that employees working from home are no less in touch than employees who work on the employer's premises. Home working will not suit everybody and management needs to monitor the situation very closely. Some employees need to be in the company of others to work effectively and feel part of the team or organisation, while others are self-motivated and can adapt to what is in effect a lone working environment. Management must ensure that home workers do not become encapsulated in the home and avoid venturing out to meet clients or visit the office. There can also be home life conflicts where members of the family want to take part in an activity and expect the home worker to stop work and participate in the activity.

Nonetheless, the employer's responsibility for the health and safety of his employees, particularly as set out in *s* 2(2) of the *Health and Safety at Work, etc Act 1974 (HSWA 1974)*, extends to home workers, and such employees should not be disregarded when producing the diverse employees' policy.

Voluntary/charity workers   1.8

Despite the increasing importance of volunteering (22 million people volunteer each year), the legal obligations of organisations towards their volunteers with regard to health and safety are less clear than they are for employees. Nevertheless, organisations do have legal obligations towards their volunteers. It is clearly good practice to treat volunteers with equal consideration when it comes to health and safety. A volunteer' is defined as someone who commits time and energy for the benefit of others and who does so freely, through personal choice, and without expectation of financial reward, except for the payment of actual out-of-pocket expenses. Most voluntary organisations are employers and as such will have a duty towards persons who are not in their employment but who may be affected by their undertaking', such as clients and volunteers (*s* 3 of the *HSWA 1974*). This duty extends to the health and safety of those persons in the same way as with paid employees.

Agency workers   1.9

This group is diverse for completely different reasons in relation to employment law. This is due to the fact that they lack additional protection in the employment law arena. There is still much debate as to whether the agency or the company who requests their services is their employer, although agencies should work on the basis that they that are the employer.

Disabled   1.10

This group of employees are probably the most obvious in their diversity, as they will normally have a physical, mental or sensory condition, which may impede the usual way of working. There are obviously health and safety issues here. But there are also employment law issues. Disabilities, whether physical, mental (which would include those with learning difficulties, such as dyslexia) or indeed newly discovered disabilities, be it illness or injury, require that an employer should treat an employee in a particular manner. This is both in relation to discrimination and making reasonable adjustments to the role and, if necessary, the equipment and premises, as well as ensuring that the company's policies do not add further damage, for example a highly restrictive sickness policy.

Young workers   1.11

Young workers are those employees between 16 and 18 who are outside the compulsory education age bracket, ie they have completed Year 11 of High School. Obviously this is a vulnerable group of employees, who should be treated carefully in relation to undertaking long hours or arduous and heavy work. They do receive some additional protection under employment law, but are afforded far more in relation to health and safety regulations (*Management of Health and Safety at Work Regulations 1999 (SI 1999/3242)*).

Race/ethnic minorities   1.12

The employees who fall into this category may also need to be considered alongside religious groups. In general, there is protection against discrimination based on colour, which can effect selection and promotion, as well as bring about the possibility of harassment. However, the situation can be made more complicated where English is not the employee's first language. The employer would need to ensure that reasonable adjustments were made in respect of performance to targets and the employee's understanding of their role and instructions.

Immigrant workers   1.13

There are two Acts which employers have to comply with regarding the employment of immigrant workers and they are:

- the *Race Relations Act 1976*, which makes it unlawful to discriminate on grounds of colour, race, nationality, ethnic or national origins in the recruitment, employment or dismissal of any person; and

- the *Asylum and Immigration Act 1996, s 8*, which makes it a criminal offence to employ a person who has not been granted leave to enter or remain in the United Kingdom or who is subject to a condition prohibiting employment.

A very important factor when considering the health and safety of the workforce is that the language barriers may not be used as a device to exclude immigrants from employment and attempts to impose language tests have resulted in allegations of racial discrimination. The problem extends not just to immigration from Asian or African countries but under article 48 of the Treaty of Rome the free movement of workers throughout the European Union is guaranteed and an influx of non-

English speaking workers from Europe cannot be excluded. Training for safety officers may well include some form of instruction in foreign languages.

Sexual orientation   1.14

Effectively every employee will fall within this category, as the issue is not whether the employee is gay but their general sexual orientation. Since 1 December 2003 employees are protected against discrimination relating to their perceived sexuality. This means that they can be discriminated against in the same ways as has been mentioned above, based on what sexual preferences someone believes them to have, not what they actually do.

Health service workers   1.15

Hospital staff, especially in Accident and Emergency departments, may experience verbal abuse or physical violence because people are kept waiting or from casualties under the effects of drink or drugs.

Community midwives/district nurses/carers/social workers are placed in a lone worker situation and although their work could be considered to be proactive, caring and of low risk they are:

- visiting clients at home;
- visiting locations that may be poor or run down housing estates;
- dealing with unknown people and situations involving domestic violence or drug/alcohol abuse;
- driving on remote country roads and in areas unknown to them;
- working at night;
- working in clinics/health centres in the evenings and at weekends, when there are fewer staff around;
- encountering domestic violence; and
- having to remove children from abusive parents.

Public workers   1.16

There are serious implications for a number of public workers as regards personal safety due to the nature of their work or their lone worker status, which make them diverse. These public workers include thousands of council employees throughout the country who may have to visit clients in their own homes or come into contact with clients in job centres, social services offices and rent offices, where although the employee is there to help the client, they may become verbally abusive or even physically violent due to the nature of their business with the service.

Transport workers such as bus and taxi drivers, as well as ticket collectors on trains, are also public workers, as are the police and prison officers.

Bus drivers 1.17

There are groups of people who serve the public in a general way and yet are subject to confrontation and violence. One such group is bus drivers. Today the main public transport companies are large organisations and may provide both rail and bus services. Such a large organisation may have overseas operations and in the UK has a number of operating companies. A bus company may have several hundred buses and more than a thousand bus drivers and many of those drivers will encounter times of conflict from passengers and other road users. Operating companies, therefore, need to implement a programme of violence prevention and management measures with the outcome of preventing violence to its drivers.

Taxi drivers 1.18

Another group who face the public are the drivers of around 23,000 licensed black cab' taxis in London. The black cab' drivers are mobile workers who pick up customers hailing them in the street or waiting at designated taxi ranks and the customers pay the driver at the end of the journey. Drivers who are members of organisations such as Radio Taxis also do account work or get jobs through telephone or Internet bookings and money does not change hands if an account is used.

Police 1.19

Having reviewed the problems faced by staff groups who are in the caring professions or undertaking work that would not normally be considered to place them in a violent situation, there are groups who face violent confrontation as a matter of course. The most obvious are police officers who have a duty to protect and safeguard property. The nature of their job means that it is normal for an officer to be in contact with potentially violent people.

Prison officers and other staff 1.20

Prison staff can be considered diverse by nature of the alien environment in which they work with the constant threat of potential violence by inmates.

There are risks of violence to others, in particular teaching staff, as all prisons have some kind of education facility, usually for formal education as well as vocational-type training. A prison may have some full-time staff to provide this, but it is usually supplemented by contracts with local education providers, such as further or higher education colleges. Clearly the training providers also have a duty to their employees under *s 2* of the *HSWA 1974*. Teachers are frequently not familiar with the prison environment and may not have had an induction or even basic personal safety training. Voluntary and charity workers also visit prisons on a regular basis, such as the Citizens Advice Bureau and prison visitors, all of whom will encounter similar risks to those of prison officers and education staff.

Security staff   1.21

Unlike the police, security staff are not employed to go into confrontational situations and their main function is to undertake security patrols and control of access to buildings which is generally carried out by lone workers. Some staff may also have key-holder responsibilities, which means they lock up buildings when staff have gone and may be called to a building on their own if an incident occurs.

Nightclub stewards   1.22

Another group of people who have to face confrontation are nightclub stewards. A city nightclub will be licensed to hold a predetermined number of members of the public and the key nights for clubbing are generally Thursday, Friday and Saturday nights. Clubs that are well run will have a strong policy on dealing with drugs on the premises and establish a reputation as a drugs-free' zone. Clubs employ a range of staff including stewards who work at the door and patrol inside the club. Some clubs have a nurse on duty and staff should be trained in first aid.

Stewards often face threats and abuse from customers waiting to get into the club, particularly by potential customers who are drunk. A main part of their duties is to manage violent situations and that requires staff to intervene in fights or remove troublemakers and they may be assaulted while carrying out this activity. If the stewards are male there may be situations where there are claims of sexual harassment by female customers and there is a potential for robbery with staff handling large amounts of cash.

Window cleaners   1.23

Self-employed window cleaners carry out a variety of domestic and commercial work and develop a regular customer base. Generally payment is collected from domestic customers by visiting their houses after completing the work, while commercial clients are called upon during daytime working hours. The problems faced by window cleaners include grievances from customers, which can include, for example, access problems to a customer's house, ladder marks on a customer's lawn and accidental scratching of windows and sills. Some customers do not value the window cleaner's work and have the attitude You're only a window cleaner' and as a consequence are more likely to be aggressive or impolite.

Shop workers

In large shops there will be a number of staff on duty at any one time, however there are many shops where staff will, at some point, spend time working alone. Some shops are going to be more vulnerable than others, such as those that sell expensive items that are highly desirable may be more at risk from robbery. A shop that sells alcohol can be a target and businesses, such as rural post offices, are subjected to the threat of theft. Staff may also have to face verbal abuse from rude, angry and frustrated customers, in particular when there is non-authorisation of credit card purchases. The list of incidents that shop workers may have to endue will be extensive and often over what can be trivial matters, such as when a customer reacted angrily and became verbally abusive when a delivery was 20 minutes late. In another situation the member of staff activated the panic alarm because of a drunk and disorderly customer in the shop.

Service engineers

Service engineers deal with commercial and industrial premises, as well as domestic homes. The operatives work away from the office and are, therefore, considered to be mobile. Working in environments such as private homes, factories, shops and offices, some of which may be isolated properties, and carrying expensive tools and equipment. Service staff encounter all manner of confrontational situations and in one case a screwdriver was put to an engineer's face while working in a probation hostel and the same engineer was threatened by a Stanley knife taken from his bag. A real problem is thieves who break into engineers' vehicles parked outside jobs, usually for their tools, equipment or mobile phones.

Sales and field representatives

Field sales involves cold calling' on potential customers, which requires staff to knock on doors to advise potential customers about the benefits of changing their gas, electricity or phone supply to the company they represent. The staff will normally work alone, but in built up areas other team members and the manager are likely to be nearby. They usually work from noon to eight in the evening, which means that sales staff are particularly at risk when working at night, although the level of risk varies depending on the location.

Field representatives' work involves dealing with customers who have not paid their bills. In most cases this is going to be a confrontational situation because they are asking for payment of debts and that carries with it an inherent risk of violence. This is particularly so in certain geographical areas which have a higher risk of violence. Staff generally make the first visits alone where they knock on the door and ask customers if they are willing to pay their bills and are able to offer customers an opportunity to pay the outstanding bill by different methods. A warrant visit' is carried out as a last resort, enabling forced entry to a property using a magistrate's warrant and staff should never work alone on these visits.

Bullying   1.27

Bullying at work can very often be the catalyst for vulnerable or diverse employees and is one of the more frequent causes of stress and other work-related illnesses which would normally, but not necessarily, stem from the actions by senior members of the workforce. Frequently, bullying is caused by some form of interpersonal conflict and can take a number of different forms, apart from physical violence. Subtle forms of bullying can take place when someone in authority deliberately withholds essential information or makes belittling or offensive remarks, unwarranted criticism, public humiliation, unnecessary threats, veiled hints of inadequacies and generally undermining confidence are other examples which can have an adverse reaction on the person bullied. The end result can be an increase in work-related illnesses, causing absenteeism, low morale, poor performance and possibly accidents. The problem is probably more widespread than is generally realised.

Why are these employees diverse?   1.28

A diverse employee does not fit into the stereotype of the normal employee, who is deemed to be a white, English, fully able, male and of a middle class background. As we live in an ever-expanding multicultural society the likelihood of any workforce fitting this category is slim.

The diverse employee is at risk of harm. Employees of all backgrounds, ages, sexes and sexual orientation fill the workplace. The need is to ensure that they are afforded full protection both in relation to their employment rights and their safety during employment.

The Health and Safety Executive's (HSE) best available statistics, the *1995 Self-reported Work-related Illness (SWI) Survey* found that one in ten 25-34 year old women workers have been physically attacked by a member of the public at work, which means that attack rates are generally a third higher than for men. The survey showed that hazards traditionally associated with male industrial work are also commonplace in the jobs that women do. More than a quarter of women have to lift or move heavy loads at work and one in five are exposed to dust, fumes or other harmful substances. The survey also identified that the jobs with the highest rates of skin disease, for example hairdressing and repetitive assembly work, are jobs employing a predominantly female workforce. The GMB union guide on women's work hazards cites a HSE report which found that:

> 'Unavailability of, or improperly fitting, personal protective equipment has been shown to be a significant cause of some workplace injuries to women.'

The TUC's 1999 report, *A Woman's Work is Never Safe*, is based on official statistics and identifies the following:

- women are more exposed to repetitive and monotonous work and to stressful conditions;

- young women are more likely than men to be physically assaulted at work; and

- women are more likely than men to experience back strain, skin diseases, headaches and eyestrain.

UK statistics show that in 1998 women made up nearly half of the workforce (44 per cent, or 11.7 million workers). The great majority (86 per cent) worked in the service industries, such as health, education, hotels and restaurants and the retail trade, compared to 59 per cent of men. Only one in seven women (13 per cent) work in construction and manufacturing, compared to 37 per cent of men.

Equal Opportunities Commission (EOC) statistics found that in 2001, out of 1,434 potential tribunal cases involving pregnancy/maternity related discrimination, 1,387 involved some breach of health and safety legislation. It is shown that problems arise when employers are uninformed or confused about their legal duties to pregnant employees or new mums. The *Equal Opportunities Review*, a legal journal, reveals that the employers increasingly have to pay higher awards in sex discrimination cases and the average compensation payout for a case involving dismissal due to pregnancy is £9,871. It is an important fact that there is no limit to how much a company could be ordered to pay in compensation.

The number of complaints received and investigations initiated by HSE in the last five years

Year	Complaints	Investigations
1997/1998	79	10
1998/1999	89	13
1999/2000	94	26
2000/2001	67	8
2001/2002	67	3
TOTAL	396	60

Compensation payouts awarded, compiled by the Equal Opportunities Review (EOR no 108/Aug 02)

Average award for dismissal due to pregnancy	£9,871
Average award for injury to feelings in sex discrimination cases	£4,349
Range of awards for aggravated damages in sex discrimination cases	£2,000 to £50,000
Awards for personal injury in sex discrimination cases	£1,000 to £17,000

The Department of Trade and Industry statistics on new and expectant mothers at work show a considerable number of women who fall in the criteria

Approximate number of pregnant women working per year	350,000
Approximate number of women who return to work after giving birth	240,000
Percentage of women who returned to work	69%
Recruitment saving costs if number of mothers returning to work increased by 10 percent	£39M

How should organisations manage diverse employees?   1.29

The idea of this book is not to tell an employer how to run their business. Day to day role management is not an issue. The issue here is how to deal with the wide and varied levels of diversity amongst employees.

The most important place to start is of course at the beginning. That is, the start of a possible employment relationship. Not just when an employer is setting up a new business, but at any time when recruitment is an issue for an employer. The employer must ensure that they have a comprehensive Equal Opportunities Policy. This should not just be a record of the cross section of applications received, but a comprehensive guide to dealing with a variety of issues which having employees necessitates.

The policy should be able to advise employees on what will happen in relation to their particular need, for example if they are paraplegic. The policy should, therefore, be more than just a way of separating black, white, Indian and others within the applications received. If this is all the policy does, then the employer is at risk of discriminating immediately. Yes, it is important to know about the ethnic diversity of a company's application base and employee pool, but such a policy should go much further.

An effective Equal Opportunities Policy should aim to create a workplace and workforce which is fully diverse across the complete spectrum of society. The aim should be to have a variety of cultural and racial backgrounds, including religion and sexual orientation. Ensuring that there are men and women of all ages, at all levels within the business, including at managerial level. The policy should also encourage everyone to make important contributions to the organisation and such contributions should be supported.

Once there is a sound Equal Opportunities policy and an employer is ready to recruit, they must ensure that the job advertisement is completely non-bias in relation to age (although not yet a British litigious issue), sex, disability and race. The employer will also need to ensure that, unless there are justifiable reasons, there is no religious or sexual orientation bias either.

Once the employer has managed to ensure that the job advert and Equal Opportunities Policy are in order, they will need to ensure that, at interview stage, the interviewers are fully trained and able to ask questions that could have no discriminatory overtones. For example, not to ask a woman in her mid/late twenties whether she plans to have children or even whether a person's illness means that they have a poor sickness record.

It is very important to ensure that interviewers are aware of what should and should not be asked. They must also be aware of issues that need to be addressed, tactfully, such as a person's disability, and know that they must keep a full and informed record of the reasons for rejecting a prospective employee. It is important to bear in mind that such reasons for rejection should be noted and kept in respect of all applicants, whether or not they are actually interviewed. This is particularly important where the employee is of a group which has anti-discrimination rights.

Once someone has been selected and employed, it is important to ensure that they are given a full and detailed induction to the firm. This should not just include a quick trip round the office. It should include awareness training in respect of their or their colleague's disabilities. Ensuring, if they are disabled, that all the relevant and necessary adjustments are made, whether to the premises or the equipment and policies. The employee should also receive a contract of employment, together with a staff handbook if necessary, and these should be explained to them and signed by both the employer and employee. There should also be a health and safety risk assessment, particularly where the job involves repetitive activities or movements, computer work, heavy machinery or lone working. Health and safety training is obviously something that each employee should undergo, irrespective of previous training, as no workplace is ever the same. Health and safety training will take place at induction and when anything changes, ie new processes or new equipment or new skills are required.

Changes to company policy have been discussed in this section. It is important to ensure that sick policies and any benefits included within those policies do not discriminate against someone with a disability. For example, someone with cancer, who has been deemed to be disabled within the *Disability Discrimination Act 1995*, and is likely to have long term treatment, should not be penalised or disciplined for those absences connected to their illness. Whereas someone without a sufficient medical reason for long or persistent absence should be disciplined.

Spiralling costs of sick leave and pay   1.30

Most contracts allow for a portion of paid sick leave, ie full pay for a period of time, for example one to six months. This may or may not include an element of

Statutory Sick Pay (SSP). Some employers may only pay SSP, but whatever the situation is, SSP is not necessarily recoverable from the government.

Where sickness absences are only short, it may not be necessary to obtain cover for the person off sick. Their workload may be distributed amongst their colleagues. However, this is not always possible. It may be necessary to obtain cover from colleagues within the company, which could result in additional wages being paid, whether overtime or basic salary, or it may even be necessary to obtain cover from an agency, resulting in considerable expense, as hourly rates charged are more than those paid to regular employees.

Should there be long-term absence, cover will then be necessary whether internal or otherwise. If the cover is by someone who does not normally perform the absentee's role, then additional costs will be incurred, as training is likely to be required.

The return of the employee after their sickness absence may not bring about the end of the employer's expense. If the absence was long term, there may have been the need to obtain medical reports or medical records. However, the additional costs are more likely to arise from any adjustments required to enable the employee to return to work, including a staggered/staged return. Here, cover would still be needed for the employee's role, but the employee would also be entitled to be paid for the time they spend in the office.

It may well be the case that an employer can budget for the long-term absence, particularly if their sick pay policy makes provision for it. However, the cost on the employer, which cannot be budgeted for, is the employee who plays the system. The most common example is where an employee takes their paid sickness as additional holiday entitlement. It is possible to discipline employees for persistent unexplained absences and if necessary dismiss them. This would obviously result in costs in relation to recruitment, however, in the longer term, the employer would be better off.

In the modern workplace, the greatest cost on employers is stress-related absences. It has been suggested that 10 per cent of all employees are off work with stress at any one time. The only way for an employer to deal with this is to ensure that they have a sound and comprehensive monitoring policy and ensure that there is supervision at all levels, together with detailed and regular appraisals. It is vitally important in trying to combat stress and, therefore, the cost of stress related illness on employers. The employer needs to be aware of heavy workloads and be able to assess the risks of these on the employee.

To ensure that a stress related illness is not exacerbated, and even that it does not reoccur, the employer should ensure that they undertake full and detailed return to work interviews and have expert advice in relation to rehabilitating the employee back into the workplace.

Impact of employment tribunals 1.31

Unfortunately, we are moving toward a highly litigious society. Therefore, the likelihood of being sued in the tribunal is increasing. Unfortunately, regulations do not yet deal with striking out every misconceived claim at the beginning before costs are incurred. It may well be necessary to defend every claim that reaches the employer's desk (provided the employer has a defence!).

Although, if employees take legal advice some claims can be stopped, this is not always the case. It is possible to ensure that a claim be struck out before it reaches a final hearing. If the employee, for example, is bringing a claim for unfair dismissal, but does not have 12 months' service, the employer can notify the tribunal of the position and they will either strike the claim out under their own powers or ask the applicant to give good reasons as to why the claim should not be struck out. In such cases, there is room to request an award of costs against the employee. However, the situation is at present that such costs are only awarded in relation to the fees of a lawyer and not for the employer's time and legitimate business expenses.

As the number of cases increases, so does the number of stress claims. It is, however, becoming exceedingly difficult to sue an employer for damages for stress. An employer obviously owes the employee a duty of care, but in many cases the link between the illness and the employer's duty to the employee is often blurred and hard to prove. However, in such cases, even if the employee loses the claim, there is no guarantee that the employer would obtain the costs of defending the claim.

Unfortunately, tribunals will tend to only have a negative effect on the employer's business. This is not to say that the tribunals are doing a bad job, which is far from the case, as over 70 per cent of all claims which reach the tribunal are found in the employer's favour. It is the cost of defending claims which affects the employer's business. It is not just legal costs, for which employers can obtain insurance (as can employees). It is the time of the employer's staff in preparing papers, providing witness statements and attending the tribunal that ultimately has the biggest effect. This has an obvious monetary impact on the business, as time is being spent on matters which do not bring in an income, whilst the employee or manager is still being paid.

However, as the vast majority of cases settle, the employer can ensure that the costs of the tribunal claim are kept to a minimum. If it is a dismissal claim, the employer should ensure that there are clear notes, a clear disciplinary procedure (which is correctly followed) and sound reasons for the dismissal and the decision on appeal. If necessary, the employer should follow the conciliatory route through ACAS or if necessary reach an amicable and economic financial settlement.

If the claim is for constructive dismissal or discrimination, the employer should ensure that there is a comprehensive grievance procedure and that any disciplinary action required against other employees is completed properly.

Managers should be fully trained and know how to deal with the situations that could arise.

These methods may not stop a claim being sent to the tribunal, but they will ensure that the claim comes to a swift end. If the claim does end in the tribunal, conducting proper investigations and grievance procedures will increase the chances that costs may be awarded.

How will this book be relevant to the HR manager?   1.32

Any HR manager or general manager whose designated responsibilities include the HR function will have come across situations which they find new and challenging. As we have seen within this introduction, the myriad of ways in which an employee can be considered diverse is ever growing, with new legislation being introduced to ensure that discrimination in the workplace is brought to a minimum. The successful HR manager of the future is someone that can accept any difficulties and complications that diversity may bring as part of the human condition and adapt their management style to handle these effectively, using them to their advantage.

Whether the HR manager belongs to an organisation that is very forward thinking and already embraces diversity as a benefit to the company or whether the HR manager finds themselves as an ambassador amongst their peers in highlighting the opportunities a more diverse workforce can bring, this book will be of relevance to them.

For those who fall into the former category, the book provides opportunities to refer to case studies and compare best practices. There is a cradle to grave' approach within **CHAPTER 4**, which covers the majority of areas of an employee's working life, from pre recruitment through to dismissal, including absence, disciplinary and grievance and post employment referencing. Health and safety are also the subject of extensive focus, as one of the key ways an employer can fail its employee is by not ensuring the provision of a safe workplace. The final chapter is particularly useful, as it covers forthcoming legislation so that pro-active measures can be taken in order to begin planning adaptations to policies and procedures.

For those who fall into the latter category, the book is beneficial in two ways. Firstly there is the means to look at the best practice methods other organisations use to manage diversity within their workplaces and to study advice and checklists which provide guidance on how to establish procedures, should they be lacking, within the employer's own company. This includes the relevant legislative references to aid the employer in recognising the areas needing specific focus and perhaps policy revisions or introduction and helping the employer to emphasise the importance of embracing diversity to colleagues and management teams.

Secondly, if policies and procedures are in place, but infrequently or poorly used, then the book provides clarity on what the current legislative position is and how best to update practices to reflect this. Some organisations adapt to changes in regulations less effectively then others, which can be due simply to absence of key personnel, lack of information or poor management emphasis on what is to be achieved. Whatever the reasons, the following chapters provide information on both current regulations and those which are forthcoming and hence give the opportunity to ensure all procedures are completely up to date.

In short, anyone with any HR function will find this book of relevance, simply because it provides an easy reference guide to the numerous responsibilities an employer has to all its employees, particularly those who can be considered diverse.

How will this book help the HR manager fulfill their responsibilities? 1.33

The responsibilities of an HR manager are wide-ranging and this book will cover what these include in more depth in **CHAPTER 4**, but in summary it is about creating a balance between business responsibilities, while ensuring that all the needs of the workforce are met. While certain general policies and procedures may apply to all, there is increasing pressure to ensure that no section of the workforce is in any way treated differently to any other and while sometimes this may be easy to achieve, there will inevitably be occasions where some form of framework and guidance over and above that which is in existence is necessary to fulfill this aim.

This book will help to fulfill the HR manager's responsibilities, by identifying exactly where the gaps in the management framework of their organisation exists and providing methods to ensure that these gaps are filled in order to protect both the organisation and the employees.

The content of the book is divided between explanations of legislation, case studies, analysis of theoretical situations and practical advice, including checklists for real life situations. The aim is that this combination should not only advise the HR manager of general action to take in particular circumstances, via the checklists and advice, but also provide some background information on the regulations that govern the various aspects of working life, including highlighting case history which may have set precedents or added additional clarification. The authors have tried to cover many different scenarios, both in case studies and general examples given, but it is obviously impossible to look at all likely situations that may occur. However, with the practical advice and the legislative background, the HR manager should be able to take the general guidelines and tailor them to the specific situations that they may encounter in the day to day running of their organisation.

In summary, when dealing with diversity in an organisation, although the benefits are great, there will inevitably be some conflict or problem arising. It may be that although the organisation has a comprehensive policy it is not something which the HR manager has dealt with in reality and would like to refer to some practical advice. Or it may involve something with which the HR manager has dealt previously, but has since had regulations passed concerning action to be taken. Either way, the book provides both angles from which to gain an insight into the correct course of action to be taken. Even if the issue has not specifically been addressed in the relevant section, the legislative background and best practice advice relating to that particular point will provide a basis around which to formulate a course of action both practicable and appropriate to each situation.

2
Legislation, Regulation and the Employer

Introduction 2.1

This chapter intends to highlight the employment regulations that protect the groups of employees set out in **CHAPTER 1**. In some cases the employees will receive nothing more than the basic protection, whereas others will be covered by a wide variety of regulations.

This chapter will attempt to highlight any loopholes in the current regulations and whether they favour the employee or the employer as the relevant regulations are dealt with.

A Human Resources Manager should be aware of the regulations which govern all employees, even if only as an overview. Obviously, the larger the employer the more likely the Human Resources Manager will come across a wider spectrum of diversity. However, all should make themselves aware of the regulations, as they can apply from the initial stages of recruitment through to post-termination references.

It should be noted that some of the regulations mentioned in this chapter are relatively new and have not yet been challenged or tested in the tribunal system. Over the next two years claims relating to the rights brought about by the *Employment Act 2002* should be monitored carefully particularly in relation to flexible working and discrimination on the grounds of sexual orientation and religion.

This chapter is intended to be a rough guide for Human Resources Managers in how to deal with employees, from in house issues and problems through to dismissal.

Employment law protection

How are these diverse employees protected under employment law? 2.2

There are two main pieces of legislation that apply to all employees irrespective of their diversity. These are the *Working Time Regulations 1998 (SI 1998/1833)* and the *Employment Rights Act 1996*. The former applies to all workers and is not just restricted to employees. Therefore where employment law did not make, for example, lone and home workers diverse, it does afford them some protection under these regulations. (These regulations do not apply in Northern Ireland.)

A worker, under these regulations, is deemed to be someone who enters into or works under a contract of employment (therefore including employees) or any other contract. This contract could be verbal or in writing or even implied by law. The individual undertakes to do any work or services for another person or party, who is not deemed to be a client or customer. That is to say, that anyone who is self-employed is not normally seen as a worker, unless they work exclusively for one organisation. In this particular case, the boundaries are somewhat blurred. In *Byrne Brother (formwork) Limited v Baird [2002] IRLR 96* a self-employed carpenter claimed holiday pay from the company he worked exclusively for. He won his claim as the tribunal felt that his contract was mutual and exclusive. The tribunal also decided that he was working on a personal basis, not as a company. In the case of *Syers v Kirkwood Contracts Limited ET Case No. 2300459/00* the applicant was self-employed. However, he was unable to work elsewhere and would not send a substitute when he was unwell or on holiday. The company provided him with all his equipment and his insurance. He was also disciplined by them. The tribunal found that he was a worker within the terms of the *Working Time Regulations 1998*.

It should be borne in mind that all employees are workers and therefore the *Working Time Regulations 1998* apply to everyone, but not all workers are employees. Therefore the national minimum wage and the right to accept or reject work apply to everyone. However, only employees can be protected from unfair dismissal.

The *Working Time Regulations 1998* afford certain protection, which compliments, in many ways, the protection afforded by the *Employment Relations Act 1999 (ERA 1999)* and the various health and safety regulations. In particular the *Working Time Regulations 1998* set out the bare minimum which an employer should comply with, such as the hours of work which an employee should be limited to during a day, week or 17 week period. The *Working Time Regulations 1998* also set out the amount of paid holiday each employee/worker is entitled to receive.

The *Working Time Regulations 1998* deal with the issue of working time. This has caused much debate in relation to call out and stand by time. Where an employee works in an area which involves being on call, the time spent on call only counts toward their working time where they are:

● working;

● at the employer's disposal; and

● are carrying out their duties.

Unless all three of these apply to the situation at hand, the employee's time will not count. It has been suggested in case law that the third part of the test can only be met where the employee is on the employer's premises, or on such premises where they must undertake their duties (in the case of vets on call – see *Sindicato de Medicos de Asistencia Publica (Simap) v Conselleria de Sanidad y Consumo de la Generalidad Valenciana [2001] All ER (EC) 609*.

Working time is deemed to be the time spent undertaking the duties of an employee or worker. It does not include travelling to or from a normal place of work. Neither are lunches and tea breaks included as working time.

The greatest significance is in relation to the 48-hour week. Following the implementation of the European Directives, the 48-hour week was brought in in an attempt to protect workers and employees from injury and abuse. There are some obvious exemptions to this rule, such as trainee doctors. (The Armed Forces are also exempt from these Regulations.) However, the vast majority of workers are affected by the rule. The calculation is made over a 17 week period. Holidays and sickness are excluded from the calculation. Employees can opt out of the 48 hour week rule by signing a form. Generally three months notice is required to opt back in to the ruling. The 48-hour week was introduced to prevent exploitation and long hours, which could result in injury. However, the employer owes a duty to all workers in regard to health and safety. It is not just the individual who should be protected, but his or her colleagues also. A tired and overworked employee or worker is as much a risk to others as he is to himself. The specific compliance guidelines are found at *Regulation 4(2)* of the *Working Time Regulations 1998*. Employers should also keep records of the hours worked by their employees and not destroy them for a period of two years (in accordance with *Regulation 9*).

It should also be noted that the Regulations set out rest break periods. These are particularly important in relation to health and safety as well as employees' legal rights. An adult (ie someone over the age of 18) should have 11 clear hours rest per day. They should also have 24 hours uninterrupted rest in a 7 day period (or 48 hours in a 14 day period). In addition, they should also have on duty rest breaks. Where a shift or normal working day exceeds six hours, there should be provision for a 20 minute rest break. The employee is entitled to be away from their workstation.

It is possible to be sued for breach of the *Working Time Regulations 1998*. Not just in relation to the 48 hour week, but for not allowing sufficient rest breaks. However, the employee must have had a request to take a break refused before they can bring a claim in the tribunal. In *Fraser v Carter Refrigeration & Retail Services Limited Employment Tribunal Case No. 2202270/00* the employee had been on duty through the night. He went home at 8am, but was called back into work before his 11 hour break had finished. The tribunal decided that there had been no breach of the Regulations because Mr Fraser had not asserted his right to the break. However, had he done so, then the company would have been at risk of paying damages for insisting that he forego his right to rest.

Although an employee can voluntarily forego their rest break, the employee is under a duty here, to ensure that they are not putting themselves or others at risk.

Regulation 8 makes special allowance for work of a monotonous nature. This is particularly the case where the work pattern puts the worker at a health and safety risk. In this situation, there is a specific duty on the employer to give the employee adequate breaks. This is in addition to the rest breaks mentioned above and laid down by *Regulation 12*. For example, in 1994, Bernard Matthews Evisceration Department, Holton, worked a 10 hour shift from 6am until 4.30pm. The shift included one 30 minute unpaid lunch break. However, as the work was monotonous and the speed was 36 birds per minute, additional breaks were included of one 20 minute and one 15 minute break together with job rotation.

The *Working Time Regulations* set out the right to annual paid holiday. This is currently four weeks. Unless governed separately by a contract of employment, this holiday entitlement is not in addition to bank holidays. Neither can it be carried into another holiday year. Once the holiday year is over, any holiday which has not been taken is then lost (unless the contract is terminated at that time, in which case the holiday can be paid in lieu).

It is important to be aware that an employee on long-term sick leave does not automatically lose their right to take holiday. If the employee requests holiday whilst on sick leave they are entitled to be paid for it as holiday, not sick leave. This was decided in the case of *Kigass Aero Components Ltd v Brown & Others [2002] IRLR 312.*

Night workers   2.3

Those employees who work night shifts are afforded additional protection by the Regulations. To be deemed to be night work, the shift must be at least seven hours long and include hours between 12am and 5am. At least three hours of their day must be during this period as a normal course. If this is the case they have an implied contractual term inserted into their contract. This is that their normal hours will be on average 8 in 24. The average is worked out over a 17 week period. They can work more than 8 hours. If the work is more hazardous, then they can never work more than 8 hours in 24. For example, if the work is non-hazardous the employee could do 3x12 hour shifts per week, which would average less than 8 in 24 over a 17 week period, but if the work is hazardous they could only work 8 in 24, regardless.

Night workers also require regular health assessments, which should at the very least be annually. If it is discovered that they are suffering from health problems connected to night work, they should be transferred, where possible, to a day shift. Again employers are under a duty to keep records of hours worked for at least two years.

It should be noted, that where someone works rolling shifts the daily rest break will not apply if there cannot be an 11 hour period between a change of shifts, or the employee works split shifts. However, the employer must provide compensatory rest breaks where possible.

Young workers   **2.4**

The Regulations are slightly different in respect of young workers. They are afforded slightly more protection than adult workers in respect of working hours and night work. The actual night work regulations are the same as those for adults but are subject to the changes in working hours. Every young worker should have 12 hours rest in 24 hours. They are also entitled to a 30 minute break in a six hour shift. Employers should use great caution when employing young workers to work past 10 pm, particularly when they are still at school or college.

It should be noted that there are separate regulations for children under the minimum school leaving age. They are protected by the *Children (Protection at Work) Regulations 1998 (SI 1998/276)*, however, these are not considered for the purpose of this book.

All employees are afforded protection under the *ERA 1999*. This sets out the basic terms of an employment contract, in particular setting out the position in relation to notice. The *ERA 1999* only applies to employees and not workers. Therefore people who work from home as telesales or piece workers may not be protected under this Act. Agency workers working in a company's premises are not afforded protection under this Act. They are protected against the treatment of the Agency, but as the company is not their employer, they are not responsible for their contract terms.

The *ERA 1999* defines an employee as 'an individual who has entered into or works under (or, where the employment has ceased, worked under) a contract of employment' (*section 230(1)*). Employers owe a duty and responsibility to their employees and may be liable for the actions of their employees. In this relationship there is a duty on the employer to provide work and on the employee to work. No such duty exists between employer and worker. The most important protection given by the *ERA 1999* is protection against unfair dismissal. Therefore the *ERA 1999* governs the disciplinary and grievance process to ensure that employees who are dismissed are only dismissed for a fair reason. Protection from unfair dismissal is not an issue which is to be dealt with at length in this book. We will be looking at the issues of grievance procedures and, where necessary, the correct use of the disciplinary procedure following a grievance. Suffice to say, procedure in relation to disciplinary, capability and grievance procedures should all be fair in light of the *ERA 1999*, as failure to undertake a fair procedure could result in claims for unfair or constructive dismissal.

The *ERA 1999* deals with the basic grievance and disciplinary procedures. These were originally brought in by ACAS through their Code of Practice leaflet in 1985. This Code has been expanded on over the years and tribunals tend to apply the Code to disciplinary situations where an employer has not used or does not have a disciplinary procedure to decide whether the actions were fair. The *ERA 1999* particularly stipulates that an employee should be accompanied by a colleague, or union representative, to meetings of a disciplinary nature or in relation to a grievance procedure.

The *ERA 1999* also governs continuity of employment. Where an employee works occasionally, unless the break is over a week (ie a period of time which is deemed to start on a Sunday and finish the following Saturday) their continuity is not broken. Where, for example, they finish their last shift on a Tuesday and do not work again until a week Friday, they have maintained continuity of employment in regard to any rights they might receive under the *ERA 1999*. Continuity will not be broken where there is absence due to sickness or injury (disabled employees); due to a temporary cessation of work or lay off and where the employee is absent due to an arrangement or custom, for example an agreed career break (see *Jenkins v The Captain's Wife EAT 69/83*).

In brief, the *ERA 1999* covers the following additional situations: redundancy payments and calculations; disputes relating to written terms and conditions of employment and payslips (or lack thereof, which is also now governed by the *Employment Act 2002*); maternity, paternity and parental leave; flexible working arrangements (not requests); protection from detriment under the Health and Safety regulations and whistle-blowing (see the *Public interest Disclosure Act 1998*); the right to time off for public duties; and written reasons for dismissals.

In **CHAPTER 1** a number of groups are described which only come under the definition of worker. These include lone and home workers; temporary contract and agency workers; and apprentices. Unfortunately students and, in most cases, voluntary workers are not protected by any regulations in the Employment arena as they are not deemed to be workers or employees due to the fact they are not paid. It should be noted that public workers as set out in **CHAPTER 1** are not dealt with separately in this chapter, as the regulations that apply to them depend on their individual circumstances and they may in most cases fall within one of the other groups identified.

Young workers are also afforded little protection in addition to those issues discussed above, unless they fall by circumstance into one of the other groups. There are then seven pieces of legislation that have an impact on the employer/employee relationship when dealing with diverse employees. The next part of this chapter will deal with the specific regulations and legislation that affect the employees who are diverse from an employment law perspective.

Women   2.5

As mentioned in **CHAPTER 1**, women are afforded a great deal of protection depending on their circumstances. Equal pay was mentioned, which is governed by the *Equal Pay Act 1970* and the *Equal Pay (Amendment) Regulations 1983 (SI 1983/1794)*, together with the subsequent amendments by the *Employment Act 2002*. This is to protect employees (whether male or female) from being treated less favourably in relation to their level of remuneration. The ethos being equal pay for equal work. This legislation does not just apply to women, as men are also able to bring claims. However, case law shows that women bring the vast majority of cases. This is not, per se, an issue of diversity as such. That said, employers should ensure that their pay structures reflect the work individuals undertake on their behalf. Should one employee be paid more than another for like work, the employer must be able to justify this. It should be noted that an employee can bring an equal pay claim at any time during their employment and have six months after leaving to issue proceedings, unlike the three months in other cases.

Discrimination 2.6

Sex discrimination is one of the biggest issues in relation to women. Although, as with equal pay claims, men can bring a claim under the *Sex Discrimination Act (1975) (SDA 1975)* it is nowhere near as common. The issue here would be positive or indirect discrimination, this is not an issue which will be discussed at length.

When dealing with issues of sex discrimination it is important to ensure that the managers involved are sensitive to the feelings of the employee. Ideally a female manager should interview the female employee, as this may assist the employee in providing some details she may previously have felt embarrassed to disclose to a man.

Discrimination in this case is defined as treatment which is less favourable on the grounds of the employee's sex. There are two types of discrimination, direct, which is by word or action; and indirect, which can be attributed to the policies of the company (for example changing shift patterns). This situation may affect a woman with children more than a man with children.

Direct sex discrimination can be anything from office banter, which the employee takes offence at, to inappropriate behaviour of a sexual nature. In the case of *Carver v SK (Sales) Limited (ET Case No. 1500623/2001)* the applicant was the only woman in a male sales orientated industry. She brought a claim for sex discrimination and constructive dismissal. She had received text messages from one of the directors which portrayed cartoon characters in the middle of sexual acts. In addition to these unwanted text messages, she claimed that her manager also made lude sexual remarks to her in respect of the way she dressed. The applicant argued that the behaviour suffered was degrading and discriminatory as her manager and the Director were in positions of authority over which she had no control. This claim was settled out of court. However, it shows that behaviour between men in the office, which is deemed to be light hearted, is not necessarily going to be accepted in the same way when a woman is put in the situation.

It is important to bear in mind that the treatment the employee suffers is in fact unfavourable, not just something she does not like. In relation to *Carver v SK (Sales) Limited (ET Case No. 1500623/2001)* the text messages could be deemed to just be an issue she did not like. However, the lude comments in the office could have been examples of less favourable treatment.

Indirect discrimination is brought about by a condition that the employer has applied to both sexes, but where one sex is less likely to be able to comply with the condition than the other. In many cases the condition may not be justifiable irrespective of the sex of the employee or it causes a detriment to an employee as they cannot comply with it. The question that must be asked in these situations is whether the employee would have been treated in the same way, but for their sex (*James v Eastleigh Borough Council [1990] ICR 554*). If part of a job specification holds a condition that few women could comply with, but most men would be able to, the employer must justify that the requirement is not in relation to sex. For example, if the requirement is strength related, it is likely that women will not be as strong as men. Provided the reasoning behind the condition is due to the heavy lifting involved in the job's role, then this should be a justifiable reason for the condition. However, if the condition is merely there to prevent women applying, there can be no justification.

It is important here to ensure that when considering conditions, you compare like with like. In the case of *Bullock v Alice Ottley School [1993] ICR 138 CA* the domestic staff (who were mainly women) were to retire at 60 years of age. The handy men/gardeners were to retire at the age of 65 years. This group were mostly men. It was found that there was no discrimination here as to the two roles were very different. If the retirement age had been different for men and women within the domestic staff, then it is possible there would have been an issue of indirect discrimination.

The main reason for justification is that the condition is based on 'objectively justified grounds, which are other than economic, such as administrative efficiency, in an organisation which is not engaged in commerce or business (*Rainey v greater Glasgow Health Board [1987] ICR 129 HL*). In other words the need for the condition must be real, appropriate and necessary for the running of the business.

When someone alleges discrimination they must show that they have somehow suffered a detriment. Obviously abuse of a physical or psychological nature would fall within the definition of detriment. However, it is enough that the treatment endured, or the condition imposed, amounts to something an employee could reasonably and justifiably complain about. A detriment is not necessarily any physical or economic consequent of the act complained of (*Shamoon v Vhief Constable of Royal Ulster Constabulary [2003] UKHL 11*).

It is also important to bear in mind that you cannot discriminate against a person because they are married. This is something that is more likely to affect the view of women than men. Unfortunately it is often still the case that an employer will have reservations about employing a woman (particularly if married) between the ages of 20 and 35 if they do not have children, as the assumption is that they will do so and the employer will be responsible for the costs of the maternity leave.

As mentioned in **CHAPTER 1**, a prospective employee can bring a claim for discrimination due to their treatment by a prospective employer at the application and selection stage. Unless there is a fully justifiable reason to request only single people to apply, such advertisements or selection procedures will be deemed to be discriminatory. It is important to ensure (as mentioned in **CHAPTER 1**) that an applicant is considered on their merits only, ie their skills, qualifications and experience.

Grounds to bring a discrimination claim can arise at the following times:

- when an employee is considered for a position, or a position is offered; and afterwards a difference in salary arises;

- by refusing or omitting to offer a prospective employee a position, or an existing employee a promotion;

- by reducing chances for promotion by imposing particular conditions which for example, young mothers cannot comply with; and

- by dismissing the employee or subjecting them to a detriment.

If gender is a consideration at any of these occasions, employers are opening themselves up to the risk of a claim for discrimination. It is worth noting that there is currently no cap on damages for discrimination claims.

Where the discriminatory act amounts to harassment, it is for the employee to state whether it caused offence or was unacceptable. Sexual harassment is deemed to consist of actions or words which are not welcome to the recipient. The harassment is deemed to undermine their dignity and create a hostile and offensive place to work in. It is in this case, as mentioned above, where it is for employee to decide what she considers is acceptable or offensive (*Reed & Anor v Stedman [1999] IRLR 299*). Here the employer's duty is to investigate the matter and ensure that any disciplinary action against the perpetrator is undertaken properly and to the correct level of the disciplinary process. Where the discrimination is gender-specific, as in the case of harassment, there is no need to show a male comparator (*British Telecommunications plc v Williams [1997] IRLR 668*). As is often the case, the harasser is someone in a more senior position than the employee being harassed. In such cases the harasser is likely to deny the treatment or state that the employee was a willing participant. Therefore, it is important to consider whether any reasonable person would understand, by the employee's comments or actions, that they were rejecting the conduct. If so, this would amount to harassment (see *Reed*, above).

There are ways to discriminate which would not amount to a claim for discrimination. If the condition is for health and safety reasons, the employer is acting in the best interests of the employee by preventing them from undertaking certain duties.

The next issue affecting women, as identified in **CHAPTER 1**, is pregnancy and motherhood. Before moving to the regulations, which are specifically made for these situations, it is important to note the conditions under the *SDA 1975*, which apply to pregnant women and new mothers. An employer cannot compare the treatment of a woman on maternity leave with a man on sick leave when considering whether the treatment of the woman was discriminatory. As a man can never be on maternity leave this is not a true and fair comparison. However, following the implementation of the *Employment Act 2002* in April 2003, it may be possible, in the future to compare the treatment of a woman on maternity leave with the treatment of a man on adoption leave.

It should be obvious to all employers that they cannot refuse to employ or promote a woman because she is pregnant (*Ministry of Defence v Williams EAT 0833/02-ZT*). However, this is not necessarily the case where a pregnant woman applies to undertake maternity cover.

It should also be noted that pregnancy related sickness, provided this is notified to the employer, would not count toward any sickness related disciplinary proceedings. A woman cannot be dismissed due to a pregnancy related illness (*Brown v Rentokil (Case C – 394/96) ECJ*).

As mentioned, discrimination is allowed on health and safety grounds. Although this issue does cross over with the matters discussed at **CHAPTER 3** it is important that employers are aware of the impact of the *SDA* on this issue. *Section 51 of the Health and Safety at Work etc Act 1974*, allows that in certain circumstances women can be discriminated against. In particular, pregnant women and women of reproductive age and capacity must not work where they may be exposed to lead or ionising radiation. However, this has been challenged by the European Courts (*Mahlburg v Land Mecklenburg-Vorpommern (2 February 2000)* and *Habermann-Bellermann v Arbeilerwohlfahrt, Bezirksverband Ndb/Obf e V (Noc-421/92)*). The European Court of Justice has ruled that the fact that health and safety regulations prevent the employment of pregnant women in certain roles, does not prevent the employment of pregnant women for those roles (provided the role is permanent) if they are the better candidate. The employer would then be under a duty to place the woman in a suitable alternative role until her maternity leave begins. Or, if a suitable role is not available, employ her then suspend her until the risk to her passes.

It is also important to bear in mind the issue of gender reassignment when dealing with sex discrimination. Particular as there is now more access to the necessary drugs and surgery to assist employees with such issues. Employees can be discriminated against on the grounds of their gender in these circumstances. However, the issue is often defined by what stage in the 'process' the employee is at. The Court of Appeal recently decided in the case of *Croft v Royal Mail Group Plc Court of Appeal, 2003 EWCA Civ 1045* that the employee had not suffered unreasonable treatment when asked to use the disabled toilets rather than the women's toilets when she was in a pre-operative state.

The *SDA 1975* does cover gender reassignment cases, but the application of the Act will depend on the stage of the reassignment. In this case, the employer had done everything reasonable to accommodate the needs of the employee, who was presenting herself as a female employee. Had the operative stage of the treatment been completed it is possible that the request that she use the disabled toilets would be discriminatory. When dealing with such cases it is important to bear in mind the needs and wishes of the employee, but also their colleagues. In the case mentioned, the employee's female colleagues did not feel comfortable having a preoperative transsexual using their toilets.

Part time employees 2.7

It is a fairly well known fact that the majority of part time employees are women for one reason or another. Therefore, the *Part Time Workers (Prevention of Less Favourable Treatment) Regulations 2000 (SI 2000/1551)* are dealt with here, in relation to women. These regulations were put in place to ensure that part time workers were treated exactly the same as full time workers. The issue here is to ensure that part time workers' benefits are the same as their full time counterparts. Previously full timers were paid holiday and part timers were not. This is no longer the situation, all are entitled to four weeks paid holiday. The only difficulty is the calculation of bank holidays as most part time employees' hours do not fall on every bank holiday. For ease, the normal calculations would be:

$$\frac{\text{Average weekly hours} \times \text{number of bank holidays not falling on a normal working day}}{\text{Five days}}$$

This should provide you with the number of hours pay or additional holiday due to each part time employee.

Where there are other contractual benefits, such as health care and pension, the qualification for these must be the same. For example where there is a qualification of six months employment in the full time contract, the period must be the same in a part time contract.

These regulations apply to workers as well as employees, therefore casual and Saturday workers are also entitled to qualify for benefits and holidays under these regulations. It is no longer the case that part time workers can be chosen first in redundancy situations, each redundant employee must be chosen on the same criteria, where their full or part time status is irrelevant.

Failure to comply with the regulations could result in a claim for wrongful and unfair dismissal as well as sex discrimination if the part time employee is female.

That said, if the benefits are different depending on the person's position in the firm, then there is no need to consider whether they are in breach of these regulations unless there are full time and part time employees in that particular position.

Maternity leave and pay 2.8

The most important regulations for a woman are the *Maternity Regulations* which were amended by the *Employment Act 2002*. Also see the *ERA 2002 part VIII; section 7, Schedule 4 part 1* of the *Employment Relations Act 1999, (Maternity and Parental Leave etc Regulations 1999 (SI 1999/3312)* and *Maternity and Parental Leave (Amendment) Regulations 2001 (SI 2001/4010)*. The Regulations came into force on 6 April 2002. Where previously maternity leave was a complicated calculation between ordinary and additional leave, the rights are now far easier to calculate.

It is important to establish how to calculate when the right to maternity leave and pay take effect. Initially it should be noted that there must be a sound prospect of childbirth for the right to maternity leave to arise, this was established by the *ERA* under *section 235(1)*. Therefore, where a prospective mother miscarries, they are not entitled to claim any maternity benefits if the miscarriage is before the 24th week of pregnancy. They are of course entitled to claim protection on the grounds of pregnancy related illness for any time required convalescing.

Childbirth is therefore the birth of a child, whether living or dead, after the 24th week of pregnancy. In the situation where an employee's child is still born, after the 24th week of pregnancy, they are entitled to take the full maternity leave due to them should they wish to do so.

The important date when determining rights to maternity leave is the expected week of confinement. This is deemed to be the week in which the child is due, beginning on the Sunday before hand and ending at midnight on the following Saturday.

The employee is under a duty to notify the employer with the details of their expected date of birth at the earliest opportunity. This should include a certificate confirming the date of birth from either their doctor or midwife. The employee must also by the 25th week of pregnancy, notify the employer of when they would like their maternity leave to begin. Failure to do so could result in the employee forfeiting their right to maternity leave and even pay.

Pregnancy related sickness does not count toward any absence records. However, the duty is on the employee to notify the employer that the reason for their absence was due to their pregnancy. They should also notify the employer of any risks to their pregnancy from their role within the company.

The company should also arrange a health and safety risk assessment at the earliest opportunity to ensure that they are complying with their duty of care to the employee. It should be noted that if the role could be a risk to mother or child, the employer should try to find a suitable alternative. Failing this, the employee can be suspended on full pay until the risk ends or their leave period begins. This would not effect any of their employment rights.

Once notified of a pregnancy, the employer must within 28 days confirm in writing the start and finish date of the maternity leave. If this is not dealt with, the employer will be unable to prevent the employee from returning early or discipline them for returning late.

Maternity leave is now for a period of six months. This is called ordinary maternity leave. Every employee is entitled to ordinary maternity leave irrespective of their length of service. This leave period cannot start before the 29th week of pregnancy (ie 11 weeks before the expected week of confinement), unless the baby is born prematurely. In such cases, leave would start immediately. However, the employee must have provided notice of their expected date of confinement, or should do so as soon as possible, as this determines their entitlement to leave and pay.

Pregnant women also have the right to have reasonable time off for antenatal care. This time off should be paid. It is not however, unreasonable to ask employees to try to arrange appointments at the start or end of their day so as to avoid as much disruption to their place of work as possible. Should a particularly appointment be inconvenient for justifiable reasons, an employer can refuse to give permission for the employee to attend. However, the refusal must be reasonable. If the employee attends the antenatal appointment without permission, the employee can be disciplined, as this would be deemed to be an unauthorised absence.

Where an employee does not wish to take all of their maternity leave, they can return to work, subject to reaching an agreed return date with their employer. However, there is a portion of compulsory maternity leave. This is two weeks immediately after the date of birth, or four weeks for factory workers. Where an employee wishes to return to work before the end of the 26-week period, they must give 28 days notice of the date on which they wish to return. If the notice period is not complied with, then the return date can be postponed to the end of the 26-week period. Refusal to return early can only be made with a fully justifiable reason.

An employee on ordinary maternity leave is entitled to all the normal terms and conditions of their employment. This includes where applicable: pay reviews, pension contributions and bonuses. Bonuses are calculated as if the employee were still at work and performing to the same level as when their maternity leave began. The employee will accrue benefits and holiday in accordance with their contract. On returning to work the employee has the right to return to the same position, at the same level and salary as they would have been, had they not taken maternity leave.

The employee does not have to give notice of their return date if they wish to use all of their leave. Neither does the employee need to notify the employer if they do or do not, wish to take their additional maternity leave entitlement. If the employee does not wish to return to work after either period of leave, they must resign, giving the amount of notice set out in their contract, or the required statutory period (ie one week for each complete year of service, to a maximum of 12 weeks), should they not have a contract of employment.

Additional maternity leave is also a 26 week period, which follows directly on from the ordinary maternity leave. The same rules apply in relation to returning from leave early or otherwise. The main differences are that this leave period is unpaid in its entirety; the employee only accrues statutory benefits ie they accrue holiday at a rate of 1.66 days per month rather than at the rate of any enhanced holiday agreements in their contract of employment; and finally, although they have the right to return to work, if their original position is no longer available, they must be prepared to accept a suitable alternative. They would remain on the same terms and conditions as previously. Any bonus system in place would only take account of the ordinary maternity leave period.

To qualify for additional maternity leave, the employee must have been employed 26 weeks at the 25th week of pregnancy, ie they were employed by the employer one week before they fell pregnant.

Where the employee is unwell at the end of their maternity leave period (whether ordinary or additional), their maternity leave will be deemed to have finished and they should be placed on sick leave.

An employee will be entitled to received statutory maternity pay provided they were employed one week before they fell pregnant. That is to say that the employee must have been employed for 26 weeks at the twenty five week of pregnancy. Statutory maternity pay is currently 90 per cent of the employee's salary for the first six weeks and then approximately £100 per week for the remaining 20 weeks (the amount will depend on the level of the employee's salary).

As mentioned, the employee has the right to return to their old position, or such suitable position as is practicable after additional maternity leave. They do no have the right, as appears to be a common misconception, to return to work part time, unless they were part time when they went on leave.

However, there is a possibility that the refusal to allow an employee to return to work part time after maternity leave may amount to indirect sex discrimination. This was discussed in the case of *Sibley v The Girls' Day School Trust, Norwich High School for Girls EAT, 20.5.03 (1369/01)*, where a teacher wished to return part time after completing her maternity leave. Her request was refused and the decision was upheld by the Employment Appeal Tribunal (EAT) as they felt that the reasoning behind it was justified. However, it is possible that in future the reasoning may not be, therefore amounting to sex discrimination.

Flexible working 2.9

The *Flexible Working (Eligibility, Complaints and Remedies) Regulations 2002 (SI 2002/3236)* and *section 47* of the *Employment Act 2002* give employees the right to request part time working or a change in their working hours. This provision may enhance any future chances for employees to claim sex discrimination if they feel that there request was unreasonably refused. However, there are particular qualifications which must be met for an employee to be able to apply to change their hours. An employee can apply provided that he/she has 26 weeks' service with the employer; are the mother (or father), adopter, guardian or foster parent of the child, or is married to, or the partner of such a person; and has or is expected to be responsible for the upbringing of the child. All employees who return from maternity leave should qualify (it should be noted that Agency Workers do not qualify to apply for flexible working).

An employee can make an application to change their hours provided their child is under 6 years old or 18 years if the child is disabled. However, the last possible date for an application is 15 days before the child's 6th or 18th birthday (respectively).

There is a form which the DTI suggest be completed when an application is made. However, it is not compulsory. The important thing is that the application contains the correct information. The applicant should make the request in writing. The application should state that it is an application under the *Flexible Working Regulations*; state the change in hours and when the applicant would like these to start; explain how the applicant feels it will affect their work and the employer's business; and how the applicant feels the conditions could be met. If an application has been made previously, this should also be mentioned together with the date. The application should also be signed and dated.

It is important to ensure that the employee is aware that any change in hours is permanent. The only way to change them would be to make another application. An employee can only make one application in any rolling 12 month period.

If an application is successful the employee will effectively stay on the same contract, but any benefits will be on a pro rata basis.

There is a specific procedure, which must be followed, both by the employee and the employer. Once an application is received, provided it fulfils the provisions above (otherwise it is not an application and nothing need be done by the employer), the employer must respond setting a meeting within 28 days of the date of the application. This time limit can only be extended if the person who is considering the application is off sick or on holiday when the application is received.

If the change in hours can be agreed, there is no need to call a meeting. The decision would merely need to be confirmed in writing and the changes implemented.

Following the meeting, a decision is required within 14 days. This should be in writing and signed. If the change is agreed, this should be confirmed and the date from which it is effected should be stated.

If the application is rejected the letter should state the reasons in full and give a specific explanation as to why this is the case. The employee should also be notified of the appeal procedure.

An application can be rejected, but there are specific reasons, which are deemed to be reasonable:

• The cost burden on the employer's business.

• Possible and likely detriment to the customer.

• The inability of the employer to reorganise the business to accommodate the change.

- The inability of the employer to recruit a replacement.

- The possible or likely negative effect on the quality of work.

- The possible or likely negative effect on performance.

- The fact that the suggestion amounts to insufficient working hours.

- If there are already in place planned structural changes, which cannot accommodate the suggestion.

These reasons must be expanded upon in detail applying them to the particular business of the employer. Previous decisions made should also be considered. If the business is small, changes to hours for other employees may make further changes uneconomical. However, the larger the firm the less likely the employer would be able to argue that previous changes mean the new request cannot be accommodated. If the decision was unreasonably refused an employee can bring a claim in the employment tribunal. If the tribunal agree with the employee the employer can be ordered to reconsider the application, and/or pay compensation.

If the employee wishes to appeal the decision, they must do so within 14 days of the date of refusal. A hearing must be set within 14 days of the appeal being received and the decision of the appeal made and confirmed in writing, with detailed reasons, 14 days thereafter.

An extension to the time limits can be made, but must be mutually agreed between the parties. The extension should then be put in writing and signed by both parties and a copy sent to the employee.

At every meeting the applicant is entitled to be accompanied by a trade union representative or colleague. The employer is also entitled to have a witness at the meeting.

An employee can withdraw their application at any time. An employer should only treat the application as withdrawn where the employee has indicated this either verbally or in writing; they have failed to attend a meeting regarding the initial application or appeal more than once; or the employee has refused to provide information to the employer which is needed to consider the application fully. The employer should confirm in writing that the application has been treated as withdrawn.

The employee cannot then make another application for 12 months. It should also be borne in mind that if the request is granted, the employee must make another application to change their hours back to full time, as any agreement is permanent. The same rules would apply to this as to the reduction in hours.

Parental leave 2.10

Although this also applies to fathers, again, it is more likely that mothers will take parental leave. It is important that both employees and employers are fully aware of what parental leave entitles the employee to do. An employee can add parental leave to the end of their maternity leave period. This will not affect their right to return to their normal position provided they do not take more than four weeks' leave. If more than four weeks are taken (normally only with the express permission of the employer) then the employee would only be able to return to their normal position, if it is reasonably practicable.

Parental leave is unpaid. An employee can only take 13 weeks in the first five years of their child's life. The time is to care for the child only and should not be taken as unpaid leave.

The employee must give 21 days notice of the date they would like the leave to start and the length of time they wish to take. Unless their child is in receipt of disability living allowance, the employee can only take time off in week long blocks. If the request is not financially feasible, the leave can be postponed.

Time off for dependants   2.11

This entitles the employee to time off work during normal working hours to give emergency care to their child. The guidelines were set out in the case of *Qua v John Form Morrison Solicitors [2003] IRLR 711 EAT* below and relate to the right to time off to deal with unexpected and unforeseeable events, in order to make arrangements to provide for the care of the child:

- This is not a right to take time off to provide care personally, beyond that the of the immediate emergency.

- The needs of the business and the employer are irrelevant when determining what is a reasonable amount of time off for the employee.

- The employer is not entitled to daily updates.

- Where previous problems have arisen and it is known that these could reoccur, the reasonableness of the request and the need for time off may be affected.

Religious groups   2.12

As mentioned in **CHAPTER 1** these groups are now protected under the *Employment Act* and the *Employment Equality (Religion and Belief) Regulations 2003 (SI 2003/1660)*. The regulations came into effect on 2 December 2003. This will of course run beside the race discrimination regulations, which are discussed below.

It should be noted that the *ERA* protects employees from being dismissed for not wishing to work on a Sunday. In this regard the 12 month qualifying period does not apply and a claim for unfair dismissal could be brought immediately, together with a claim for discrimination on the grounds of religious belief should this be the reason for the refusal to work.

These regulations cover both employee and the wider group of workers. The regulations are deemed to cover any 'religion, religious belief or similar philosophical belief'. They do not cover political beliefs. The important points which are likely to be considered when deciding whether there is a religion or belief include that there be a clear belief system, collective worship and a profound belief affecting the person's way of life or view of the world. There need not be a god involved. However, the regulations have not yet been put to the test, so it is not possible to know what will ultimately be defined as a religion or belief other than the already very established religions.

There are, as with all discrimination regulations, types of discrimination such as direct and indirect discrimination. Direct discrimination would be treating an employee less favourably by word or deed (including harassment) on the grounds of their religion. Indirect discrimination will be harder for the employer to avoid. For example, this would be a criteria or condition for a position, which places people with a religious belief at a disadvantage. For example, this could include the change of working practices to a rolling shift. This would automatically take in weekends thus affecting the ability of a Christian, Jew or Muslim to undertake their duties properly due to their practice of not working on their holy day.

Such acts of discrimination may be justifiable in the same way as with indirect sex discrimination, if it is in the best interests of the business.

There are two main exemptions from the regulations. Firstly where the applicant or employee needs to be of a particular religion or belief, for example, to work in a Jewish/Catholic School teaching about that belief; and secondly, where the employer has an ethos based on a particular religion or belief.

As with all the discrimination regulations there must be a comparator for the treatment. It is not yet clear whether someone without any beliefs is covered under the regulations ie an atheist or agnostic.

Dress codes will be affected under the indirect discrimination element of these regulations. It is important to consider the individual's religious grounds for their inability to comply with the standard dress code before making any decisions on whether their type of dress does not or cannot conform to the company's code. Unless the reason for the code is health and safety related, it is unlikely that a refusal to accept a variation will be justified.

Where particular hours need to be worked due to the need of the business or their customers (as per the example above) it is likely that enforcement of those hours, will not be discriminatory.

At this time, the regulations do not require the employer to provide somewhere for religious practices to take place. For example, the requirement of the Muslim to pray three times per day. However, the employer must consider whether the refusal to provide a safe place to pray may be seen as discriminatory, particularly if reasonable changes are possible.

Disabled employees   2.13

The current position is that employers with less than 15 members of staff are not covered by the *Disability Discrimination Act 1995* (*DDA*). Those employers that are, must not discriminate against an employee on the grounds of their disability, thereby treating them less favourably or placing them at a disadvantage. This will change from October 2004 when all employers, irrespective of size, must not discriminate against the disabled, whether there is a mental or physical disability.

For an employee to be covered under the *DDA* they must have a physical or mental impairment which has long term and substantial effects on their ability to undertake normal day to day activities.

A mental impairment must be a clinically well-recognised illness. Currently stress is not a mental impairment, unless it is coupled with depression or another psychiatric illness. The issues relating to stress will be addressed in more detail in **CHAPTER 4**. For the disability to be long term, it must have lasted or be likely to last, more than 12 months.

Where an impairment ceases to have a substantial long term effect, it will be treated as continuing if it is likely that the impairment will recur. For example, in a situation where treatment is currently controlling the condition, but if the treatment were to stop, the impairment would return completely.

There has been much debate as to what constitutes day to day activities. For example some activities are only undertaken by women for example, putting on makeup or straightening hair. However, case law has agreed that activities only undertaken by one sex can amount to a normal day to day activity provided it is common within that sex. Therefore the inability to run five miles per day is unlikely to be a normal activity, as few members of the general public would consider it.

Impairments are generally deemed to affect someone's day to day activity, where it affects a person's ability to be mobile. This is not just physical mobility, but can also include the ability to use public or private transport. Others include: manual dexterity; the ability to lift or carry everyday items; physical co-ordination; speech, hearing and sight; continence; memory or concentration; and the perception of risk or physical danger.

Where the illness is progressive, for example muscular dystrophy, the impairment may not be sufficient to be deemed a disability immediately. However if the effects will worsen over time and then have a long term substantial effect, the condition will be deemed to have immediate effect and thereby be protected under the *DDA* (*Mowat & Brown v University of Surrey [2002] IRLR 235 EAT*).

As with the *SDA 1975*, a refusal to employ someone must not be on the grounds of their disability. Again, if the refusal is for health and safety reasons, due to the nature of the work, then the *DDA 1995* will not apply. This would be in such situations where the modification of equipment or the ability to make adjustments to the place of work would not be economically viable for the business. For example, where the employer is in a listed building and the employee needs the use of a lift to reach floors above ground level. It would not be possible to make the required changes in this case and therefore the employee would not have been discriminated against if they were not successful with their application despite their disability being the reason for it.

Again, as mentioned in **CHAPTER 1**, the wording of any job advertisements should be clear and not make any comments which could be deemed to put a disabled person on an unequal footing.

When dealing with the interviewing of a disabled employee it is important that the interviewer has some awareness of the situation. In some cases it may not be possible, as the applicant may not have been advised of their disability before hand. During the interview, once it has been carefully established whether there is a disability, you would then need to address whether there are any specific requirements or adjustments needed. This should be dealt with carefully and not lingered over.

Where an employee is deemed to be disabled in accordance with the *DDA 1995*, the employer is under a duty to make reasonable adjustments (*section 6(1), DDA 1995*). This is not just to the place of work, but to the employee's hours and possibly the employer's policies. The employer must ensure that the disabled employee is not at a disadvantage. *Section 6(3)* of the *DDA 1995* sets out what adjustments are reasonable by an employer. These are some examples:

- Physical adjustments to the premises; provide a reader or interpreter; provide supervision; modify procedures for assessments and company policies or reference manuals; provide training; allow reasonable time off (paid) for rehabilitation, assessment or treatment; acquire or modify equipment.

- Where the disability has occurred since the employee's employment began, the employer should also consider:
    - the allocation of some duties to a colleague;
    - transferring the employee to fill another vacancy;
    - altering their working hours; or
    - assigning them to a different place of work.

From October 2004, it is anticipated that there will be additional changes expected of the employer. These are likely to include that the employer provide training to 'able employees' regarding the disabilities within the firm and on any equipment required; as well as there being an opportunity to receive external support.

When considering what reasonable steps/adjustments the employer can make, the employer must also consider the extent it will affect them financially and practically. As well as the disruption to the current workforce and work practices. The employer must also consider to what extent the adjustments will prevent the disabled person being at a disadvantage.

The employer is not expected to make all the adjustments available to them. Neither are they expected to make adjustments which they could not possibly have been aware of. If in doubt, there is no reason why the employer cannot ask the employee what they feel would assist them.

There are limits to this duty to make adjustments. There is no requirement to make such adjustments as would assist the disabled generally. The adjustments are in relation to the needs of the specific employee, not the community as a whole. If the adjustment only gives the employee a minor advantage, there is no requirement to follow that route.

Where the employer could not have known about the disability or could not have known that it would have a substantial effect on the employee, there is no duty to make adjustments.

In addition, the duty does not require the employer to make the best possible adjustment to the role or premises. Neither will the employer be required to provide material or equipment, which the employee could reasonably be expected to already own for their personal use. Nor, is the employer expected to remove and reallocate crucial duties, which fall within the employees remit.

The employer receives further protection if they fail to make reasonable adjustments where they based their actions on advice, which appeared to be from a reputable source, for example a medical specialist. Or, where the employer had made reasonable efforts to obtain information about the condition and any appropriate adjustments, but remained unaware of some other possibilities.

The employer must show that they have made serious attempts to address the problem. In the case of *Kenny v Hampshire Constabulary [1999] IRLR 76* a new employee, who suffered from cerebal palsy required assistance when going to the toilet. The employer asked for volunteers to assist the new employee, but none were forthcoming. It was not practical for the employee to work from home where he was able to deal with himself. The manager applied for assistance with a support worker, but the funding exceeded the managers authority. As there was no quick solution, the employer withdrew the offer of employment as there was an urgent need to fill the vacancy. The tribunal found in favour of the employer in that they had acted reasonably and had, at no time discriminated against the applicant.

Another issue which needs to be considered in relation to disabled employees is illness. This is an issue for two reasons, firstly, the disability causes periods of recurring or long term sickness which affect the business and, two, the reason behind the long term sickness has resulted in a disability, for example stress leading to clinical depression.

The main question for employers to answer is: can a disabled employee be dismissed for long term or persistent sickness or even lateness? The answer to this is yes. However, the employer must ensure that they have tried every possible avenue before dismissing the employee. In *Dennis v Impress Metal Packaging Limited ET Case No. 1500471/2003* the applicant was dyslexic, but recently suffered from panic attacks, which resulted in a long term absence. On returning to work he found that these attacks meant that he could not travel more than 30 miles by car. He was unable to use public transport and struggled to go to public places.

The employer had a very strict attendance and lateness policy. An employee had to call at least one hour before the start of their shift if they were to be absent or late. Due to the type of illness from which the applicant suffered, he was rarely able to comply with this reporting obligation. He would often have attacks on route to work and not be able to continue his journey. By the time the attack was over it would often be too late to call the factory on time and on some occasions reach work in time to clock on.

The applicant was disciplined on numerous occasions due to his failure to comply with the company procedures. Eventually the applicant was dismissed. He brought a claim for Disability Discrimination. The tribunal found that although the employers had not modified their reporting policies to accommodate the applicant (as the machines ran on a 24 hour basis and changes were not practical), if the applicant had not been disabled he would have been dismissed some eight months earlier.

In relation to dismissals of this type, they will be lawful provided an able bodied employee is not treated more favourably. The dismissal can be due to the disability if the employer can show that another employee would have been dealt with sooner. However, generally it is better to deal with the issues that do not relate to the disability itself, for example, where the reason for the illness is not related to the disability.

Disability related illness can cost businesses a lot of money. However, it must be treated carefully, much in the same way as pregnancy related illnesses. The employer, should the period of illness be very long, may be able to use capability as a reason for a dismissal. However, it is important to bear in mind that the ultimate reason for the dismissal is the person's disability. Therefore the employer must have tried every possible avenue to encourage the employee back to work. The needs of the business should also be considered when making a decision. However, first it is important that the employer obtain a medical report on the condition so that they are aware of all the problems and if necessary ask the medical expert for advice on how to get the employee back to work if possible. A dismissal should not be considered until after these routes have been exhausted.

Where an employer has requested a medical report, but the employee has refused their consent, the employer is entitled to make a decision based on the information they have to hand.

Discrimination on the grounds of disability can be justified provided the failure to comply with the duty to make reasonable adjustments is 'both material to the circumstances and substantial' *(section 5(4), DDA 1995)*.

As with the case of *Dennis* (See *section 6(1), DDA 1995* and above), there was a justifiable reason for the dismissal. There are ways of justifying a failure to comply with the *DDA* under *sections 5(3)* and *5(5)*. Examples would include where, as in the case of *Callagan v Glasgow City Council [2001] IRLR 724* an employee has a number of sickness absences over an extended period (in this case due to depression and stress). The employer made every effort to work with the employee to deal with his extended absence. The employee persistently failed to co-operate. He was dismissed and the dismissal was deemed to be fair, even though the employer had not considered what reasonable adjustments could have been made to help the employee back to work.

Where an employee has had extended absences and is then reintroduced to the workplace, he can be warned that further absences could result in disciplinary action and even dismissal. Where further absences occur, the employer is within their rights to dismiss *(Christey v Cummins Inc ET case No. 6400202/00)*.

Where an employee is a full time senior member of a team and a job share or part time hours would not be appropriate following a long period of sickness, a dismissal would be reasonable particularly when the employee does not know when they will return *(Sillifant v North and East Devon Health Authority ET Case No. 1401241/97)*.

It should also be noted that the *DDA* applies to agency or temporary workers too. In the case of *Burton v Higham t/a Ace Appointments [2003] IRLR 257 EAT* it was decided that an agency worker could sue an employment agency for discrimination. The *DDA* in particular defines the group to which it applies in the same terms as the *ERA* defines 'worker'. It is not relevant that the work undertaken by the worker is for the client, not the agency. It is important to remember that this decision does not make agency workers employees.

Race 2.14

The *Race Relations Act 1976 (RRA 1976)* sets out the guidance in relation to the treatment of people of a different race or ethnic origin. This can now be run hand in hand with a claim under the Employment Act for discrimination on grounds of religion, particularly where dress is a fundamental part of the religion and culture, for example a Sikh turban.

The *RRA 1976* is very similar in scope to the *SDA 1975*, only relating to colour, race, nationality, and national and ethnic origins.

Again there can be direct and indirect discrimination, including harassment. Discrimination can occur as with the *SDA 1975* and the *DDA 1995* at the recruitment stage. It is therefore important to ensure that and advertisements or recruitment practices do not bear any elements, which could be deemed to be discriminatory.

Where there is direct discrimination, the employer must have treated the employee less favourably on racial grounds. To establish discrimination you must compare like with like. In the case of *Dhatt & anor v McDonald's Hamburgers Limited [1991] ICR 238 CA*, the two applicants brought a claim of race discrimination as they had been asked to provide work permits. However it was McDonald's practice to ask all employees for a work permit. Therefore the request was not a discriminatory one.

Furthermore, the act by the employer must be more than just poor or deplorable. It must be established that just that particular employee was treated badly. It was argued by the respondent in the case of *Chapman & Anor v Simon [1994] IRLR 124 CA* that he treated everyone appallingly and not just the applicant. He was found to have not discriminated against the applicant.

Indirect discrimination here is deemed to be the imposition of a condition or requirement, which cannot be satisfied by an employee by reason of his or her race. To establish this, the tribunal would consider the number of people within the employee's ethnic or racial group who could comply with the condition. The requirement also cannot be justified on non-racial grounds and the applicant has suffered a detriment as they cannot comply with it.

The employer would need to justify the condition. There needs to be objectivity when considering the needs of the employer and any effect the condition may have on the employee. The condition must be justifiable for some other reason than race. In *Board of Governors of St Matthias Church of England School v Crizzle [1993] ICR 401 EAT* the school were able to justify the condition that the Head Teacher had to be a committed Christian as they would need to administer communion. Although this condition excluded Asians, it was justifiable in regard to the needs of the school.

Justification is of course allowed in regard to health and safety or hygiene. For example, a religious need to have long hair could result in a sufficient reason to refuse employment in the catering industry. However as this is particularly related to dress, it was found in the case of *R v Birmingham City Council ex parte EOC [1989] IRLR 173 HL* that there was not a health and safety reason behind the prevention of a Sikh bus conductor from being able to wear his turban.

As with the justification reasons under the religious discrimination, if there is a genuine occupational reason, then it is unlikely that discrimination will be found. For example, a greek waiter or manager in an authentic greek restaurant.

When dealing with issues of racial discrimination caused by racial language, it is important not to confuse what is offensive and what is racist. As decided in the case of *Law Society and ors v Bahl {2003] IRLR 640 EAT* it is quite clear that all racist language is offensive, however, not all offensive language is racist. Therefore when facing a similar situation, it must be established exactly what was said to make the matter racist rather than to what the employee took offence.

Sexual orientation   2.15

The regulations are particularly carefully defined as to what is covered. Discrimination on the grounds of sexual orientation applies to same sex, the same and opposite sex and opposite sex relationships. However, the issue is not what sexual orientation the employee is, but what they are perceived to be. It should be noted that sexual tastes and practices are not covered here and therefore paedophilia is not protected under the regulations.

The *Employment Equality (Sexual Orientation) Regulations 2003 (SI 2003/ 1661)* apply to workers not just employees and therefore agency workers are protected here also. As with all the discrimination Acts, protection continues after the period of employment ends. This will be discussed more in **CHAPTER 8**, however, it is important to be aware that a reference which is discriminatory could result in a claim in the county court and the employment tribunal.

As with the other discrimination Acts, there are two types of discrimination, direct and indirect. There can be no justification in law for direct discrimination, i.e. not employing someone because they are gay. This is irrespective of whether the persons discriminating are also gay.

The discrimination does not necessarily have to be directed at the employee, but could be directed at a member of their family. As with race claims where it is unlawful to discriminate against someone due to their spouse's race, here it would be unlawful to discriminate because the employee's father is gay.

It is also important to deal with homosexual and heterosexual employees in the same way. It has been suggested by the Christian Institute that they would not have a problem employing non-practising homosexuals as it is the act of sex outside marriage that is frowned upon. However, if sex between unmarried heterosexual couples is overlooked but gay sex is not, this could amount to direct discrimination. Furthermore, if the argument is that extramarital sex cannot be allowed, the employer could be guilty of indirect discrimination as gay couples cannot marry (*IDS Brief 740 September 2003, p 14*).

There is a defence of genuine occupational requirement. An employer can refuse to employ or even dismiss an employee for this reason. This defence has two camps: one, which applies to all employers; and the other, which applies only to religious organisations. The first, is very difficult to see. Unless it could be argued that only gay people should work in gay clubs there is no reason for the genuine occupational requirement to be enforced. However, in relation to religious organisations, it is easier to see how this could be argued. The defence would relate to strongly held religious convictions of the group or followers. This does not mean that faith schools such as Catholic, Church of England, Jewish etc should be able to refuse to employ a gay teacher. In a House of Lords debate it was decided (although not implemented into the definition of the regulations) that a role 'for the purpose of organised religion' involved working in a church, synagogue or mosque, not a school, which is for the purpose of education not religion. However, if a similar situation arose to *Crizzle* (see *Sillifant v North and*

East Devon Health Authority at [**2.13**]) in relation to sexual orientation, it is possible that the same defence could be used in that a committed communicant was required and therefore a practising homosexual would not be appropriate. This is of course an issue for future debate and case law.

With regard to indirect discrimination, employers will need to be more careful with how they phrase advertisements. As with the other Acts, wording here is very important. An advert could not ask for married couples in the present climate, as that would instantly put gay men and women, who cannot currently marry at a disadvantage. In the same way, benefits should not be dependant on whether the employee is married. For example, a death in service pension should not automatically be payable only to a widow or widower. There should also be an option to pay the life partner, not only because gay couples cannot marry, but more and more people are not getting married and therefore should not lose out because of this. However the situation currently is that married people are protected from being put to a disadvantage in comparison to unmarried people. The regulations do not currently work in reverse.

What does the HR manager need to know and do in order to comply with the law and regulations? 2.16

As mentioned throughout the section above, training is essential for all managers, not just those in HR. To prevent discrimination it is important to ensure that the actual needs of the position advertised are specified without the use of words such as 'able', 'energetic', or such other words which could amount to a discrimination claim.

The employer's equal opportunities policy needs to comply with all the new regulations, as should the terms and conditions of employment, the staff handbook and the company's dress code.

Every HR manager should ensure that they are kept up to date on the law by email updaters, magazines or bulletins from a local solicitors firm. Employment law changes quickly and keeping up to date could prevent a company falling foul of the regulations.

Managing grievance procedures 2.17

The basic procedure an organisation should use is set out in the ACAS code of practice. However, once a grievance procedure is in place it is important to ensure that all employees are aware of it.

The procedure should have a number of levels so that an employee does not have to raise a grievance with the person who has caused them distress. In many firms and businesses, the grievance procedure is applied literally rather than logically.

For example, an employee is being bullied by their manager, the grievance procedure states that they must raise a grievance with their manager who will then investigate and make a decision. Until this stage is completed, no one else can be involved. Obviously this could not work properly and the relationship between the two people could only worsen.

The ideal situation would be that the employee raises their grievance to the HR department and it is dealt with outside of the employee's department or area of work.

The ultimate reason for the grievance procedure is to stop any claims in the employment tribunal arising. Therefore the procedure must be fair and reasonable. An employee who feels that they are being bullied should not be made to face their bully if they do not think that they can do so.

Grievances must be dealt with promptly and carefully including a full and frank investigation, where the person who is being investigated is suspended if necessary, whilst the investigation is underway. The employees on both sides should be allowed witnesses to all meetings (witnesses should be a colleague or trade union representative, as in the case of disciplinaries). Minutes at meetings should be taken and copies provided to all those attending so that they can be agreed (witnesses need not have a copy).

Whatever the outcome of the investigation the findings should be put in writing with reasons for them. If disciplinary action is necessary the complaining employee should be made aware of exactly what action is being taken so that they are satisfied with the outcome. If disciplinary action is not necessary, it may well be reasonable to move one or both of the employees so that the situation could not arise again.

It is important to ensure that, when dealing with grievances, there is a paper trail. An employee who brings a claim for discrimination will have a harder time proving that their employer was liable for the actions of their colleagues if the employer can show that they did everything possible to deal reasonably with the employee's complaint.

Under the *Employment Act 2002*, there are proposals for dispute resolution. This should have been implemented in October 2003, but to date is still in abeyance. However, once implemented an employer or employee who has failed to properly deal with, or raise a grievance, could be financially penalised at any subsequent tribunal proceedings.

If an employer can show that they took the complaint seriously and did everything possible to investigate and resolve the complaint, more often than not the employer would not be found responsible for the actions of their employees.

3
Legislation, Regulation and Health and Safety

Introduction 3.1

Diversity and protection of vulnerable people in the workplace is not new and has been evident in health and safety extending back to the nineteenth century, when legislation was introduced to provide protection to workers. The *Health and Morals of Apprentices Act 1802* was introduced in an attempt to provide some regulation for pauper children in the textile industry. At this time children were exploited as cheap labour. In 1819 the introduction of the *Factory Act 1819* ruled that children under nine years of age were not to work in cotton mills. Furthermore, children working in other factories were restricted to an 11-hour maximum working day. It was not until 1833 when Althrop's *Factory Act* limited the hours that children could work and established four factory inspectors to oversee the Act. By 1842, with the introduction of the *Mines Act 1842*, the employment of women and children under the age of 10 to work underground was prohibited. It still showed the exploitation of the vulnerable in high-risk manual labour work and there was no consideration given to women of childbearing age. Further progress was made in 1901 with the introduction of the minimum working age being set at 12 years. In the same year trade boards were established to set minimum wages in specific industries. It was to be 36 years before the *Factories Act 1937* was introduced, which restricted workers under 16 years of age to a 44-hour working week. But it was not until 1974 that the *Health and Safety at Work, etc Act 1974 (HSWA1974)* provided legal protection to all workplaces. Exposure of vulnerable people to workplace hazards can be identified throughout history and even today there are those who are exposed to risks to their health and safety, albeit in different circumstances to earlier years.

The Health and Safety at Work, etc Act 1974 3.2

The *HSWA1974* emanated from a committee of six, chaired by Lord Robens. He was chairman of the National Coal Board, a post he held from 1961 until 1972. During that time he had taken to writing personal letters to the widows and mothers of those killed in the pits. During his time deaths at work reduced in number, but he considered that there were still too many accidents. This first hand knowledge and experience provided him with the credentials he needed to chair the committee.

The committee determined that there was a need to move away from prescriptive legislation to adopt a self-regulating system, which focused on the need to have better systems of safety organisation, management initiatives and more involvement of the workforce. The emphasis was that with health and safety, good management should be normal management, and that effective management will encompass detailed policy and objectives within an effective organisation. The *HSWA 1974* provides the UK with a framework of legislation placing a duty on employers, the self-employed and employees to conduct their activities in such a way that those who could be affected by the activity of the business are not harmed. This extends to those who are not connected with the activities, such as members of the public. The *HSWA 1974* provides the tool for the Health and Safety Executive (HSE) and local authorities to carry out their work, which seeks to balance their duties of giving advice, inspecting, undertaking enforcement action and investigating complaints and accidents.

Although there is no specific health and safety legislation relating to diverse employees, the *HSWA 1974* and many of the subsequent regulations apply to all groups of workers.

Section 2 of the *HSWA 1974* has a general duty on employers to their employees in that the employer has a duty to ensure, so far as is reasonably practicable, the health, safety and welfare at work of all of his or her employees. The duty extends to include so far as is reasonably practicable:

- the provision and maintenance of plant and systems of work that are safe and without risks to health;

- arrangements for ensuring safety and absence of risks to health in connection with the use, handling, storage and transport of articles and substances;

- the provision of such information, instruction, training and supervision as is necessary to ensure the health and safety at work of employees;

- maintain the place of work under the employer's control in a condition that is safe and without risks to health and the provision and maintenance of means of access to and egress from it that are safe and without such risks; and

- the provision and maintenance of a working environment that is safe, without risks to health and with adequate facilities and arrangements for employees' welfare at work.

Where five or more people are employed, employers have a duty to prepare and revise as often as appropriate a written statement of general policy with respect to the health and safety at work of the employees and the organisation, arrangements for carrying out that policy and to bring the statement and any revision of it to the notice of all of the employees. The policy will need to reflect the needs of diverse employees.

There already exists, within the *HSWA 1974,* offences for individuals including directors, managers, employees and others. A *HSWA 1974, s 36* offence is where there is the fault of another person through vicarious liability while a *s 37* offence is a corporate offence for directors, company secretaries and managers. *SS 7 & 8* are used for individual employees. These four offences include a wide and diverse range of people who owe a duty of care to others with sanctions available when they fail in that duty.

Section 36 Offences due to the actions of another person 3.3

Offences due to the actions of another person, *HSWA 1974, s 36* occurs where the commission of an offence by any person is due to the act or wrongdoing of another person, that other person will be guilty of an offence. That person may be charged and convicted of an offence even though proceedings may not have been taken against the first person.

Section 37 Offences by directors, managers and secretaries 3.4

Offences by directors, managers, secretaries, *HSWA 1974, s 37,* occurs where the offence is committed by a corporate body and is proved to have been committed with the consent or connivance of, or is attributable to any neglect on the part of any director, manager, secretary or other similar officer of the corporate body, or person who was purporting to act in such a capacity. That person, as well as the corporate body, will be guilty of the offence.

Section 7 General duties of employees at work 3.5

Employees can be prosecuted under the *HSWA 1974, s 7* as they have a duty to take reasonable care for the health and safety of themselves and others who may be affected by their acts or omissions at work. This offence covers a wide range of issues, such as a supervisor who supports an employee in undertaking an unsafe act, that supervisor could be prosecuted. An employee who through an act of horseplay or skylarking while at work, causes another to be injured, that employee could be prosecuted.

Section 8 A duty not to interfere with or misuse things provided pursuant to certain provisions 3.6

Anything provided for the protection of health, safety and welfare identified as being required to meet legal requirements must not be interfered with or misused. Any person who breaches this duty could be charged with the offence.

Management of Health and Safety Regulations 1999

3.7

The *Management of Health and Safety at Work Regulations 1992 (MHSWR 1992) (SI 1992/2051)* was implemented as a result of the EC Directive (89/391)(EEC) 'on the introduction of measures to encourage improvements in the safety and health of workers at work'. The original Regulations have had to be amended four times since 1992.

Significant additions are to be found in the *Management of Health and Safety at Work Regulations 1999 (MHSWR 1999) (SI 1999/3242)*, which incorporates the Approved Code of Practice and guidance. It is important to note that the Regulations are law and the approved codes of practice are not, with the following proviso:

> 'Approved Code of Practice and guidance have been approved by the Health and Safety Commission, with the consent of the Secretary of State. They give practical advice on how to comply with the law. If you follow the advice you will be doing enough to comply with the law in respect of those specific matters on which the Code gives advice. You may use alternative methods to those set out in a Code in order to comply with the law. However, a Code has a special legal status. If you are prosecuted for breach of health and safety law, and it is proved that you did not follow the relevant provisions of a Code, you will need to show that you have complied with the law in some other way or a court will find you at fault. The documents also include other, more general guidance not having this special status. The guidance is issued by the Health and Safety Commission. Following the guidance is not compulsory and you are free to take other action. But if you do follow the guidance you will normally be doing enough to comply with the law. Health and safety inspectors seek to secure compliance with the law and may refer to this guidance as illustrating good practice.'

The MHSWR regulations are based upon a 'Safety Management System' and the requirement for undertakings to have in place a health and safety policy statement and the organisation, responsibilities and arrangements for putting that policy into practice. There is also a requirement to identify and manage risks through the process of risk assessments of health and safety hazards present in the workplace. This is not a new concept, legislation governing the use of asbestos, lead and noise all imposed duties on the employer to assess the risks from specific workplace hazards and then identify and implement appropriate measures to reduce the risks. The *MHSWR 1999* extend that requirement to all employers (and the self-employed) and to all workplaces covered by the *HSWA 1974* from the simplest office to the most hazardous process. Other Regulations requiring risk assessments include:

- *Control of Substances Hazardous to Health Regulations 2002 (COSHH 2002) (SI 2002/2677);*

- *Personal Protective Equipment Regulations 1992 (PPE 1992) (SI 1992/2966);*

- *Manual Handling Operations Regulations 1992 (SI 1992/2793);*

- *Health and Safety (Display Screen Equipment) (SI 1992/2792),* amended by the *Health and Safety (Miscellaneous Amendments) Regulations 2002 (SI 2002/2174).*

Fire risk assessments are also required under the *Fire Precautions (Workplace) Regulations 1997 (SI 1997/1840).*

The first step is to recognise the hazards and risks that are found in a particular work environment. It is the responsibility of the employer to identify hazards and ensure that there are arrangements in place to remove or control the risk. While this is important in every workplace, its emphasis becomes far more important where there are diverse and vulnerable employees. The arrangements will require a system to be in place that will include the effective planning, organisation, control, monitoring and review of the preventive and protective measures. In addition to risk assessments, there is a requirement for employers to undertake health surveillance of its employees, which means having regard to the risks to their health that are identified by the assessment. The employer has a duty to have health and safety assistance by appointing one or more competent persons to assist him or her in undertaking measures he or she needs to take to comply. That person will have to be competent and have sufficient training, experience, knowledge and other qualities to enable him or her to properly assist. It is also a duty for the employer to provide procedures to manage serious and imminent danger and to identify and control danger areas. These can include a written emergency action plan and a procedure for identifying foreseeable events that need to be covered and what action needs to be taken. Employers have to provide information to employees that is relevant, understandable and achievable for:

- any risks to their health and safety identified by the assessment; and

- the preventive and protective control measures.

Estimates attribute up to 80% of accidents to human factors, with human error being an element in many major incidents. In the past placing blame for incidents on human error was seen as a viable explanation and beyond the control of an organisation's management. This is not acceptable and the human element needs to be managed in the same way and with the same seriousness as technical and systems failures.

Regulation 3 – Risk Assessment   3.8

Employers are required to make suitable and sufficient assessment of the risks to the health and safety of employees and others who are not in his or her employment but could be affected by the activities of the organisation's undertaking. The assessment will identify the measures needed to comply with the requirements and prohibitions imposed upon the employer by or under the relevant statutory provisions and by *Part II* of the *Fire Precautions (Workplace) Regulations 1997.*

General principles and purpose of risk assessment 3.9

Because of the importance of risk assessment in all organisations, the Health and Safety Executive has produced a guidance leaflet, *5 Steps to Risk Assessment* that contains information designed to help management in understanding what is required and how to set about undertaking risk assessments. The leaflet contains a blank risk assessment form that can be adopted by most businesses and industries, focusing on topics of hazards, who might be harmed, identifying if the risk is adequately controlled and what further action is necessary to control the risks. The requirement for risk assessments in an organisation employing less than five persons is, that the findings do not have to be recorded and where there are more than five employees only significant findings need to be recorded. This is a very important point because if there is an accident the evidence to show that risks have been assessed can only come from risk assessments that have been recorded and held on file. It is strongly recommended that risk assessments are carried out and that they are recorded no matter the size and type of business. An important part of the risk assessment process is that employers have to identify the capabilities and competencies of its employees and provide training, where necessary with the emphasis on health and safety. This can he achieved by providing adequate health and safety training when employees are recruited and when they are exposed to new or increased workplace risks. Assessments for diverse employees may require more detail proportionate to the risk.

All employers should carry out a systematic general examination of the effect of their undertaking, their work activities and the condition of the premises. A risk assessment is carried out to identify the risks to health and safety to any person arising out of, or in connection with, work or the conduct of their undertaking. It should identify how the risks arise and how they impact on those affected. This information is needed to make decisions on how to manage those risks so that the decisions are made in an informed, rational and structured manner, and the action taken is proportionate to the risk.

Suitable and sufficient 3.10

The Regulations state that the risk assessment should be suitable and sufficient 'Suitable and sufficient' is not defined in the Regulations. In practice it means the risk assessment should identify the risks arising from or in connection with work. The level of detail in a risk assessment should be proportionate to the risk. Once the risks are assessed and taken into account, insignificant risks can usually be ignored, as can risks arising from routine activities associated with life in general, unless the work activity compounds or significantly alters those risks. The level of risk arising from the work activity should determine the degree of sophistication of the risk assessment.

An example of a risk assessment could be the routine activity of a competent motorist driving a car to work then exchanging the vehicle for a mini bus which is carrying passengers who are perhaps physically disabled or have learning difficulties and driving without support from caring staff who can manage the passengers. Any assessment will need to be reviewed by the employer if there are reasons to suspect that it is no longer valid or there has been a significant change in the matters to which it relates.

Risks assessment in practice 3.11

There are no fixed rules about how a risk assessment should be carried out, indeed it will depend on the nature of the work or business and the types of hazards and risks. The risk assessment process needs to be practical and take account of the views of employees and their safety representatives who will have practical knowledge to contribute. This consultation with employees will be an important aspect of the assessment process for activities undertaken by diverse employees. It should involve management, whether or not advisers or consultants assist with the detail. Employers should ensure that those involved take all reasonable care in carrying out the risk assessment. Where employees of different employers work in the same workplace, their respective employers may have to co-operate to produce an overall risk assessment.

Identifying the hazards 3.12

First, identify what the hazards are. It will be useful to produce an inventory of what and who has to be assessed. The inventory will not be definitive, but it will be a useful tool in getting started. If there are specific Acts or regulations to be complied with, these may help to identify the hazards. Some regulations require the assessment of particular risks or types of risks. If these particular risks are present, they must all be addressed in the risk assessment process.

Identifying who might be harmed and how 3.13

Identify people who might be harmed by the hazard, including employees, other workers in the workplace and members of the public. Do not forget office staff, night cleaners, maintenance staff, security guards, visitors and members of the public. The employer should identify groups of workers who might be particularly at risk, such as young or inexperienced workers, new and expectant mothers, night workers, homeworkers, loneworkers, disabled staff and other groups already mentioned as being diverse or vulnerable.

Evaluating the risks from the identified hazards 3.14

There is a need to evaluate the risks from the identified hazards. Of course, if there are no hazards, there are no risks. Where risks are already controlled in some way, the effectiveness of those controls needs to be considered when assessing the extent of risk which remains. The diversity of employees will need to be taken into account when identifying the likelihood of harm occurring and the worst possible consequences. There is also a need to observe the actual practice which may differ from the works manual, it is important that the employees concerned or their safety representatives are consulted and record what actually happens in the workplace or during the work activity; and take account of existing preventive or precautionary measures. If existing measures are not adequate, the issue will be to identify what more should be done to reduce risk sufficiently.

Recording   3.15

Employers must record the significant findings, which should represent an effective statement of hazards and risks, which then lead management to take the relevant actions to protect health and safety. The record should be retrievable for use by management in reviews and for safety representatives or other employee representatives and visiting inspectors. Where appropriate, it should be linked to other health and safety records or documents, such as the record of health and safety arrangements and the written health and safety policy statement. It may be possible to combine these documents into one health and safety management document. This record may be in writing or recorded by other means, such as a computer system, so long as it is retrievable and remains retrievable even when, for example, the technology of electronic recording changes. The record will often refer to other documents and records describing procedures and safeguards.

The significant findings should include a record of the preventive and protective measures in place to control the risks, what further action, if any, needs to be taken to reduce risk sufficiently and proof that a suitable and sufficient assessment has been made. In many cases, employers (and the self employed) will also need to record sufficient detail for the assessment itself, so that they can demonstrate, for example, to an inspector or to safety representatives or other employee representatives that they have carried out a suitable and sufficient assessment. This record of the significant findings will also form a basis for a revision of the assessment.

Review and revision   3.16

The regulation requires employers and the self-employed to review and, if necessary, modify their risk assessments, since assessment should not be a once-and-for-all activity.

Assessment under other regulations   3.17

Other regulations also contain requirements for risk assessment specific to the hazards and risks they cover. Where an employer is assessing a work situation or activity for the first time, an assessment is particularly useful to identify where a more detailed risk assessment is needed to fulfil the requirements of other regulations.

Health surveillance   3.18

Health surveillance has to be provided by the employer having regard to the risks to the health and safety of their employees which are identified by risk assessment. The risk assessment will identify when health surveillance is required by specific health and safety regulations, such as *COSHH 2000*. Health surveillance should also be introduced where the assessment shows that there is an identifiable disease or adverse health condition related to the work concerned and that there are valid techniques available to detect indications of the disease or condition. It should identify if there is a reasonable likelihood that the disease or condition may occur under the particular conditions of work and that surveillance is likely to further the protection of the health and safety of the employees to be covered.

Employees identified as being at risk of ill health should be given an explanation of, and an opportunity to comment on, the nature and proposed frequency of such health surveillance procedures and should have access to an appropriately qualified practitioner for advice on surveillance. A competent person acting within the limits of their training and experience should determine the type and frequency of health surveillance.

The objective of health surveillance should be to detect adverse health effects at an early stage enabling further harm to be prevented. The results of health surveillance can provide a means of checking the effectiveness of control measures, providing feedback on the accuracy of the risk assessment and identifying and protecting individuals at increased risk because of the nature of their work.

Health and safety assistance   3.19

Every employer is required to appoint one or more competent persons to assist in complying with the requirements and prohibitions laid down by relevant statutory legislation.

Employers should look to appoint one or more of their employees with the necessary competence to provide the health and safety assistance required. If there is no relevant competent employee in the organisation, the employer may engage the services of an external consultancy. Professional bodies hold registers of safety practitioners. In some circumstances a combination of internal and external advisors might be appropriate, recognising the limitations of the internal competence. Some regulations contain specific requirements for obtaining advice from competent people to assist in complying with legal duties.

Employers who appoint occupational health practitioners to advise them of the effects of work on employee health or to carry out certain procedures, for example health surveillance, should first check that such providers can offer evidence of a sufficient level of expertise or training in occupational health. Similar registers of competent health practitioners are maintained professional bodies.

The appointment of health and safety advisers does not absolve the employer from responsibilities for health and safety under the *HSWA 1974* and other relevant statutory provisions and under *Part II* of the Fire Regulations. It can only give added assurance that these responsibilities will be discharged adequately. Where external services are employed, they will usually be appointed in an advisory capacity only.

Competence does not necessarily depend on the possession of particular skills or qualifications. Simple situations may require only an understanding of relevant current best practice, an awareness of the limitations of one's own experience and knowledge and the willingness and ability to supplement experience and knowledge, when necessary, by obtaining external help and advice.

More complicated situations will require the competent assistant to have a higher level of knowledge and experience. More complex or highly technical situations will call for specific applied knowledge and skills which can be offered by appropriately qualified specialists. Employers are advised to check the appropriate health and safety qualifications (some of which may be competence-based and/or industry specific) or membership of a professional body or similar organisation. They should always check the level of membership in an appropriate part of health and safety to satisfy themselves that the assistant they appoint has a sufficiently high level of competence.

Information for employees   3.20

Employers must provide their employees with information on the risks to their health and safety identified by the assessments and the preventive and protective measures.

Prior to employing a child, employers must provide a parent of the child with information on the key findings of the risk assessment and the control measures taken before the child begins work. (A child is considered to be under the statutory school leaving age.) This information can be provided in any appropriate form, including verbally or directly to the parents or guardians or, in the case of work experience, via an organisation, such as the school, the work experience agency or, if agreed with the parents, via the child, as long as this is considered a reliable method.

The risk assessment process helps to identify information which has to be provided to employees under specific regulations, as well as information relevant to risks to employees' health and safety. Employees will also need to be given information to help them ensure their own and others' health and safety. The information provided should be pitched appropriately, given the level of training, knowledge and experience of the employee. It should be provided in a form which takes account of any language difficulties or other diversity. Information can be provided in whatever form is most suitable in the circumstances, as long as everyone can understand it. For employees with little or no understanding of English, or who cannot read English, employers may need to make special arrangements. These could include providing translation, using interpreters or replacing written notices with clearly understood symbols or diagrams.

Capabilities and training 3.21

The employer, when delegating tasks to employees, must take into account the employees' capabilities as regards health and safety and ensure that the demands of the job do not exceed the employees' ability to carry out the work. Employers should also take account of the employee's training, knowledge and experience. The employer must provide health and safety training when employees are recruited and if they are exposed to new or increased risks.

Managers should be aware of relevant legislation and should be competent to manage health and safety effectively. Employers should review their employees' capabilities to carry out their work, as necessary. If additional training, including refresher training, is needed it should be provided. Training needs to be repeated periodically where appropriate and training needs to take place during working hours.

Employees' duties 3.22

Employees' duties under *section 7* of the *HSWA 1974* includes co-operating with their employer to enable the employer to comply with their statutory duties for health and safety. Under these regulations, employers, or those they appoint to assist them with health and safety matters, need to be informed without delay of any work situation which might present a serious and imminent danger. Employees are required to use any equipment, machinery, vehicles and dangerous substances in a manner consistent with training, written and/or verbal instructions.

Employees have a duty to inform the employer or fellow workers of any work situation which a person with the employee's training and instruction would reasonably consider represented a serious and immediate danger to health and safety and of any matter which a person with the employee's training and instruction would reasonably consider represented a shortcoming in the employer's protection arrangements for health and safety. It is important to note that the duties placed on employees do not reduce the responsibility of the employer to comply with duties under the *HSWA 1974* and the other relevant statutory provisions. In particular, employers need to ensure that employees receive adequate instruction and training to enable them to comply with their duties.

Workplace disability discrimination 3.23

When employers are filling vacancies, promoting and selecting people for jobs they have to be aware of the requirements of the *Disability Discrimination Act 1995*

(DDA 1995), which will have an impact on the business because people with a disability have to be integrated into the business to allow them to do their work. This means that it is unlawful for an employer to discriminate against a disabled person. There are three specific points to be considered:

- in the arrangements made for determining to whom should be offered employment;
- in the terms on which employment is offered; or
- by refusing to offer, or deliberately not offering, employment.

Further, it is unlawful for employers to discriminate against a disabled person:

- in the terms and conditions of employment;
- in opportunities for promotion, transfers, training or any other benefit; and
- by dismissing him or her or subjecting him or her to any detriment due to their disability.

The main question is to determine what is discrimination? The basic answer is that a person discriminates against a disabled person if:

- for a reason which relates to the person's disability, the employer treats him or her less favourably than the employer would treat others to whom that reason does not apply; and
- the employer cannot show that the treatment is justified.

Further, it can also be seen as discrimination if an employer fails to make reasonable adjustments to the premises or disabled person's working conditions and if the employer cannot show that the failure to comply with the legal requirements is justified. In these circumstances the burden of proof is on the employer to show that the less favourable treatment is justified, but the reason must relate to the circumstances of the particular case and not be trivial. The employer needs to remember that, depending on the circumstances, less favourable treatment may be justified if:

- the disabled person is not suitable for employment;
- the disabled person is less suitable for employment than another person and that other person is given the job;
- the nature of the disabled person's disability significantly impedes the performance of any of his or her duties;
- in the case of training, the nature of the disabled person's disability would significantly reduce the value of the training; and
- it would be unsafe for the disabled person to attempt the work.

An important factor is that each individual circumstance must be taken into account and it should not be assumed that, for example, all blind people are unable to type or use computers. Another important factor is that a person who is off work sick because of a disability cannot be dismissed solely for that reason if their level of absenteeism is not substantially less than other employees. Employers need to be aware that an overall concern for health and safety requirements should not over-ride the need to consider the individual circumstances of a disabled person, however, the employer cannot opt out of health and safety requirements. An assessment of the risks should be made for each individual case.

The employer has a duty to make adjustments so that any arrangements made or any physical feature of premises occupied for the purpose of work do not place the disabled person at a substantial disadvantage in comparison with persons who are not disabled. It will be the duty of the employer to take such steps that are reasonable in all the circumstances for him or her to take in order to prevent the arrangement or feature having that effect.

The employer will have to take a proactive approach to cater for those with disabilities and focus on issues such as:

- making practical adjustment to premises;
- allocating, if appropriate, some of the disabled person's duties to another person;
- transferring them to fill an existing vacancy if suitable and practicable;
- allowing him or her to be absent during working hours for rehabilitation, assessment or treatment;
- giving the person training so as to make best use of their abilities;
- acquiring or modifying equipment to meet specific needs;
- modifying instructions or reference manuals to encompass disabled persons; and
- providing appropriate supervision.

It is for the employer to determine if it is reasonable to take any particular actions and alterations, and that will depend on:

- the extent to which taking the action would prevent discrimination;
- the extent to which it is practicable for the employer to take action; and
- the financial and other costs which the employer, in taking the action, would incur and the extent to which it would disrupt any of his or her activities.

The requirement of an employer to make 'reasonable adjustments' does not require an employer to make the best adjustment possible, nor to adapt workplaces to make them accessible in anticipation that a disabled person may be employed at some future time. Further, an employer will not be expected to alter the job or provide items which a disabled person could reasonably be expected to have already for their personal use.

Even when a disabled person has been taken into employment, they can be dismissed on health or safety grounds, but that places a considerable burden on the employer to show that a full appraisal of all the facts has been made and, in particular, that all possible suitable alternative employment options were explored before contemplating dismissal. It is important that the employers must familiarise themselves with the job, the disability and the hazard, and must make extra efforts to accommodate a disabled person.

For the employer, health and safety matters in the workplace involving a disabled person will always highlight special problems. Examples could be where a deaf person will not be able to hear fire alarms or warning cries, a blind person will not find their way to escape routes and a physically disabled person will not be able to react with the necessary speed to emergency situations, all of whom will require assistance. The duties owed by an employer to employees are personal to each employee and so special attention will need to be applied to the situation and systems be put in place to cater for the particular disabilities of the employees. The essential point is that safety factors will override all other considerations, apart from the duty of the employer to act reasonably when handling employees who have any type of disability. Usually this will mean taking medical advice and identifying suitable employment, as well as personal protective equipment.

An important case, *Farmiloe v Lane Group Plc [2004] All ER (D) 08 (Mar)*, that addresses many of the factors discussed above highlights how health and safety legislation can override both employment and disability law. This case involved an individual who was unable to wear appropriate personal protective equipment (PPE) determined necessary by the company's risk assessment process. The employer allowed the employee to wear his own footwear and not PPE because of his foot condition. The local authority's environmental health officer insisted that all employees were to wear PPE recognised by the risk assessment. The company sought medical advice and reviewed the possibility of having special protective footwear manufactured but were unable to find an appropriate resolution. They also faced an additional difficulty because they were unable to offer alternative employment that did not require the use of personal protective footwear and, as a result, had to terminate the employment of the individual.

In 1996, following a risk assessment, Lane Group Plc adopted a policy that all persons working in their warehouse were required to wear safety footwear. Due to his medical condition an exception was made for Mr Farmiloe and he was permitted to wear his own sturdy, but soft-leather, Clark's shoes. Mr Farmiloe had for a number of years suffered from psoriasis. One effect of that condition was that he was limited in the type of footwear which was suitable for him and ordinary protective working boots exacerbated the condition on his feet.

On 27 August 2001 Mr Farmiloe suffered an accident at work when he was hit on the back by a gate chain and on 11 October 2001 Christine Bartlett, a senior health and safety officer with North Somerset Council, carried out a routine health and safety investigation at Lane Group Plc premises. During that visit, having reviewed the accident reports, including that relating to Mr Farmiloe, Ms

Bartlett learned that he did not wear either protective footwear or headwear in the warehouse due to his skin condition. On being informed that an exception had been made in his case Ms Bartlett told Lane Group Plc's safety manager, Stuart McFarlane, that an exception could not be made. In her words: 'You cannot opt out of health and safety.'

As a result of Ms Bartlett's visit, Mr McFarlane arranged a meeting with Mr Farmiloe. During the meeting it was explained that the company had decided, based upon information received from the authorities, that he must wear protective footwear in the warehouse, where he worked mainly as a forklift truck driver, otherwise he could not continue working in the area. On the recommendation of Ms Bartlett, the company was to conduct a medical assessment of Mr Farmiloe to ensure that appropriate footwear could be provided so as to comply with the company's health and safety policy, whilst not exacerbating his medical condition. In the meantime it was decided to suspend Mr Farmiloe on full pay pending an examination by the company's occupational health expert.

Mr Farmiloe was examined and, as a result, advised that the steel toecap on protective footwear tended to press on Mr Farmiloe's toes, causing pain, and he required slip on shoes so that he could slip them off in order to allow fresh air to ventilate his feet. It was concluded that he required protective shoes made of sufficiently thin fabric to keep his feet free from sweating. If this did not solve the problem of complying with the need to wear protective footwear then alternative employment had to be considered for Mr Farmiloe in areas where protective footwear was not required.

The company made a number of attempts to obtain suitable protective footwear for Mr Farmiloe so that he could comply with their safety policy. None of the standard footwear available on the market was suitable for his condition and the only possibility appeared to be for footwear to be designed specifically for his needs. A firm, Bolton Bros, agreed to produce a pair of shoes costing £350. However, following discussions between Mr Farmiloe and the medical advisor it was agreed that the shoes would not work. In these circumstances the company did not order the shoes. After reviewing the situation it was decided that no suitable alternative position was available for Mr Farmiloe within the organisation where he would not be required to wear PPE. Attempts to find suitable footwear were exhausted and so the company had no option but to dismiss Mr Farmiloe, which was done by way of a letter.

Mr Farmiloe appealed against his dismissal on two counts, firstly that the company should make adjustments to its stringent health and safety policy and secondly that the company should approach Ms Bartlett to obtain an exception in special cases such as that of Mr Farmiloe. The company did communicate with Ms Bartlett but her position was uncompromising and she informed the company that if they did not have a policy requiring the wearing of PPE in the warehouse (which they did) then North Somerset council would carry out an inspection. If they determined there was a risk of damage to feet associated with manual handling and mechanical handling in the warehouse they could serve a notice requiring that appropriate PPE be worn. If an employee then refused to wear PPE he or she could be guilty of an offence. There were no provisions under health and safety regulations to allow an employee to opt out unless the risk of injury could be controlled by equally effective means (which was not applicable in this case). Further, an employer cannot opt out of the obligation to protect the safety of employees by agreeing with them to opt out of wearing PPE and that an employee's medical condition cannot exclude the use of PPE and if it is not worn the individual cannot work in the relevant area.

The company had to abide by the requirements of health and safety legislation, in particular *section 33(1)* of the *HSWA 1974*, which makes it a criminal offence for a person to contravene any health and safety regulations and to contravene any requirement or prohibition imposed by an improvement or prohibition notice. If there is a failure to comply there are sanctions that can be imposed which include a fine and, on indictment, imprisonment for up to two years.

The *Personal Protective Equipment Regulations 1992 (PPE 1992), regulation 4* states:

(1) Every employer shall ensure that suitable personal protective equipment is provided to his employees who may be exposed to a risk to their health or safety while at work except where and to the extent that such risk has been adequately controlled by other means which are equal or more effective.

(3) Without prejudice to the generality of paragraphs (1) personal protective equipment shall not be suitable unless:

  (a) it is appropriate for the risk or risks involved and the conditions at the place where exposure to the risk may occur;
  (b) it takes account of ergonomic requirements and the state of health of the person or persons who may wear it;
  (c) it is capable of fitting the wearer correctly, if necessary, after adjustments within the range for which it is designed;
  (d) so far as is practicable, it is effective to prevent or adequately control the risk or risks involved without increasing overall risk.'

There is the question in this case as to whether Mr Farmiloe was a disabled person within the meaning of *s 1* of the *DDA 1995* and that issue was resolved in favour of Mr Farmiloe by a differently constituted Employment Tribunal through a decision following a Preliminary Hearing. The relevant medical condition was psoriasis and there has been no appeal against that finding.

Mr Farmiloe complained that the company had unlawfully discriminated against him by:

• failing to make reasonable adjustments to the company's health and safety policy to avoid the disadvantage caused to the applicant by him not being able to wear protective footwear or footwear of a particular specification;

- failing to make reasonable adjustments to the protective footwear by supplying or arranging for the supply of the clog footwear from Bolton Bros; and

- dismissing him for a reason relating to his disability and confirming that dismissal on appeal.

The Employment Tribunal had found that the company was in breach of their duty under *s 5(2)* of the *DDA 1995*. They declined, in these circumstances, to consider the separate issue raised under *s 5(1)*, having made all necessary findings of fact to determine that question. Section 5(1) provides:

'For the purposes of this Part, an employer discriminates against a disabled person if–

(a) for a reason which relates to the disabled person's disability he treats him less favorably than he treats or would treat others to whom that reason does not or would not apply; and
(b) he cannot show that the treatment in question is justified.'

Section 5(2) provides:

'For the purposes of this Part, an employer also discriminates against a disabled person if–

(a) he fails to comply with a section 6 duty imposed on him in relation to the disabled person; and
(b) he cannot show that his failure to comply with that duty is justified.

The appeal found that the complaint of disability discrimination failed and was dismissed and formally remit the complaint of unfair dismissal to a fresh Employment Tribunal for a new hearing, bearing in mind that the disability discrimination complaint was regarded as having been seriously undermined.

The appeal court dismissed Mr Farmiloe's complaint of disability discrimination against the company and confirmed that North Somerset Council cannot be liable to Mr Farmiloe and the Council was dismissed from the proceedings. The judgment found that Ms Bartlett acted properly throughout and in accordance with the statutory duty under the *HSWA 1974*. It was highlighted that as Ms Bartlett had stated 'You cannot opt out of health and safety' it makes it clear that health and safety legislation takes precedence over the protection against disability discrimination, provided that all reasonable steps have been taken to accommodate the particular needs of the individual worker, as they had been in this case.

Safe system of work   3.24

The term *safe system of work* is broad based and includes the precautions that have to be made to account for the safety of the workers at all times, this includes having sufficient persons to do the job. These persons must be competent and capable of undertaking the work tasks. In addition, the term extends to those not employed who have to be safeguarded against harm caused by the activities of the undertaking. The definition of a *safe system of work* is most effectively dealt with by the examination of cases that have progressed through the appeals system. While it is not definitive, it does provide the details of what the management failed to do in ensuring the health and safety of the employee and the legal determination.

A leading case for *safe systems of work* that explores this concept is that of the Appeal to the House of Lords in 1952 of *General Cleaning Contractors Ltd v Christmas [1952] 2 All ER 1110.* This case involved a lone worker, a window cleaner, who was employed by General Cleaning Contractors Ltd to clean the outside of the windows of a club. This was a job with hazards and, therefore, a risk assessment would identify a number of precautionary measures that the employer should have taken. The facts of the incident were that there were no fittings to which he could attach a safety belt so he stood on the sill of the window, a method commonly used by his colleagues. A defective sash window fell on his hand, causing him to let go and fall. He was awarded damages against both the employer and the occupier of the premises. However, the decision against the occupier was reversed on appeal because the defective window was not an *unusual danger* of which the occupier was bound to warn the window cleaner.

The employer appealed to the House of Lords. The House of Lords ruled that where the practice of ignoring an obvious danger had developed, it was not reasonable to expect the individual employee to take the initiative in devising a system of work against the danger. This is regardless of the fact that other systems of work were not practical. General Cleaning Contractors Ltd were still obliged to consider the situation, to take reasonable steps to provide a system that would be reasonably safe having regard to the dangers inherent in the operation and to ensure that its employees were instructed on how to prevent accidents in their work, including providing the implements. The employer had not done so and had not discharged its duty to the employee and, therefore, the appeal was dismissed.

This case explains the relationship between the duty of care owed by employers and the obligations on workmen to take reasonable care for their own safety. It is the responsibility of the employer to take the initiative in devising and using safety precautions and the workman is not expected to do so himself. This is very important where the employee may not understand the need for safety precautions. If a man is doing work as specified and expected by his employer and there has been a failure to take adequate safety measures, then the blame should not rest on the man. The main issue is whether the employer has taken responsibility with reasonable care to provide a safe system of work for the employees. Where a practice of ignoring an obvious danger has developed then it is not the workman's responsibility to devise a system to overcome it. The decision as to what is reasonable the employer must take into account the conduct and long established practices in the trade. In the case of a window cleaner, he or she will work outside of the confines of the employer's premises and direct control and there is a reliance on the individual to follow procedures and carry out the work safely. This would be good in an ideal world but in the real world there is a great deal of trust imposed on the individual to get it right.

Lord Oaksey highlighted the key issues in the case and stated:

'It is the duty of an employer to give such general safety instructions as a reasonably careful employer who has considered the problem presented by the work would give his workmen.'

He continued to state:

'It is well known to employers ... that their workpeople are very frequently, if not habitually, careless about risks which their work may involve. It is for that very reason that the common law demands that employers should take reasonable care to lay down a reasonably safe system of work. Employers are not exempted from this duty by the fact that their men are experienced and might, if they were in the position of an employer, be able to lay down a reasonably safe system of work themselves. Workmen are not in a position of employers. Their duties are not performed in the calm atmosphere of a boardroom with the advice of experts. They have to make their decisions on narrow sills and other places of danger and in circumstances where dangers are obscured by repetition.'

Lord Reid said in the same case:

'Where the practice of ignoring an obvious danger has grown up I do not think that it is reasonable to expect an individual workman to take the initiative in devising and using precautions. It is the duty of the employer to consider the situation, to devise a suitable system, to instruct his men what they must do and to supply any implements that may be required.'

The general consensus of the legal ruling and commentators regards the definition of what is a safe system of work is that it is broad and open to interpretation and in the event of an accident it will be a matter of fact and for the Judiciary to determine. However, it does place the duty for the development of a safe system of work with the employer and places the duty on the employer to inform the employees of what is required. Where there are members of staff who have some form of impediment, literacy problems or a poor understanding of English then the employer must take those factors into account and ensure that there is a real understanding of what is required.

Existing disability   3.25

Vulnerable employees may not always be apparent and employers need to look at individuals beyond the obvious physical impediments and the type of work they are required to undertake and hazards that could affect them. An important case that highlights the need for proactive risk assessment involved an employee who had a partial disability and because of a failure in the management of health and safety to identify potential harm outside of what may be expected the employee was completely disabled.

The case was the House of Lords appeal in 1950 of *Paris v Stepney Borough Council [1951] AC 367* which involved a one-eyed garage worker who became completely blind after a chip of metal entered his good eye. It was not usual practice for Stepney Borough Council to provide protective goggles to its employees working in garages on the maintenance and repair of vehicles, so no protective equipment had been given to Mr Paris. After the accident Mr Paris claimed damages from his employer, alleging negligence. The claim was successful in the High Court but the Court of Appeal reversed the decision. Mr Paris then appealed to the House of Lords who held that where an employer is aware that an employee has a disability which although does not increase the risk of an accident occurring but does increase the risk of serious injury, special precautions should be taken if the employer is to fulfill its duty to take reasonable care for the safety of its employee. The condition of Mr Paris' eyes, the employer's knowledge of his condition, the likelihood of an accident occurring and the gravity of the consequences should an accident occur were all to be considered in determining whether the employer took reasonable steps to protect its employee's safety. It was determined that Stepney Borough Council owed a special duty of care to Mr Paris and had been negligent in failing to supply goggles to him, even though such equipment was not given to other employees.

In this case Lord Morton stated:

> 'There are occupations in which the possibility of an accident occurring to a workman is extremely remote, while there are other occupations in which there is a constant risk of accident. Similarly, there are occupations in which if an accident occurs, it is likely to be of trivial nature, whilst there are other occupations in which [...] the result [...] may well be fatal [...] there has to be in each case a gradually ascending scale between the two extremes [...] the more serious the damage which will happen if an accident occurs, the more thorough are the precautions which an employer must take.'

An individual can be assigned to what could be described as requiring a basic level of competence, but the employer has to evaluate the work task against the person who is going to do it. An employee may have little or no perception as to any hazards and the risks that they face. If the employee is not instructed in a way that he or she understands, both in the carrying out the work tasks and the need for personal protective equipment, then the employer could be exposing that employee to unnecessary risks of harm. The reality is that employers and safety advisors have to assume that there is little understanding of what is safe practice and put in place effective measures to provide a safe system of work. Equally important is that once a system is established, the employee understands what is required and the implications of not complying and the employer has to ensure that the procedures are followed.

Duty of care 3.26

The care of young persons is paramount and failure to manage any activity can have serious consequences, none more so than the case of Paul Ellis. The prosecution of Paul Ellis, a teacher from Fleetwood High School, for manslaughter was brought by the Crown Prosecution Service, following the death of Max Palmer, a 10-year-old boy, in May 2002. Max was with his mother, who was an educational assistant helping with a trip from the school to the Lake District organised by Paul Ellis. Mr Ellis led an outdoor activity. It was alleged that he had not taken reasonable care of other people, including Mrs Palmer and a pupil from the school who were airlifted to hospital suffering from hypothermia. Mr Ellis was also charged under *s* 7 of the *HSWA 1974*. He pleaded guilty to the manslaughter of Max Palmer and was jailed for 12 months.

The incident occurred while Ellis was taking a group from Fleetwood High School on an adventure weekend to the Lake District. Max was swept to his death in a river. The weather that weekend was poor, with rain and low temperatures which had 'curtailed much of the planned activity'. Ellis was keen to do some form of activity to prevent the trip being a 'complete washout'. Ellis wanted the party to jump into a pool from a height. A 13-year-old pupil jumped first and found it so cold he struggled to move. Max followed and jumped into the water and was immediately seen to be in difficulty. Ellis jumped into the water to try and rescue the boy but he was unable to help due to the extreme cold. Mrs Palmer then jumped into the pool to attempt to rescue her son. She got hold of Max and managed to hold his head above water but found the current too strong to swim with him. Struggling in the cold water she managed to get him to the side of the pool and keep him above the water. Unable to maintain her hold, Max's body then slipped out of her grasp and back into the water, from where he was pulled out of the pond and attempts were made to resuscitate him.

The HSE takes the view that outdoor adventure trips are of great value in developing young people and offers an excellent opportunity for risk education. The vast majority of such activities take place without serious incident. It is essential that the activities are planned properly, carried out safely and involves competent people. Teachers must put the safety of their pupils at the top of their agenda and follow good practice. Information is available through the Department for Education and Skills and the Health and Safety Commission, who have produced comprehensive guidance for organisations that conduct adventure activities. The guidance will assist schools in setting up systems and procedures that better support teachers and others leading adventure trips.

Employment agency 3.27

Staff who are engaged through an employment office often have no prior knowledge of what to expect or what is expected of them. The duty falls on the employer to ensure the health, safety and welfare of such employees. This did not happen in the case of Simon Jones, who was a 24-year-old Sussex university student, who died on his first day at work on 24 April 1998 whilst employed by

Euromin Limited at Shoreham Docks. On arrival at the docks, Simon was directed to work unloading a cargo of bagged stones from inside the hold of a vessel. He was given no training. The cargo was to be lifted out of the hold by a crane owned and operated by Euromin limited. Jones was sent as casual labour to a job at the docks by an employment agency. He was tasked with attaching bags of cobblestones to hooks which had been welded to the inside of the open grab. The conventional method would have been to attach a hook to the crane but employees stated that the company was reluctant to change the crane from grab to hook and back again because it cost time and money. Jones received only a few minutes training and there was no briefing on health and safety.

A critical factor was that the banksman was Polish and did not speak English, a fact known by the managing director. Two different attachments were supplied by the crane manufacturer, although only one could be attached to the crane at any one time: one was 'the grab' which was used to lift loose aggregates and the other a lifting 'hook' with chains which was used to lift objects. The managing director had, however, personally ordered hooks to be welded to the column inside the grab in order to avoid the delay in changing the attachments. Although the safety instruction of the crane manufacturer warned that it was not safe for anyone to be within the work area of the grab, the new welding arrangement meant that any worker doing Simon's work would have to put his head close to the grab. On this occasion the jaws of the grab closed around Simon's neck killing him. The trial of Euromin Ltd and Richard Martell was held at the Old Bailey and on 29 November 2001 the company was found guilty of two breaches of the *HSWA 1974*. The company was ordered to pay fines of £50,000 and costs of £20,000. Richard Mantell was cleared of manslaughter.

Provision and use of personal protective equipment

3.28

Another case of an employee following instructions but given no support or protective equipment was the case of Jackson Transport (Ossett) Limited who was convicted in 1996 of corporate manslaughter and fined £22,000. Its director, Alan Jackson, was convicted of the individual manslaughter of one of his employees and jailed for 12 months and fined £1,500. The case centered on 21-year-old James Hodgson, an employee of the company who died less than an hour after being splashed with a deadly chemical while cleaning the inside of a chemical tanker at Jackson Transport's base in West Ossett, Yorkshire. Mr Hodgson was carrying out the dangerous cleaning job protected only by a pair of overalls and a baseball cap. Special suits for protection against chemical risks were only provided to the tanker drivers of the vehicles. The protective suits that were available on the company's premises were in poor condition and there were no hats, visors or goggles.

The trial judge, Mr Gerald Coles QC, determined that if Alan Jackson did address the subject of safety clothing he failed to do so adequately. The fact that the deceased was not concerned to wear safety clothing made it all the more important that he should have made sure that he not only had it, but that he also wore it. This is an important issue in that not only does the employer have a duty to provide adequate and suitable personal protective equipment, he or she has to ensure that it is used and used correctly. In this case the judge found that Jackson was totally indifferent to the statutory duties in that he failed to address the issues of a system of safety and that he failed to take precautions against inevitable disasters. The failure to provide a safe system of work was only the last in a long catalogue of deficiencies.

In summary, there was a lack of PPE, there were no trained first aiders nor was there first aid equipment provided by the company. There were no procedures to ensure safe entry to the tank or rescue equipment for use in an emergency. It was ironic that the failings were made worse in that the company had drawn up a manual detailing safe methods of cleaning out tankers. That manual had been produced six years before Hodgson's death and had been put in a drawer and forgotten, however the management had identified the hazards and associated risks and failed to implement a safe system of work.

Young person 3.29

Failure to supervise and take account of an employee's inexperience is highlighted in the case of Adrian Rickwood, who at 17 years of age was working at Jack Moody Limited's waste recycling plant in Shareshill, Staffordshire, when he was involved in an accident on the 14 February 2003. Rickwood was working on the waste recycling line operating a hard-core screener that separates bricks and rubble from soil. The system operates by a conveyor that transports soil after it has been separated from the rubble so that the soil can be fine sifted and packed for sale. On the day of the accident, the conveyor belt had moved out of alignment because of a build-up of soil on the roller that powers the belt. Rickwood decided to remove the soil using a shovel but this was too big to reach the roller so he decided to use his hands instead and it was while he was attempting to clear the roller, which was still running, that his left arm was dragged into the in-running nip, the area where the belt and the roller meet. Although the conveyor belt slipped off the roller, which may have prevented his arm from being severed, it continued to operate, trapping Rickwood's arm and crushing his chest against the frame of the conveyor. He was trapped but was able to gain the attention of a colleague working nearby who turned the machine off and released him. He suffered bruising to his arm and chest as a result of the incident.

Although the company had carried out a risk assessment for the operation of the hard-core screener, it was inadequate and failed to identify that there was a risk of workers being trapped in the conveyor's unguarded end rollers. Had a suitable risk assessment been undertaken then it would have identified that the hard core screener needed to be fitted with suitable protective guards to prevent employees from coming into contact with the conveyor's in-running nip areas. An important factor was that the company failed to take into account the relative inexperience of young workers at the site.

Child at work   3.30

The case of Jamie Bryant is an example of bad management and a disregard of the individual's experience and capabilities, which had a serious outcome. Jamie Bryant was 13 years of age when he was working on a casual basis during the school holidays at D Davies and Company's egg packing plant in Shawbury, Shropshire, when an accident occurred on 27 August 2002. Bryant had lied about his age to obtain a job at the plant, which was picking eggs from a moving conveyor belt and packing them into boxes. However, as the belt restarted following a routine break in the picking cycle, Bryant's left forefinger became caught between a moving guide wheel and chain situated under the conveyor belt. The top half of his injured finger was later amputated in hospital and he now has problems playing school sports, riding his bike and using computers.

A partner in the company failed to ensure that suitable protective guarding was installed on the conveyor to prevent workers coming into contact with its moving parts. Further, a warning alarm fitted to the conveyor belt which is designed to alert workers when the unit is about to start operating was not loud enough to be heard by all workers in the packing area. The partner also failed to carry out an adequate risk assessment covering the employment of school age children at the site. Although the business policy was that all casual workers should be aged 14 or over, Bryant had put down a false birth date on his application form to mislead managers at the site into thinking he was 14. The HSE's investigation into the incident also found that there were a number of other school age children working at the site who were aged 13. The partners should have established a system of work for monitoring and supervising young workers to ensure that they were physically capable of carrying out the work safely. They should also have provided the parents of children working at the site with information on the type of work their children would be carrying out and the measures in place to ensure their safety.

The HSE considers that young persons below the age of 18 are at risk in the workplace because of their inexperience and lack of risk awareness. They may also be physically or mentally immature. This means that employers who intend to employ school age children in workplaces should carry out a young person's risk assessment and inform parents what the risks are and what preventative measures are in place.

4
Managing the Employment Aspects of Diverse Employees

Introduction 4.1

There are numerous issues involved in managing diverse employees. CHAPTER 2 and CHAPTER 3 set out the regulations that HR managers need to be aware of in regard to working with diversity. The intention of this chapter is to assist HR managers and officers in dealing with the day to day issues that arise and how, as a whole, the workforce can be managed to the best advantage of both employer and employee. Before doing so it is important to establish what the key responsibilities of a HR manager are.

What are the responsibilities of the HR manager? 4.2

The key responsibility of the HR manager is to strike and maintain a delicate balance between the needs of the employer and those of the employee. On the one hand, they must ensure that they function productively in the economic context of the business in which they work, ensuring that their key areas of impact, such as absence and labour turnover, are managed effectively so that that negative costs are minimised. On the other hand, the HR manager must weigh their obligation to the welfare of the workforce and afford them due protection where necessary. In summary, the HR manager must be fair and considerate to all employees while maintaining a business perspective.

This said, as the workforce grows ever more diverse, its needs grow greater, with more care and consideration necessary to ensure that all members of the workforce are treated in a fair and consistent manner and with reference to a clear equality and diversity policy. Therefore, areas where the HR manager needs particular depth of understanding to manage this diverse workforce would include:

- a broad based knowledge of employment law;

- a good understanding of the existing policies and procedures of their organisation;

- working methods which cover all aspects of employment, ensuring no discrimination occurs;

- a system in place to identify and address any employee relations concerns; and

- experience in negotiation, in order to ensure best practice amongst peers and management teams in general.

The majority of these points, if not already in place, can usually be covered by either amending existing policies and procedures and working practices or by introducing simple checklists to use, for example, when conducting return to work interviews after a sickness absence. Therefore, to assist in fulfilling the above responsibilities, the following will be discussed in this chapter:

- the employer's duty of care;

- how to set up a HR policy for managing diverse employees;

- recruitment guidelines and checklist to ensure no discrimination occurs during selection;

- communications best practice, both internal and external;

- best practice management of sickness absence;

- management of rehabilitation; and

- best practice management of grievance, disciplinary and capability procedures.

Employer's Duty of Care 4.3

The employer has a duty of care to all of its employees. There are a number of duties, which the employer must adhere to, including the duty to pay wages, provide work and provide the facilities for further development. More important are the employer's duties to:

- exercise care;

- treat the employee with respect;

- deal promptly and properly with grievances;

- provide a reasonably suitable working environment; and

- provide a fair and reasonable reference on request.

An employer has a general duty of care to its employees in relation to health and safety, which is to provide a safe place of work, a safe system of work and competent colleagues. These are duties which arise under the law of negligence. This means that a failure by the employer in his or her duty to take care could result in a claim for damages by an employee who has suffered an injury due to the employer's failure to comply with this duty. This failure could arise by reason of the employer's flagrant disregard of the regulations or by a fellow employee's incompetence or tomfoolery.

Where an employee undertakes a role for an employer which could be deemed hazardous, for whatever reason, the employer must ensure that there are reasonable precautions in place. For example, where an employee works through the night in a 24-hour petrol station, it is reasonable to assume that the employee might be at risk of attack or injury, if working alone.

What are considered to be reasonable precautions depends on the level of risk an employee is exposed to and the likelihood of them suffering physical or mental harm. The size of the organisation should also be considered. In *Dutton & Clark Ltd v Daly [1985] ICR 780* the employee was a cashier in a bank. She claimed that the employer's safety precautions were insufficient to protect her from harm. During her employment the bank had suffered two armed robberies. However, by the time of the second, which resulted in the cashier resigning and claiming constructive dismissal, the bank had installed steel plating from floor to counter, a glass screen above the counter and panic alarms at each position. The bank also made enquiries into the installation of bullet-proof glass. However, the costs outweighed the benefits as it would only have protected against shotgun pellets and the profit margin of the branch was not very high. The Tribunal felt that there was very little else that the employer could have done and, therefore, the claim was dismissed.

Much of this duty will be governed by health and safety regulations, as discussed in **CHAPTER FIVE**. However, it is important to be aware of the employment law impact on situations of this type. Employers must undertake risk assessments where there is a possibility of harm to the employee when undertaking their reasonable duties. If the employer fails in their duty to protect the employee they are at risk of a claim for constructive dismissal.

These regulations are long established, as is shown by the case of *Keys v Shoefayre Ltd [1978] IRLR 476*. A shop assistant had been on duty during two armed robberies at her place of work. As with *Dutton & Clark Ltd v Daly [1985] ICR 780*, she resigned and claimed constructive dismissal after the second robbery. However, in this particular case, despite the employee's complaint to the manager after the first attack, there was no attempt to protect the employees. There was no telephone in the shop and no panic alarm. The Tribunal, needless to say, found in the applicant's favour, as the employer had failed to take any protective measures whatsoever. This was despite knowing that the shop was in an area which was known to have a high crime rate.

The issue in relation to protecting employees does not end with taking reasonable precautions. It is important to ensure that the employee is treated carefully and reasonably after they have been the victim of an attack.

It should also be noted that if an employee perceives that there is a reasonable possibility of their being harmed, due to a serious threat of imminent danger, they are entitled to refuse to work and not return until the danger has passed. If an employee is dismissed in such circumstances they will have an automatic right under the *Employment Rights Act 1996 (ERA 1996)* to claim unfair dismissal, irrespective of their length of service.

Also under the duty of care, the employer must provide a competent work force. If another employee could put members of staff at risk, then they must be removed. In this regard, grievances raised by employees about other members of staff, or even equipment they use, should be taken seriously and investigated.

The next two duties, in relation to respect and grievances, would tend to go hand in hand. The duty of respect is an implied term in every contract of employment and is often referred to as 'trust and confidence'. Most claims for constructive dismissal are brought on the grounds of 'respect' or 'trust and confidence'. This occurs where the employee feels that the employer's treatment of them was so poor that it lacked respect and, therefore, resulted in a loss of trust and confidence in the employer. This would be deemed to be a fundamental breach of contract brought about by the unreasonable behaviour of the employer.

Many of these claims arise due to the employer not dealing promptly and properly with grievances that have been raised. Particularly in regard to issues of discrimination or harassment, as discussed in the case of *Carver v SK (Sales) Limited (ET Case No. 1500623/2001)* in **CHAPTER 2**. However, all employees have the right to raise a grievance, for whatever reason, and have this dealt with properly and promptly. Even if there is no real grounds for the grievance, there is no reason for there to be a delay in dealing with an employee's complaint.

In the case of *Goold (W A) (Pearmak) Ltd v McConnel [1995] IRLR 516* problems arose for two salesmen who worked on a commission based pay scheme. The way the commission was calculated changed when there was a change to the sales method. The salesmen tried to raise a grievance. However, the company lacked a proper procedure to register their complaint. Therefore, they tried to raise the grievance with their manager and the managing director on a number of occasions, but with no results. In a final attempt to be heard, they requested an interview with the company chairman. This was refused so both men walked out and claimed constructive dismissal. Both the Tribunal and the EAT upheld that the men had been constructively and unfairly dismissed. The EAT went on to say that the failure to hear the grievance was a fundamental breach of the implied term in the contract and such would be sufficiently serious to justify the employees terminating their employment.

What should be in a grievance procedure and how it should be used is discussed in **4.4** below. Reference should also be made to **CHAPTER TWO**.

HR Policy for managing diverse employees   4.4

Bearing in mind the duties an employer owes to its employees and following on from what has been outlined in **CHAPTER 1**, the benefits of having clearly defined and publicised policies are numerous. They include:

- a clearer understanding by individuals of their responsibilities in given situations;

- a framework around which to build working methods and practices;

- a stronger belief by employees that there is a structure in place to support their working life; and

- an increase in morale, as the workforce feels confident that disputes and grievances can be dealt with more effectively.

A diversity policy, in particular, provides reassurance to more vulnerable workers and ensures a clear path to follow when dealing with all aspects of diversity as an employer.

So, what would need to be considered when establishing a policy for managing diverse employees?

Obviously the grounding for such considerations will be based in legislation, which has been covered in **CHAPTER 2** and **CHAPTER 3**. However, initially it is important for a HR manager to look at how a policy should be shaped and used to ensure it is applied practically within the workplace. It is no good defining every aspect of the policy to the last letter if the end result is impossible for all members of the workforce to understand! Therefore, what must be kept in mind is that a policy, which is to be established, maintained and utilised effectively within an organisation, must be clear and simple to understand, avoiding any ambiguity. Hence, a clear definition of exactly what comes under the heading of diversity is a key primary point, see **CHAPTER 1**. The language used within the policy must be accessible to all levels, particularly to ensure it does not alienate any of those employees it encompasses. It must be laid out in a straightforward fashion to avoid any grey areas, which may imply a lack of commitment by the organisation to the policy. In large corporations, it may be necessary to consider having the policy contained in other mediums than just a written document. For example, a Braille guide or even an audio tape. Those employees who have sight or reading difficulties may well benefit from access to an audio script of the company's guidelines.

Having laid out how the policy is best established, it is important to stress that unless maintained and actually employed in daily use, a well-written policy can be worse than pointless and may appear to be merely a token gesture. Simply having a policy does not in itself provide any protection against the possibility of a discrimination claim. What must also be in place is the organisation's commitment to that policy through reference to points covering its use and how any required updates would take place. The establishing of a policy is seen as the agreement by the management of an organisation to be bound by its contents. Therefore, essential considerations include how employees and managers alike should receive training in relation to the policy and how access to the policy should be given and maintained.

It is advisable that once the policy has been created, members of management and key personnel have a comprehensive training session to familiarise themselves with the content and intentions of the policy. In order to ensure that all members of staff are aware of the policy, it is essential that there are training sessions ensuring that every staff member is aware of their responsibilities, that the policy is included in inductions and it is recommended that a copy is placed on the staff notice board and inserted into any staff handbook. Updates should be made as and when changes in legislation cause the policy to become outdated, or even where existing policies can be 'touched up'. Again, any changes must be notified to all members of the organisation, so that they are aware of any change in their responsibilities and of the protection afforded to them under the law.

When setting up such a policy it is important for the HR manager to ensure that it complies with all the regulations set out in **CHAPTER TWO**. It is also important to ensure that all information gained through the use of this policy is monitored and stored in accordance with the *Data Protection Act 1998* (*DPA 1998*). Some of the information gained may be of a highly sensitive nature, as defined by the *DPA 1998*. This would include reference to criminal convictions, health and religion. Such issues, unless disclosed willingly by an employee to their colleagues, are highly confidential and should at no time be made public without the employee's consent.

Such a policy should bear in mind issues of equal opportunities, which are at the heart of any policy. It is important for the HR manager to monitor areas which are of particular concern in regard to issues of discrimination. This would include disabilities, race, sex, marital status, etc. By monitoring these issues, normally via the recruitment process, an organisation can ensure that, at least in regard to the makeup of their workforce, they are not seen to be discriminating. Such issues should also be borne in mind in regard to selection for promotion or even training.

A policy should also contain definitions of what the organisation considers to be discriminatory behaviour. Much in the same way as a disciplinary procedure will set out examples of gross misconduct. It is also important to ensure that the employees are aware of who is responsible for updating and complying with the policy.

Grievances are discussed in **4.24** to **4.27**. However, it cannot be stressed enough, that the provision of and compliance with a grievance procedure is a fundamental part of any policy, whether relating to issues of diversity or general matters of staff care.

The implementation of the grievance policy is also important. Training is a fundamental part of any policy. Where an organisation is large, a working party can be set up to ensure that the policy is implemented and made known throughout the company. This can be particularly important in companies and organisations where there are a number of small branches across a wide spread area. As many HR managers will be aware, it is difficult to ensure that all of the company's managers comply with the one policy in relation to recruitment, promotion and disciplinary and grievance issues.

Recruitment checklists and guidelines   4.5

Whether the organisation is well established with low labour turnover and limited recruitment requirements or a new company just setting up or a company that simply has high recruitment needs, it is vital not to underestimate the importance of managing diversity, even at this early stage of the working relationship.

There is a common misconception that discrimination can only start once an individual has commenced employment. However, it must be noted (as mentioned in **CHAPTER ONE** and **CHAPTER TWO**) that even the job advertisement can give rise to a discrimination claim up to three months after the advert has been removed. Therefore, it is important to establish a checklist of each point of recruitment and the key considerations and possible pitfalls at each and every stage.

Stages of recruitment include:

- advertising;
- screening;
- selection;
- interview;
- decision;
- offer; and
- induction.

Advertising a vacancy

Placement   4.6

The placing of the advert is very important. There are a wide range of mediums that can be used to advertise vacancies:

- internally, within the organisation;
- externally within the locality using, for example, boards or flyers;
- job centre networks;
- Internet job sites;
- specialist publications for the industry;
- local and national press; and
- specialist agencies.

Obviously some of the above incur significant costs and, therefore, may not be practical for all organisations. However, what must be considered is whether the medium with which the company wishes to advertise reaches all sections of the 'local' catchment area, however widely that is defined, and is appropriate to the area in which the company is based. An example, which highlights how important this is, is where a new supermarket was opening in the Leicester area and recruitment was primarily by word of mouth. The initial white staff base drew strongly on their own culture, which resulted in a highly disproportionate ethnic split in the workforce.

This is a good example which highlights ethnicity. But equally consideration of the whole community should be given even when, for example, advertising for trainees within local schools. It is important to ensure adverts are placed in all schools in the area, ensuring no possible discrimination against a particular gender in, for example, single sex schools or against people with disabilities in special needs schools.

Wording 4.7

One of the most important issues when advertising a vacancy is to take great care when wording the advertisement. Words and phrases once in common usage should now be avoided, for example advertising for a foreman without the clarification that the post is open to both genders, and asking for someone 'fit and healthy'. In regard to the latter, the company's intention may not be to discriminate against the older applicant or even the disabled applicant, but such phrases can cause offence and open the organisation up to the possibility of a discrimination claim. These may appear to be obvious examples, but it is important to ensure that only relevant and justifiable requirements are stated and that the advert be specific with regard to duties to be undertaken and hours of work required. In this way, detailing reasons for de-selection, as discussed in **4.8** and **4.9**, will become much easier.

A best practice procedure for large organisations that often have many similar vacancies to advertise would be to set up job specifications for each role that exists. A job specification should include:

- a description of the role in as much depth as practicable, ie day to day duties, tasks and responsibilities;

- hours the person may be required to work (obviously this may vary from vacancy to vacancy);

- general qualifications or specific skills required – usually technical skills – ranging from basic numeracy and literacy, through to very specific qualifications such as a degree and including perhaps skills gained in the workplace, for example competency using Windows '98; and

- particular aptitudes, often called competencies, such as organisational skills or customer service skills.

The more relevant information included on a job specification, the less likely the company is to receive unsuitable applicants to screen, particularly when these are pre-screened through either a job centre or agency. However, it is again important to stress that requirements that are not necessary for a particular role cannot be included, as this may be construed as discriminatory. For example, GCSE English may be an acceptable requirement for a secretarial post, but certainly not for a supermarket cashier.

Be very aware of the possible areas of discrimination and the fact that within the *Sex Discrimination Act 1975* and the *Race Relations Act 1976* it is possible to discriminate both directly and indirectly. It is less and less likely that adverts would be directly discriminatory, for example requesting a male worker for a mechanic position. However, it is easier to fall into the trap of indirect discrimination whereby a requirement is applied to a job specification that would either favour one gender over another, such as 'must be over 6 feet tall', or would favour one ethnic group over another.

Note, however, that a requirement can be applied that favours a gender or ethnic group provided that it is *genuinely necessary for the needs of the role*. This relates to genuine occupational qualifications (GOQs) or requirement, which is where an otherwise discriminatory specification is placed on an advertisement, often on the grounds of decency or privacy, such as a female worker in a mammogram unit. However, many industries have no justifiable GOQs, so it should not be assumed that all organisations might be able to justify the requirement should it be challenged. If there is no reasonable justification in regard to the position being advertised, then such situations should be avoided at all costs.

Screening   4.8

Screening will either occur when the closing date for a particular application has passed or at regular intervals, depending on the nature of the industry and volume of applicants. This is the point at which all applicants will either be put forward for selection or rejected due to lack of suitability. The most important issue to consider at this stage is the ground on which an applicant is rejected – this should only be if they fail to meet the specifications detailed within the job advertisement. If it is for other reasons, the HR manager must ask if they are actually genuine reasons for rejection and whether these issues could have been included in the job specification to make it more specific.

Having established the grounds for rejection, there must be a working system in place for recording reasons for rejection, whether this is on the application form, or CV, or on a separate document. Wherever this is done, it is vital for the HR manager to ensure that what is recorded is factual and accurate and does not include subjective or possibly discriminatory comments. It is also important to retain the applications that have been rejected, or at least the notes showing the reasoning behind the rejection. This (although not space saving), could provide the HR manager with all the information they require to defend a claim for discrimination. Remember that an individual can still claim discrimination even at the application stage and the HR manager may be called upon to justify the company's screening methods, either in general or relating to a specific applicant.

In addition to the recording of reasons for rejection, there is also a strong argument for adopting a monitoring system for applicants. Such a system is already a requirement on the grounds of religion in Northern Ireland, however with the introduction of the most recent legislation and with more forthcoming, the benefits of broadening this out to include all aspects of diversity are two fold. Not only does it provide an internal check to ensure that advertising and screening methods are reaching and including a representative section of the catchment area, but they are also a valuable defence against any claim for discrimination.

Selection process   4.9

Many companies now choose to include a formal selection process within their recruitment structure, often taking the form of psychometric testing and including some kind of interactive group work. Obviously a psychometric test requires very specific criteria and must be implemented only by those with the specific qualification to do so or by using a consultancy agency. Not to do so would in itself risk potential discrimination claims, as test questions must be worded and balanced to ensure no bias to any particular grouping of the population.

Where any type of testing session is used, it should be appropriate to the organisation. It is vitally important for all candidates to be informed of the type of session and the medium with which they will be assessed. This will ensure that any candidates who may require, for example, reading glasses or particular writing tools can bring the necessary items with them to avoid any likelihood that they will be unfairly disadvantaged when taking the test. It is also essential that all potential candidates be asked whether they have any particular requirements with regard to taking the test that they cannot meet themselves. It may be that they require a large print copy of any questionnaire or instructions in Braille, for example. The HR manager should also take time to consider the times of day that a session may be planned for, particularly if it is to last for several hours, as this may coincide with times of religious observance for some candidates. Such issues should also be considered if the organisation has a set application form which is used. This should also comply with the basis of the equal opportunities policy and, where necessary, should be available in different formats, such as large script or audio. Employers should also be in a position to accept audio applications where the applicant would be at a disadvantage when making a written application. Equally, should refreshments be provided, it is important that they are appropriate for all the possible dietary requirements of the group, not only for those with specific customs, but also for anyone with a disability which may define what they can and cannot eat or, for example, a diabetic who may need more frequent refreshment breaks.

For the purposes of consistency, if there is a chosen recruitment tool, it should be used equally for all candidates. However, it should not be so rigid that a change to the test is not agreed where it may constitute a reasonable adjustment for someone with a disability. Therefore, it is again important to consider the impact of diversity on the possible outcomes or scores for each candidate. For example, with a written test an applicant for whom English is not their first language may have perfectly adequate skills to complete the tasks required for the job, but struggle to interpret and complete the questions presented. Therefore, the scores obtained from any testing must be used circumspectly and any borderline decisions should be followed up with an interview to ensure a fair decision is reached.

As discussed in **4.8**, choosing to reject a candidate must be done on valid grounds, which relate to the meeting of specific areas of the job requirements. These reasons should be recorded and monitored to ensure the company's diversity policy is working and to guard against possible claims.

Interviews

It cannot be stressed enough at this point that anyone conducting a recruitment interview should be fully aware of the relevant aspects of employment law and appropriate questioning techniques. It is often forgotten that what is said at interview forms part of the contract of employment, in addition to the terms and conditions of the job and what is stated in the offer letter. Therefore, it is vitally important that the interviewer has a full knowledge of all the details of the position they are interviewing for, such as times of work and rates of pay. This will ensure that there is no discrepancy with regard to information quoted at interview and that included within any offer letter.

In addition to these points, and with particular regard to the diverse applicant, it is important that the interviewer knows what questions are acceptable, and more importantly unacceptable, to ask at interview. In the same way as the wording of the advertisement is now less likely to discriminate directly, it is also less likely that interviewers would ask such obviously discriminatory questions as 'I see you have just got married, are you planning to have start a family soon?' However, there is still a possibility that an assumption such as this might be made and hence influence the decision making process. If an interviewer has question to doubt a candidate's suitability for a role on anything other than specific stated job requirements, it is essential that they establish why and if necessary take steps to change the environment in order that it would be suitable for any qualified candidates.

It should be borne in mind that where the position advertised is for temporary cover, in particular maternity cover, it would not necessarily be discriminatory for the interviewer to ask if the woman being interviewed was pregnant (if it is suspected) or where it is obvious that they are pregnant, not employ them for that reason. The whole purpose of the position is to cover leave of someone who is pregnant.

Having established that direct discrimination is now (hopefully) more rare in interviewing, it is important that best practice is followed to ensure any indirect discrimination is also avoided. It can be tempting for the interviewer to find out more about a candidate's background, particularly where the workforce is often part time or casual and the interviewer may wish to try and ascertain what other commitments they have on their time or their projected length of service. However, questions such as 'Who looks after your children while you are at work?' and 'Would you plan to give up work if you had children?' would be indirectly discriminatory, even if asked of all candidates. In the first instance it would be more likely to impact women, as they are still traditionally the main carers in our society. Secondly, the question would more likely be detrimental to both women and certainly some ethnic groups, where it may be traditional to leave work after having children. It is, therefore, important to remember that neither of these questions or similar are actually determining the candidate's suitability for the role and if taken to Tribunal, case history shows that such questioning techniques are unacceptable, even with the token gesture of asking all candidates.

It is important for the interviewer to also consider the body language and communication skills of the applicants. They should look beyond any difficulties with language if English is not their native tongue, this should only be considered in proportion to how important language skills are as part of the job. Cultures vary immensely with regard to appropriate body language to use in certain situations, it may be that the candidate feels eye contact is inappropriate or does not wish to shake hands. By traditional Western standards this may be seen as insincerity or disrespectful, but it is necessary for the interviewer to move away from judging candidates solely using his or her own value system.

Finally, as with the other stages, the HR manager should ensure factual and accurate reasons for rejection are detailed and available for review and feedback to candidates where necessary. These should be objective and helpful. As with all criticism, only constructive comments should be used. It may well be that an applicant would have received an offer of work but for a couple of issues that they needed to improve on. If they are told this, the next time they apply to the organisation they should be in a position to add value to it. Although this is time consuming, it is an important part of the recruitment stage, particularly where an applicant has potential for the future.

Decision   4.11

The decision making process is almost a summary of all the other stages within the recruitment process. All decisions should be made and based solely on the factual information gathered from interviews and/or selection tests. The HR manager should refrain from enforcing their own value system too heavily on candidates' performances. Although it can be important to consider issues such as less than favourable health records or times of availability to work, these could infringe on the areas covered in discrimination legislation. For example, considering health records could be discriminating under the *Disability Discrimination Act 1985* or, in relation to times of work consideration may not be given as to whether those restrictions are imposed by times of religious worship or belief as covered by the *Employment Equality (Religion and Belief) Regulations 2003 (SI 2003/1660)*. Above all, is the HR manager being fair? If the HR manager is confident that there is no flaw in their reasoning then he or she must ensure their decisions are recorded factually and accurately and are available for review and monitoring.

Job offer   4.12

Quite simply, the HR manager needs to ensure the offer letter and contract accurately reflect the terms and conditions previously discussed at interview or contained within the advertisement. If there is any possibility of change, this should be discussed immediately with the candidate to ensure that they are happy with the revised terms before they formally receive them. This ensures that they do not feel that they have been treated unprofessionally and potentially less favourably.

It is important for the HR manager to remember that every employee (old or new) should now have a contract of employment or statement of terms and conditions, in accordance with *section 1* of the *Employment Relations Act 1999*. A new employee should receive their contract within eight weeks of starting their employment. For those employees, of which there are too many, that do not return their contract duly signed, it is important to note that unless they raise a formal, written objection to the terms of the contract, those terms apply and remain in force. Where an objection is raised, it should be discussed and if possible resolved to everyone's satisfaction, even if this means that a particular clause is removed or amended.

As an aside, it should be borne in mind that an employee who brings and wins a claim in the Employment Tribunal and has never received a contract of employment (or indeed payslips) may have their damages increased by two for four weeks wages. This is capped at the same level as the maximum statutory award for redundancy. This was due to come into force in January 2004, but is likely to be enacted from October 2004 with the new regulations relating to disciplinary and grievance procedures.

Induction   4.13

This is the final stage of the recruitment process. An induction should be comprehensive enough to cover all aspects of working life, including:

- health and safety;
- absence procedures;
- pay;
- benefits;
- disciplinary and grievance procedures; and

- where the process comes full circle, their own responsibilities as employees under the organisation's defined policies, including equality and diversity.

As much as it is best practice to cover health and safety legislation at induction, not only to fulfil the responsibility as an employer and to adequately train the employees, but also to explain to the employees their own responsibilities to protect themselves and their colleagues at work, it is equally important to cover equality at work regulations. This affords good protection for the organisation, as Tribunals may find that proof of adequate training in either of the above areas absolves a company of responsibility and instead proceed against an individual who has breached regulations.

As with the selection process, thought should be given to the timing of the induction session, as this may be different to normal working hours. Consideration should also be given to any special requirements the new employees may have. Queries relating to the policies of the organisation and the employee's contract can also be dealt with at this time.

An important final note here is that while the training and development that would naturally follow on from induction in this section is not specifically dealt with in this book, what must be considered is that it would be a breach of the *Part Time Workers (Prevention of Less Favourable Treatment) Regulations 2000 (SI 2000/1551)* if any worker were to be denied access to training opportunities solely due to their part time status. Therefore, when planning further staff development, it is vital to ensure that part time workers are not excluded from this.

The HR manager may wish to use the list below as a summary of how to run the recruitment process:

- Advertisement:
  - place the advert using a medium that covers the broad spectrum of the catchment area;
  - include as much information as possible, but stipulate no unnecessary requirements; and
  - only exclusions of diverse groupings can be for GOQs.
- Screening:
  - deselect based only on failing to meet the specified criteria;
  - ensure reasons for the deselection are recorded and are factual and accurate; and
  - establish a monitoring system to check the effectiveness of the diversity policy.
- Selection Process:
  - use consistent selection method for all (only alter where reasonable adjustment required);

- o use approved psychometric testing only when trained to do so;

- o check – do candidates understand what the session requires of them, do they have any special requirements for the session;

- o do consider scores carefully – are there reasons for particularly low scores, if in doubt, interview; and

- o ensure again that reasons for deselection are recorded and are factual and accurate in all areas.

- Interview:

  - o ensure the interviewer has knowledge of employment law and information on the specifics of the position;

  - o ensure the interviewer is aware of unacceptable questioning techniques – remember the impact of indirect discrimination;

  - o do not pre-judge a candidate on communication skills or body language; and

  - o ensure reasons for deselection are recorded and are factual and accurate.

- Decision:

  - o ensure all decisions are based only on factual information and not assumptions;

  - o avoid enforcing your own value system on candidates' performances;

  - o consider negative indicators – could they relate to something covered under employment regulations; and

  - o record reasons for selection and deselection – be accurate and factual.

- Job Offer:

  - o a summary of what was discussed at interview and included in the advertisement

  - o contact the candidate should you wish to amend

- Induction:

  - o should cover all aspects of work life;

  - o should also consider any special requirements new employees may have; and

  - o should highlight the employee's own responsibilities under all company policies, including diversity.

Communications   4.14

Communication between an employer and its members of staff is fundamental to a well-oiled working organisation. There are specific areas of communication that an employer is responsible for, including ensuring that these methods of communication are carried out fairly and thoroughly so that no section of the workforce is disadvantaged. These can broadly be split into two areas:

- internal communications – either with the workforce in general covering, for example, company policies, new procedures, working practices or specific contact with employees who are absent either through sickness, maternity or unauthorised absence; and

- external communications – contacting or being contacted for references and contacting GPs or consultants or other official bodies.

Internal   4.15

The most important basis for any relationship, working or otherwise, is good communication at all levels. For too long, organisations followed their obligation to provide information to their workforce in only the most limited fashion. This meant posting policies and company information on noticeboards and in handbooks and, at most, producing periodic newsletters. Obviously there are exceptions to these generalisations and it is those companies who have recognised the value of promoting more comprehensive two-way communication that have seen the benefits of a more committed workforce. This can be seen from the example of Internet bank Egg, who have set up a consultative group called the Egg Forum, whose responsibilities include highlighting health and safety issues and discussing employee relations issues with management representatives (case study from *IRS Best Practice in HR handbook*). Taking this one step further and building on the benefits that have already been mentioned which a diverse workforce can provide, the employer needs to ensure all communications, where possible, are clear and concise. Employers can set up working parties, which will help to convey the important issues raised in their communications. It is important to ensure that these working parties include representatives from every aspect of the workforce. Obviously to deny access to any member of a diverse grouping would be outright discrimination in any case, but here employers should actively seek the benefits that different viewpoints can give. Best practice is becoming more frequently used and, therefore, through the establishment of colleague forums and the use of regular colleague 'opinion polls' and surveys, an employer will be in a better position to consider employees' views.

Once a representative group has been set up, it should be the members of that group who help to fine tune the communications processes used within the organisation. It may be something simple, such as placing company information at low level on noticeboards, to ensure that it is accessible to wheelchair users. If the company has high groupings of a particular ethnicity, it may be beneficial to produce the company newsletter in more than one language. Obviously there are many variations that can be made in communications but the most important suggestions about which will work well are usually best coming from those who may have previously been excluded.

In addition to communication with the workforce in general, there are obviously going to be many occasions where it is necessary to contact employees on an individual basis. Some of these will be more sensitive situations. The most common situations where communication of this type occurs tends to be contacting employees that are absent through sickness, or on maternity leave, or who are absent without leave.

Whatever the situation the employee is in, it is important to maintain regular communications with them. Bearing in mind that whether or not these employees have an illness that is covered by the *Disability Discrimination Act 1995*, any employee that is absent through genuine ill health must be considered to be vulnerable and careful consideration should, therefore, be given to how communications with the employee are approached.

As with all sickness policies, the employee is under an obligation to keep the employer informed. There is no obligation on the employer to contact the employee, however, the occasional telephone call to see how they are getting on should not be deemed to be inappropriate.

It is often the employer's misconception that they cannot contact an employee when they are on sick leave. However, it is not possible for an employer to run their business efficiently and effectively if they are not fully up to date on the issues affecting their employees. Therefore, it is appropriate to maintain regular contact with the employee and the projected length of absence will determine how frequent this might be. It is impossible to lay down specific guidelines to frequency. Such contact should be made as a way of supporting, not harassing, the employee. Particularly with long-term absence, the support of the employer in helping the employee return to work is often underestimated. It is wholly appropriate to investigate the health of the individual. If the length of absence is undetermined, it is useful to have occasional meetings either at the workplace or in the employee's own home where necessary, to discuss the ill health and possible return to work. It is important that the individual has a representative to provide support during the meeting, but this does not need to be a colleague in these circumstances. This is not a disciplinary situation and, therefore, a member of the employee's family, a friend or even their GP would be appropriate as their companion. Such meetings can be very stressful for an employee and, therefore, it is important for the HR manager to ensure that the setting is relaxed and issues relating to their work are not discussed, particularly in cases of stress related absence, see **4.21**.

In relation to those employees who are absent due to maternity leave, as they remain employees throughout their leave, both ordinary and additional, communications with them come within the guidelines of internal communications. In these circumstances an employee must be notified immediately, whether by letter or in person (a telephone call will not suffice) of the possibility of redundancies or restructuring in the company. Or indeed, of the possibility of a transfer of undertaking under the *Transfer of Undertakings (Protection of Employment) Regulations 1981 (SI 1981/1794)*. Any changes to the employee's salary or terms and conditions (such as bonuses) should be relayed to the employee in writing, setting out the time scale in which these changes may occur.

However, in relation to the employee's actual maternity leave, the employer does not have the right to contact the employee to ascertain whether or not the employee will be returning to work or taking additional leave (should they be entitled to it). An employee must provide the employer with notice of their intention to return to work early (ie before their 26 weeks or 52 weeks leave has expired) by giving 28 days notice. The employee must also give the employer the period of notice as set out in their contract of employment, or the minimum statutory notice if they do not have a contract, if they do not intend to return to work.

Other than for these reasons, there should be no need for there to be any communications between the employer and employee, other than to make enquiries as to how mother and baby are progressing.

In relation to those employees who are absent without the employer's authority, the situation is wholly different. The employee, by not complying with the employer's notification procedures, is in breach of contract and liable to disciplinary action. Whether or not the employee is sick, they must notify the employer, or the relevant designated person, of their absence and the reason for this.

In such cases as an employee who has suffered a bereavement and has been given compassionate leave, the employee must comply with the terms of that leave. If they fail to return to work after the leave period has expired without notifying the employer that they wish to take holiday or unpaid leave, they are at risk of disciplinary action.

The employer, when an employee is absent without explanation or authority, has the right to try to contact the employee by phone or letter. The employee should be warned that their actions could result in disciplinary action. The employer has the right to discipline the employee for their absence, whether it is justified or otherwise. The extent of the disciplinary action must be balanced against any reason given by the employee for their actions.

A summary of internal communications is shown in the table overleaf.

External   4.16

External communications can take several forms. They include:

- contacting, or being contacted by another organisation for references – either personal or business;

- contacting a medical practitioner for information on someone who is either working or off sick;

- contacting an individual who is either off sick or has taken unauthorised absence (although as they remain employees this does fall into the category above); and

- being contacted by official bodies, such as the police or social services.

Summary of internal communications

	Sickness Absence	Maternity Leave	Absence without Leave
Responsibilities of the employer	To maintain appropriate levels of contact and support a return to work	To notify employee in writing or in person of possible redundancies, restructuring or of any changes to terms and conditions	To attempt to contact the employee either in person, by telephone or by letter, explaining possible outcomes of their unauthorised absence
Responsibilities of the employee	To maintain regular contact with the employer To provide a medical certificate after 7 days	To give 28 days' notice of any intention to return to work before the end of ordinary maternity leave or additional maternity leave To provide the period of notice stated on their contract if they do not intend to return to work	To avoid the possibility of this by following absence reporting procedures at all times
Other considerations	To ensure employee has representation should a meeting be necessary		There may be genuine reasons for the situation, particularly in the case of serious illness or bereavement, where there may simply be an oversight in procedure

It is important to remember that any information held about a colleague is confidential and covered by the *DPA 1998*, see **4.4**.

When dealing with requests for references, it is essential that before any information is given out, a full check is made to ensure that the person making the enquiry is genuine and has a real claim on the information they request. Such enquiries should be made in writing in the first instance, or where information may be required more urgently, the identity of the call should be established. To enable this to be done, it would be necessary to take a caller's name and number, check their right to the information requested, often by asking the employee in question for their comment and if necessary their consent. Not until this has been done should the call be returned. By returning the call the HR manager is then able to assess whether they were calling from a legitimate and relevant source. If the HR manager is in any doubt, they should not disclose any information until they are satisfied that they can do so safely.

If the company does not respond to reference requests, or does so with only limited information, it is wise to inform the applicant company, as providing no reference is sometimes seen as a negative indicator on the individual concerned, whether or not there is justifiable reasons for such a conclusion. And as with all other areas, consistency should be maintained. Where references are given indicating performance and attendance, the same criteria should be used to judge all leavers and should be factual and accurate at all times. Oversights should be avoided in the supply of references – it is possible to bring a discrimination claim even after the employment has terminated if an individual feels that unjustifiably poor references have been detrimental to them obtaining further employment. However, this only occurs where an act of discrimination has already occurred and been found to have been discriminatory. For example, where an employee has brought a claim for sex discrimination, they later request a reference and this is poor, see **CHAPTER 8**.

That said, the employer is under a duty to provide a fair and reasonable reference. If the reference was false it could give rise to a claim for damages in the County Court. The Tribunal does not currently have jurisdiction to consider such actions unless they result from some previous claim before the Tribunal. The issue of references will be discussed further in **CHAPTER 8**.

Other external communications would include contacting medical practitioners for information on employees' health, either when they are absent, or while they are still attending work. Before a report can be obtained from an employee's GP the employee must have given their written consent to the report. However, the employee is within their rights to withhold their consent. If this occurs, the employer is within their rights to make such decisions as are necessary on the evidence before them.

It is important to note that where an employee is on sick leave due to a pregnancy related illness, the employer is not entitled to take action against the employee for such sickness absence and neither are they entitled to look further into the reasons for the absence.

When requesting medical reports, or indeed obtaining a report from Occupational Health or a company medical practitioner, it is important to ensure that the correct questions are asked, see **CHAPTER 2**. Also that the employee has had their rights explained with regard to access to their medical records, most importantly, their rights to refuse to allow access and their right to view the report.

Managing sickness 4.17

This is a particularly important issue for all employers. As mentioned in **CHAPTER 1**, there are considerable costs for employers in the managing of sickness and sickness absence.

Such absences include:

- long term sickness;
- persistent unexplained absences; and
- minor infrequent absences.

Many companies budget for a set amount of days within their business plan. However this only helps to manage some of the financial impact on the company of the absence rather than the effect on the business of the employee being unable to undertake their duties for whatever reason.

Sickness policy   4.18

Every organisation should ensure that they have a clear and consistent absence policy. Every employee should be aware of the policy and if necessary it should be included within the contracts of employment or staff handbook.

The policy should notify the employee of what they need to do when they are absent from work due to sickness. Normally this will establish a time by which the employee must notify their manager, or such other person as appropriate, of their likely absence from work, together with the reason for their absence. An employee merely stating that they are ill or sick is not sufficient reason to warrant an absence.

Short term sickness   4.19

When, in regard to short-term sickness, the employee returns to work, they should at the very least complete a return to work form, confirming the reason for their absence. This can then be held on their personnel file and used for future reference in relation to issues of attendance where necessary, but, more importantly, should there be any concerns regarding stress related illness at some point in the future.

Long term sickness   4.20

Employees returning from long term absence should attend a return to work interview. This should be dealt with carefully and a set format should be followed. It is important to establish the reasons for the absence and what, if anything, the employer, or indeed the employee, can do to prevent the absence reoccurring.

This is obviously at the end of the absence period. There are other issues to consider during the period of absence itself. An employer is allowed to contact the employee when they are on sick leave. It is also important to ensure that any period of absence over seven days is covered by a doctor's certificate. If none are forthcoming, it is necessary to contact the employee to remind them to obtain the certificate and forward this on. If no certificate appears, consideration needs to be given as to whether this is an unauthorised absence. If so, disciplinary action may be necessary.

Where the likelihood of the employee's return is not for some time, due to injury or significant illness, it is important to establish the likely date of return. In such circumstances a medical report can be obtained. The main issues to obtain clarification on are:

- how long the employee is likely to be off work;

- the details of the condition from which they are suffering; and

- what, if anything, can be done to ensure a safe return to work and no relapse.

It is important to ensure that the questions asked are measured and sensible. This is a means of obtaining important information for the organisation, as well as obtaining information on the employee's health. However, often the important point is when the employee can return to work. If it is unlikely to be for a number of months, the employer needs to consider whether it is prudent to retain the employee. If the role they undertake is an important one, it may not be possible to cover their work without replacing them for a long period of time. If this is the case, then the employee may be dismissed on the grounds of capability. This is discussed in **4.28** below. At no time is the employer expected to be a medical expert, unless of course they are one! The employee's opinion should also be sought in relation to how quickly they feel that they will be able to return to work and undertake their full duties.

However, before dismissing an employee who is on long-term sick leave, consideration must be given to the sickness absence procedure. Where sickness is paid in full for long periods, it may not be possible to justify dismissing an employee before the period of paid absence expires. That said, where there is little or no paid leave, there is no cost to the employer in retaining the employee once the period of statutory sick pay expires. Therefore, the only person retention affects is the employee, as they would be unable to gain further employment until they resign themselves.

It should also be noted that an employee who is dismissed or resigns when they are no longer receiving full pay is not entitled to receive notice at full pay. This may be paid at the discretion of the employer.

Where an employee is to return to work and the time for their return approaches, it is important for the employer to meet with the employee before their return to confirm how their return will be managed. It may well be necessary to have a staged return to work. Particularly where the work is arduous or stressful. This staged return programme should be drawn up in full consultation of the employee's medical advisor, the employee, their manager and, if necessary and appropriate, the organisation's doctor or Occupational Health worker.

In some circumstances there may be a need to vary the role into which the employee returns, particularly if their absence is the result of a debilitating illness, accident or even stress. This variation may be on a temporary or permanent basis. Such changes should be confirmed in writing and made with the employee's full knowledge and consent.

Stress   4.21

With the growing number of claims for stress, it is important to ensure that employers are aware of all the pitfalls as well as the ways to prevent employees suffering from stress or continuing to do so should they have suffered from stress in the past.

The Scale of Occupational Stress: The Bristol Stress and Health Study, a survey published by the Health and Safety Executive (HSE) in May 2000, established the belief that five million workers had, or were suffering from, high levels of stress. In February 2002 the TUC announced that stress claims had increased tenfold. The increase in the number of people suffering or claiming to suffer from stress has had a massive impact on the finances of not only the health service, but also private employers.

It is a duty of care on the part of the employer to ensure that employees do not suffer from and are not at risk of excessive and substantial levels of stress. Where as in the past, stress has been seen as an employee whining rather than having any actual concerns, it is now important to take reasonable precautions against the possibility of employees being stressed. The problem is that stress can ultimately lead to depression, which is covered under the *Disability Discrimination Act 1995*. Therefore not protecting employees at the beginning of the employment relationship, or more importantly when they first complain or show symptoms of stress and dealing with the whole process poorly could ultimately amount to a claim for disability discrimination. Not only this, but could amount to a claim for personal injury. In the case of *Walker v Northumberland County Council (1995) ICR 702* the employee had had a period of long term sick leave due to stress. The employee made the employer aware of the reason for his absence and the fact that he was extremely over worked. On the employee's return to work, the employer did nothing to change their practices or assist the employee in his role. This resulted in the employee taking a second period of stress related sickness absence. The employee ultimately brought a claim to the Employment Tribunal for damages. He was successful and the damages for injury to feeling were considerable.

The HSE have defined stress as:

> 'the reaction people have to excessive pressures or types of demand placed upon them. It arises when they worry that they cannot cope.'

Stress at Work: A Guide for Employers, HSE.

There are many symptoms, which are the result of stress. Some are obvious and some less so. They include:

- long and unexplained absence;
- lack of concentration and memory;
- poor motivation and mood swings; and
- anxiety.

A number of issues can contribute to an employee suffering from stress. These are not just work related. However, those that are should be borne in mind and monitored. They include:

- poor internal communications;

- lack of resources; and

- a decrease in staffing resulting in an increase in workload.

Having and using a good policy system within the organisation can prevent all of these issues. If the management are approachable such situations can be prevented. If necessary regular reviews should be undertaken so that employees can raise any issues of concern.

The employer is obliged to make investigations of their staff's welfare. Although the employer can take what they see and are told at face value, there are obvious signs which should spark a warning to employers to revaluate their current procedures and speak with the employee in question to assess whether anything can be done to alleviate the problem and ensure that the employee does not need to take sick leave to recover. If they do need to take leave, the employer needs then to be supportive, find out how the current situation can be changed and put those changes into practice. There is no justifiable reason to say that there was nothing to change. If necessary, splitting the work through the department or bringing in an assistant may be all that is necessary or merely reviewing the employee more regularly to monitor how they are coping and whether they need training in any areas.

An employer will owe their employees a duty to prevent any harm caused to them by stress. The indications of a problem should be plain enough that a reasonable employer will acknowledge that something needs to be done and do it.

Illness dismissals 4.22

As touched on in **4.21**, it is possible to dismiss employees due to their sickness absence. The procedure and reasons will depend on whether the dismissal is due to long or short term sickness.

Where the issue is short-term sickness, the employer should carefully consider the reasoning behind the dismissal. If there is insufficient medical evidence to support a dismissal for reasons of capability, but the employee's absence record is unacceptable, they can be dismissed by way of some other substantial reason (SOSR). This is one of the five fair reasons for dismissal.

If the reasons for the absence are merely malingering or unjustifiable then the employee may be dismissed for misconduct.

Obviously in both these situations the proper procedure must be used. In each case the employee must have been made aware that their conduct and absence record could result in dismissal.

To enable an employer to deal with absence in this way it would be necessary to have a criterion for assessment set out within the contract or staff handbook. Once a set limit of absence is reached this then would result in a review, which could lead to disciplinary action. This could also assist in the identification of a disability, which was not previously known to the employer and possibly even the employee.

When considering dismissals due to incapability, ie due to long term absence, the employer must also consider what, if any, actions can be taken to improve the situation. In the situation where the employee is not likely to return for more than six months or will never return, the issue of capability is an obvious one.

However, in circumstances where the employee has had a number of long-term absences which have affected performance, it is important to assess whether anything can be done to improve the position. As with normal issues of an employee's capability to perform a role, the employee should be given the time and opportunity to improve, before there is a further move through the disciplinary process.

Where the dismissal is due to misconduct, the employer must establish that the dismissal is based on a genuine belief following a reasonable investigation into the situation. The most obvious situation would be where the employee has claimed sickness absence when they have in fact been fit to work. This would amount to misconduct.

If a disciplinary hearing is called for any of the above reasons, the employer cannot insist on the employee attending if they are not fit to do so. To force attendance, would in itself be unfair. However, if the employee continually misses meetings due to illness, when they have been perfectly healthy until disciplinary action is mentioned, it may be reasonable to hold the hearing in their absence. However, to ensure reasonableness, it may be also be prudent to obtain medical evidence to confirm that they are fit to attend.

Managing rehabilitation   4.23

Rehabilitation follows on directly from long term absence. Once the return to work interview has been completed and the employee is back to work (even if only part time), it is important to ensure that their progress is monitored so that if any further adjustments or changes are necessary they can be dealt with before any further problems arise relating to the employee's health.

This can run hand in hand with procedures relating to capability. Although in this situation a disciplinary process would not be relevant, capability is the main issue here.

It is important that the employee knows that there is a support structure in place, not only from their family and friends and local GP, but also from within their employer's organisation.

Rehabilitation can take many forms, from counselling, regular reviews, changes in hours or, if necessary, a complete change of roles. This can be time consuming for an employer to deal with and often is best dealt with by asking for assistance from Occupational Health. However, once the employee is back to work the employer is again fully responsible for their health and progress.

It may at this point be necessary to undertake further health and safety risk assessments, as well as obtain further medical evidence as to how well the employee is improving, as the change in their health could have a large impact on how they are able to perform their normal work functions. Where hours return to normal over usually a 6 to 18 week period, targets may be reduced or waived for longer. Particularly where the recover from the illness is hindered by stress, such as heart conditions and depression.

The *Disability Discrimination Act 1995* has a massive impact on what an employer should do. Full attention should be given to establishing whether the employee suffers from a disability within the Act. If they do not, this does not reduce the employer's duty to rehabilitate, but does remove some of the pressure to make major adjustments which could impinge on the whole organisation, such as structural changes.

The use of regular review meetings should not result in criticism of the employee's performance, but should be used constructively by making suggestions on how further improvement may be attained. The employee should be allowed to make comments at every opportunity and their opinion of what they feel capable of should be heeded.

To govern rehabilitation, an employer should ensure that they have a return to work policy, which goes further than the return to work interview. This should set out the basic situation so that the employee is aware of what will happen when they return to work. The criteria should not be set in stone, as sometimes a return to work schedule of six weeks may be wholly inappropriate for one employee, but more than sufficient for another.

Review meetings may be required on a weekly basis at first, then moving to fortnightly, monthly and so forth. Should it be felt that the employee has had a relapse or does not feel that they are progressing, as they ought, it should be possible to make the reviews more frequent if necessary. Conversely, if the employee is improving better than expected, they may wish to have the reviews on a less regular basis.

When offering counselling, it is important to ensure that the employee is aware that the counselling sessions are completely confidential and will not reach their personnel file. Counselling should be offered to employees at the expense of the employer and with the employee having the ability to chose which professional counselling service they wish to use, unless there is already an arrangement set up in the organisation.

As part of the rehabilitation policy it may be sensible to provide telephone numbers of agencies which the employee may find useful, be it counsellors, support groups, social clubs or even people who can assist with debt problems.

Although notes should be taken at meetings for reference purposes, it is important to bear in mind that the content of them is deemed to be sensitive data within the *DPA 1998* and should not be made known to anyone without the employee first giving their written consent.

So, in summary, important steps to take when managing the return to work and rehabilitation of an employee are as follows:

- Ensure a comprehensive return to work interview is the first priority on the employee's first day back. This is essential to ensure that the employee is actually fit to be returning to the workplace and to give them reassurance that their return will be managed effectively.

- Complete a risk assessment where appropriate. This should ascertain whether there are any activities that the employee should not be undertaking or should undertake only with assistance and/or supervision.

- Ensure that the employee understands what steps are available to facilitate their return to work and what counselling services may be available.

- If the period of absence has been for some length of time, include a chance to update the employee on any changes that may have taken place in their absence.

- Finally, agree a progressive reintegration period, ensuring this is tailored to the individual, with the option to extend or reduce the time taken to return to full productivity.

Managing grievance, disciplinary and capability procedures

4.24

When considering the issues of diversity with these procedures it is important to ensure that there can be no possibility of discrimination, for whatever reason. Therefore, it is important to have checklists for each stage of the procedures and specific considerations that must be taken into account to ensure no discrimination takes place.

Part 2 of the *Employment Act 2002*, which comes into force in October 2004, will mean that a basic minimum disciplinary and grievance procedure must be included in every employment contract. Every employer should check their existing procedures to ensure they comply with the regulations, or use the regulations as a basis to formulate procedures where none exist. This new legislation aims to reduce the number of claims in Tribunals by making grievance and disciplinary procedures a legal requirement (see **CHAPTER 8** for more details on the changes which are to take place in October 2004). The idea being that employees and employers make every effort to resolve their disputes in house without the need for recourse in the Tribunal. Currently when considering claims, Tribunals place great emphasis on the use of the ACAS Code of Practice for Disciplinary and Grievance as a minimum by employers when handling employment issues. Currently a claim can succeed or fail based on whether an employer has followed a procedure. The extent of that procedure is not considered provided that it is fair. However, the Tribunal will also consider whether the employee would have been dismissed in any event had a correct procedure been used. With the changes due in October 2004 the damages awarded by a Tribunal will depend in part on whether the employee or employer used the procedures available to them.

Disciplinaries 4.25

Many employers are not fully aware of how a disciplinary should be conducted. In some cases, where the employee has less than one year's service, no disciplinary action is used whatsoever. As mentioned in **4.23**, from October 2004, every employee must have been taken through a complete disciplinary process before they can be dismissed. It is very important to ensure that the process is fair and followed correctly.

Disciplinary action should always aim to be corrective not punitive, the action taken should always be the minimum required to rectify behaviour or remedy inappropriate activities. Above all, it should be fair and consistent and take into account an employee's history and any mitigating circumstances.

Stages 4.26

The following is a list of stages that should be taken when disciplinary action takes place.

- A shortfall in an employee's work performance or inappropriate conduct is noticed or brought to the attention of management.

- The employee is suspended if necessary – this would be for particularly serious incidents, where the action may be deemed to be gross misconduct or where the employee or other members of the workforce may be at risk. Suspension should be on full pay and not for more time than is reasonable, this is ussually between 7 to 14 days.

- The incident should be investigated thoroughly and as soon as possible. Detailed notes should be kept and signed witness statements from those involved should be obtained where necessary. All involved should be spoken to, including the individual concerned, as there may be a simple explanation for the incident, which could save a time consuming investigation.

- The evidence gathered should then be reviewed. The HR manager should decide whether disciplinary action is appropriate or whether the situation can be resolved using less formal methods, such as reviews or counselling. The HR manager should also check that it is not in fact a capability issue (see **4.28** below). Any previous similar incidents should be reviewed to see whether a precedent for action taken has been set.

- If it's decided that the situation requires no further no action then it is good practice for the HR manager to meet with the individual to discuss how the decision was reached and to agree on any formal or informal action to be taken with regard to future conduct or work performance.

- If the HR manager decides to proceed with disciplinary action they must write to the employee setting out the date and time of the hearing and confirm to them that they are entitled to bring with them a witness, who is either a colleague or trade union representative. They must also be told exactly what the allegations are against them and be provided with any evidence. The letter should ensure that the employee has sufficient time to consider the evidence and prepare their defence.

- The disciplinary interview, if necessary, can be held in an independent location, particularly if the employee is in a senior position. The interviewer should ensure that they have a witness present to take detailed minutes. Following the meeting, these minutes should be agreed between the parties, typed and sent to the employee for their approval. This ensures that there is a true account of the meeting and enables other managers to consider what happened at the original meeting, should the employee appeal. The record should be comprehensive and cover who was present and exactly what was said. This could provide a valuable defence should the employee bring a claim in the Tribunal, to show that the correct procedures were used. All present should be introduced and their roles explained. If the employee has not chosen to bring a representative, that option should be reiterated to them to ensure that they have made a conscious decision to attend alone. The reason for the disciplinary should be clearly explained and should reflect the reasons given initially to the individual, with nothing new added at this stage. Possible outcomes should also be explained, including dismissal if this may be likely.

- The main body of interview should allow for the individual to state their case and for any questions to be posed, if necessary. It should attempt to clear up any grey areas and should any new facts emerge, time should be allowed for those also to be thoroughly investigated. If necessary, witnesses should be made available so that the employee can put questions to them.

- A decision should only be made once all questions are answered and any additional information from the employee has been collated. If necessary, an adjournment should be called to allow the disciplining manager time to reach a decision. It is best practice to call for an adjournment in all cases, even the most straightforward, as it allows time to read through any notes and consult with the management representative to ensure that a fair decision is reached. The decision should take into account:

  o   any mitigating circumstances;

  o   any decision previously reached for a similar case; and

  o   the employee's previous disciplinary record and service generally.

If the proposed action seems reasonable in light of all the above, the interview should be reconvened to inform the individual of the action taken. The decision reached should be recorded and, except in the case of no action, the employee should be informed in writing, with a copy kept on file for a designated period.

- Unless the employee is dismissed regular review meetings would normally be necessary, particularly in capability situations. These reviews would most often include a series of meetings or review sessions to ensure the conduct or work performance of the individual was returning to and maintaining at the level required.

Throughout the whole process, much as with recruitment, it is important to be mindful of the possibility of discrimination and to ask whether everything possible is being done to ensure the proceedings are fair and objective. Where the employee is upset or suffers from an illness where regular breaks are required, small adjournments are allowed for everyone's ease and comfort.

Grievance procedures 4.27

It is vital for a company to have an effective grievance procedure in order that all employees feel they have an avenue down which to pursue redress for any perceived ill treatment. However, it is important to stress that it is valuable to encourage a culture where concerns can be addressed in a less formal fashion at an early stage when they are more likely to be resolved amicably. Mediating between two aggrieved individuals is often far quicker and easier than immediately suggesting they turn to the grievance procedure to resolve their differences.

Ideally any grievance procedure should clearly state that internal complaints should first be dealt with informally, provided this is possible.

However, it must be stressed to the employees at all stages that the opportunity to raise a formal grievance does exist should they feel their complaint is not being taken seriously or not being dealt with as they would wish. This ensures that the HR manager has every opportunity to resolve their complaint. It is important to remember that the employer must act on all grievances properly and promptly. Unwarranted delays could amount to breach of contract and a claim for constructive dismissal, irrespective of the employee's length of service.

It should also be made clear to employees that unless they use the grievance procedure they may not be able to bring a successful claim in the Employment Tribunal. Although this seems an unusual thing to state, it is important for the protection of the employer. From October 2004, employees who resign and claim constructive dismissal without using the grievance procedure could have their damages reduced or even their claim struck out.

There are several key considerations when establishing and using a grievance procedure, initially the procedure should define:

- how the grievance should be submitted, ie in writing;
- who the grievance should be submitted to;

- what information should be contained in the grievance and whether evidence in support should be submitted at this stage;

- that an initial meeting will be set to discuss the position as soon as possible;

- the length of time in which the employee should expect a response following the meeting;

- whether a second meeting will then be necessary at that stage to discuss the position further;

- investigate the matter fully;

- confirm that the employee is entitled to a representative at any meetings, but they should be a colleague or trade union representative;

- the next course of action should a full response not be received or should it be deemed to be unsatisfactory, ie the right to appeal; and

- what happens if the grievance is upheld, ie whether disciplinary action will be taken against the other employee.

There should be room within these procedures for alternative routes of appeal, as it may be inappropriate for an employee to submit a grievance to their line manager if they are in some way involved, although ideally the levels of seniority should stay the same. Where the employee works for a small employer and there is no one else to hear the grievance, the manager is under an obligation to deal with it as impartially as possible.

As the grievance needs to be made in writing, it is important that any employees who do not have English as their first language are able to take advice on how and what to write from either a union representative or even a legal adviser or the Citizens Advice Bureau.

The grievance should always be thoroughly investigated and documented evidence of everything discussed should be kept. This is vital, as should the individual feel that their complaint has not been answered satisfactorily and ultimately resigns and claims constructive dismissal, then records of a thorough investigation can prove a valuable defence.

It is equally important to ensure the individual is kept informed throughout the process and provided with written conclusions once the investigation is over.

The employee should be encouraged to make suggestions on how the matter should be resolved, even if the suggestions are not practical. All of the suggestions should be considered. Where they are not appropriate, the employee should be informed of the reasons behind the decision not to follow a suggestion. This ensures that they are fully involved throughout the process. The employee may not necessarily be satisfied with the response to their grievance, but provided the HR manager is sure that a thorough investigation has taken place and that all aspects of the situation have been covered fairly, including the company's requirements under the law, with solutions and/or compromises offered where necessary, then the HR manager may feel confident that they have come to the correct decision.

When dealing with the grievance hearing it is important again to ensure that the employee is aware that they are entitled to have a witness present at every meeting. A full record of the meeting should be taken and a copy provided to the employee for them to comment on before finally having the minutes agreed. It is also sensible for the manager to have a witness to take notes, as often it is not possible to take full notes of a meeting in which they are speaking as well as listening.

The employee is entitled to explain their complaint in detail. The employer can then respond or adjourn pending further enquiries or advice. In many cases, an initial meeting would be held to take further details, then an investigation would be undertaken and a second meeting called to discuss the findings and whether any decision can be made at that point.

It is also important to ensure that when asking questions of the employee at the grievance meeting, that the HR manager is sensitive and that the questions are fully appropriate to the situation. If not, this will amount to a full appeal needing to take place. When dealing with an appeal, unless there is additional evidence being placed before the company, it may not be necessary to have a further meeting.

If the grievance is upheld, it is important to ensure that the employee is aware of what will happen next and how the person, about whom they have complained, will be dealt with.

Often there will be nothing required of the employer than to obtain an apology or move the employee whom the complaint was made about. However, if it is decided that the behaviour amounted to misconduct, then disciplinary action should be taken against the employee. In some circumstances the complaining employee may not wish to give evidence at the disciplinary hearing due to the type of complaint they made. Allowances should be made for this, for example arranging for written questions to be answered.

Where the grievance is malicious or wholly without justification it may be necessary to discipline the complaining employee.

Where the grievance stems from issues of discrimination, it is important to ensure that employees are fully aware that actions and behaviour of this sort will not be tolerated. In such circumstances leniency might result in worsening the position for the company. If an employee has been discriminated against, but they see no disciplinary action being taken, it could result in a claim for discrimination due to the fact that the organisation did not treat the grievance seriously.

When dealing with grievances, the matter does not just relate to how the grievance is dealt with, but what happens next. If the grievance is upheld, it is important to progress the next part of the complaint properly and in accordance with the organisation's disciplinary procedure.

The employer needs to retain records of any grievances made, their evidence in support, their response and any actions taken, together with the reasons for the action. A record of whether an appeal was made and the outcome should also be retained.

It is important to remember that grievances fall in the category of sensitive data under the *DPA 1998*.

Capability procedure   4.28

Capability procedures are used for two separate reasons, although the procedure itself remains unchanged. Although capability has traditionally been less widely used than misconduct in disciplinary action, it is becoming more popular as employers find it a valuable tool with which to address performance issues that do not necessarily fall under the misconduct umbrella.

The more frequent reason for a disciplinary is where an employee has done something which amounts to breach of contract. This may also include failing to do something, the failure of which results in the breach. However, capability is an issue where the individual is unable to do something properly, if at all. In such circumstances you would not use the more harsh misconduct disciplinary, which is ultimately three strikes and you are out. With an issue of capability it is the employee's ability to perform that is in question. This may have come to light due to a failure to meet targets or from regular reviews.

Where poor performance becomes an issue, it is important to meet with the employee on an informal basis to assess whether there is a reason for the lack of performance. As such, the procedure is extremely useful when dealing with a diverse workforce, as it assists in highlighting areas where an individual is not achieving, but ensures that a full investigation is instigated, with help and support offered to redress the shortfall.

The reason for the failure may be that the employee has not had the proper training, which can be resolved immediately. Investigations may also reveal that the employee is not up to the role they are in. If this were the case, the HR manager would then highlight the areas that need improving and set a period for the employee to show that they can improve. This may mean reducing their targets initially so that the goal they need to attain is not so high. A regular review should be maintained in regard to their progress. If after the allotted time, they have not improved or not improved sufficiently, then it may be necessary to use disciplinary action. This would involve setting a disciplinary hearing, putting the position to the employee in full and again asking where further assistance is required. If necessary, the employee can be given a verbal warning and a further period in which they must show an improvement. If they still do not improve, then they progress through the disciplinary process until such time as they are dismissed. If a dismissal occurs, they are entitled to receive their full notice payment, as this would not be an issue of summary, but of procedural, dismissal.

However, investigation may highlight that the reason for the poor performance is due to ill health or disability. For example, an individual in a manual job may have difficulty meeting hourly work rates. The employer may move to discipline, but within the investigation process discover that the employee is suffering from a heart condition which means that they tire more easily and simply cannot keep up with required work rates. The misconduct disciplinary procedure would then become instead the capability procedure.

Initially it would be important to obtain medical advice as to the long term effects of the illness bearing in mind the strain of the role, as well as information from the employee's GP as to what adjustments could be made to assist the employee meet his or her targets. Once any adjustments are made, a framework of regular reviews to monitor progress would be set up. As the condition may be covered by the *Disability Discrimination Act 1995*, care must be taken to make any possible reasonable adjustment, such as potentially allowing more rest breaks and the setting of a lower work rate. Should the capability path have not been followed and disciplinary action taken instead, then the employer may have placed themselves at risk from a claim for contravention of the *Disability Discrimination Act 1995*.

The benefits of using the capability process, particularly in the context of the diverse workforce, are wide ranging. Other examples might include older members of an organisation struggling with the introduction of new technology, or a shortfall in the standards of written reports by an individual whose first language is not English. The capability process also has obvious benefits for the workforce in general, as it is always more desirable to quickly address and correct any shortfalls in performance giving help and support where necessary. Unfortunately, too often the reason for not using this process is given as a lack of time, but when the benefits would include higher standards of work performance; a better valued, more motivated workforce; lower labour turnover, and above all, less risk of potential claims due to the ill handling of diverse workers, the investment is surely worthwhile.

As can be seen from the issues highlighted in this chapter, the key considerations for an employer is to ensure that they have a full and complete diversity policy, that recruitment and induction guidelines reflect this and that they utilise a practical disciplinary and grievance procedure. They must then ensure that these policies are trained out throughout the entire organisation and applied consistently and properly.

Once the organisation's employees are aware of the policies there to benefit them, the day to day running of the business should be smoother and more beneficial to both parties.

5
Managing the Health and Safety of Diverse Employees

Vulnerability in the context of health and safety   5.1

The nature of vulnerability for a large number of diverse workers is the fact that they are put in a position where they could experience both physical and mental violence.

Some such workers are discussed in **5.2**, along with the responsibilities of the health and safety manager towards ensuring the safety of those employees.

Health service workplace violence   5.2

It is for many inconceivable that hospital staff are subjected to workplace violence, because NHS staff and other healthcare workers have a right to expect a safe and secure workplace. However, the National Audit Office report *A Safer Place to Work – Protecting the NHS Hospital and Ambulance Staff from Violence and Aggression* was published in March 2003 and identifies that these staff can be as much as four times more likely to experience work-related violence and aggression than other workers. It also found that nurses and other NHS staff who have direct interaction with the public, for example ambulance and accident and emergency staff, and staff who work in acute mental health units, have a higher risk of exposure to violence and aggression. This situation is not acceptable.

It has been identified that the main factors that can create risk to staff are:

- impatience;
- frustration, due to lack of information or boredom;
- anxiety (lack of choice, lack of space);
- resentment (having no right to appeal decisions); and
- drink, drugs or inherent aggression/mental instability.

Shift working can also heighten the risk, as over 30% of the violence related incidents reported under the *Reporting of Injuries, Diseases and Dangerous Occurrences Regulations 1995 (SI 1995/3163) (RIDDOR 1995)* occurred between 10pm and midnight.

The most common types of incidents are verbal abuse and threats involving staff who are engaged in activities where there is interaction with people from all sections of society, many of whom are needy and vulnerable. Complications can arise and they trigger violent actions, which in some cases can be predictable, while in others they are not. It is the duty of employers to assess the risk of verbal and physical violence to their employees and take appropriate steps to deal with it. This is not a straight forward task and it requires full co-operation between management and staff to identify the risks, put in place acceptable and achievable measures and hold regular meetings to monitor and update procedures. The key issues would include providing training and information, better design of the working environment (such as providing physical security measures) and better design of the job.

One of the most important elements of any system is to identify what the problems are and that includes recording incidents of verbal abuse and physical violence. This will assist employers in identifying patterns and predict the type of potential incidents that could occur. The data gathered by the recording system must be taken seriously by both management and staff and seen by staff to be used proactively. A form which identifies what management deems to be an incident and linked to degree of threat and outcome will provide basic data. Staff must be encouraged and given the opportunity to complete forms. The objective is to identify and reduce incidents and great care must be taken to ensure that the level of incidents does not become acceptable because they become commonplace. The law requires employers to notify the health and safety enforcing authority if any act of non-consensual physical violence done to a person at work results in their death, serious injury or incapacity for normal work for three or more days.

Measures for dealing with violence need careful thought and a sound risk assessment. Unless there is senior management support and commitment, demonstrated in a policy which contains individual obligations, it is unlikely that the risk of violence will be taken seriously and controlled effectively. The policy should, therefore, contain an authoritative statement on how the risk will be controlled. It should enable everyone to know their individual responsibilities, demonstrating the importance of involving all levels of the workforce and consulting safety reps, regarding the proposed content, implementation, monitoring and review of the policy.

To ensure that the policy and the procedures are effective and that the risk assessment remains valid, there should be a process of monitoring the risk control measures and reviewing the appropriateness of the policy and procedures. The written policy is a statement of intent and needs to be backed up with appropriate systems and mechanisms to ensure compliance.

Senior management needs to identify the hazards facing staff and establish a framework that identifies that there is senior management ownership, the identification of the problems, how they will implement proactive procedures and what they will do following an incident.

Management Commitment	Legal requirements
A commitment to protect staff at work	The *Health and Safety at Work, etc Act 1974* Company Health and Safety Policy Statement
The definition of violence	*Reporting of Injuries, Diseases and Dangerous Occurrences Regulations 1995*
Information on risk assessment measures	*Management of Health and Safety at Work Regulations 1999*
Information on post-incident support	Post Traumatic Stress Disorder

The *Health and Safety at Work, etc Act 1974 (HSWA 1974)* and the *Management of Health and Safety at Work Regulations 1999 (MHSW 1999)*, as well as other regulations, place certain duties on employers, managers and staff. The law provides a framework and the employer has to provide appropriate information to all staff, including those who are not directly employed but work on the premises.

Responsibilities	Legal requirements
Details of the employer's legal requirements	*ss* 2 and 3 of the *HSWA 1974*
Details of the manager's legal responsibilities	*s 37* of the *HSWA 1974*
Details of the employee's responsibilities	*s 7* of the *HSWA 1974*
Details of local prevention and reduction plans	Policy, Planning, Instruction and Training
Details of local emergency procedures	Policy, Planning, Instruction and Training

It is critical that staff receive information in a way that they understand it and are able to comply with the requirements. In addition to providing information, management must obtain feedback to monitor the effectiveness of the systems and procedures. They must also modify systems and procedures where appropriate, for example:

- an explanation of staff training;

- an explanation of local reporting procedures;

- a demonstration that the policy has been communicated and implemented;

- specific precautions for staff working in the community; and

- a commitment to cultivating good relations with the local police and Crown Prosecution Service in order to pursue cases of violence.

Community midwives   5.3

The work of community midwives involves visiting clinics and clients' homes. They are predominantly involved with post-natal work, with some antenatal duties. Their duties mean that they can spend up to two hours with a client who they will generally visit every other day at the post-natal stage. The extent of the area to be covered may include inner city, council estates and rural areas. This means that they are generally outside the range of any immediate support in the event of problems.

Young workers   5.4

Every employer is required to ensure that young persons employed are protected at work from any risks to their health or safety which are a consequence of their lack of experience, or absence of awareness of existing or potential risks or the fact that young persons have not yet fully matured.

The Protection of Young People at Work Directive (94/33/EEC) has now been adopted, and was required to be implemented by Member States by 1996. The Directive requires that the minimum working age for children is not below 15, although children under that age may be permitted in certain circumstances to undertake work experience or certain light work for a limited number of hours each week.

A survey carried out by the Trades Union Congress in 2001 found that around half a million children are working illegally in the UK by:

- being too young to work;
- working too many hours; or
- working in jobs that they are banned from doing by law.

The survey identified that some of the pupils (aged 11–16) reported being too tired to do school work because of their jobs (29%) and some reported playing truant so that they could work (10%). It was identified that about half of all young people aged 13–15 get a job.

Another survey by the Child Accident Prevention Trust in 1996 found that around 20% of young people have accidents when working. The types of injury include:

- contact with moving machinery;
- injuries while handling, lifting or carrying;
- falls;
- being hit by a falling object;
- road accidents; and
- being bitten by animals.

Employers have a legal obligation to make sure that young people who have an out-of-school or holiday job don't have accidents. They have to assess any risks in the job and show how they will reduce or eliminate them. They must tell the parents or guardians of any employees under 16 the outcome of the assessment and the measures they have taken to address any risks.

The *Children and Young Persons Act 1993* states:

- children under 13 years of age are not allowed to work in any job;

- there are only certain types of job that 13 year olds can do and they cannot do babysitting or a paper round, although many do;

- school children must be issued with a permit before beginning work;

- there are a maximum number of hours that can be worked each week, which varies in different parts of the country. This can be checked with the local education department;

- children can work only after 7am and before 7pm. On school days, they can work no more than 2 hours per day; and

- children must have at least 2 weeks free from work during their school holidays.

In 2000 the European Young Workers Directive (94/33EC) was partially implemented in the UK. This says:

- children under 16 should not work more than two hours on any school day or 12 hours in any school week; and

- during school holidays, children under 15 cannot work more than 25 hours a week and 15 year olds have a limit of 35 hours.

When looking for work young people, although seeking independence, should be cautious of responding to adverts in shop windows and they should not place adverts themselves, particularly if the advert gives a name, address, telephone number or email address. Young people should be encouraged to take a parent along with them to check the employer, working conditions and safety issues.

Any young person with an after-school job should:

- make sure their employer has a work permit;

- check they are properly trained if machinery or equipment is to be used;

- know the safety rules and follow them;

- not be tempted to do extra hours; and

- say no if the they think that the job is not safe!

Employers must recognise that children are more vulnerable to injury than adults. This means that they require adequate instruction and training, appropriate to the physical and emotional maturity of the person being trained. It is prudent for the employer to have new young staff under close supervision, not as a matter of control but to advise and identify anything that may cause harm. Young people should be encouraged to question anything they consider to be unsafe. The HSE has identified a case where a 14 year old boy suffered serious head injuries when he was struck by the forks of a materials handler that was being driven by the farmer's 15 year old son. The farmer had allowed the boys to work unsupervised and were connecting a trailer to a tractor in an unsafe manner when the draw bar fell from the fork and the forks struck the child on the head. The youth had driven the handler since he was 13, having received no training other than what his father had provided. The active partner in the business was prosecuted under the *Health and Safety at Work, etc Act 1974 s 3(1)* for failing to provide adequate instructions, training and supervision to a young person which had resulted in an unsafe system of work being carried out. The partner was fined £1,000.

Immigrant workers 5.5

The Management of Health and Safety at Work Regulations, Approved Code of Practice, Paragraph 64 advises:

'The information provided should be pitched appropriately, given the level of training, knowledge and experience of the employee. It should be provided in a form which takes account of any language difficulties or disabilities. Information can be provided in whatever form is most suitable in the circumstances, as long as it can be understood by everyone. For employees with little or no understanding of English, or who cannot read English, employers may need to make special arrangements. These could include providing translation, using interpreters, or replacing written notices with clearly understood symbols or diagrams." The use of statutory safety signs will help in providing information to immigrant workers, for example: Warning, prohibition, mandatory and safe condition signs will have pictograms and be recognisable by their shape and colour.'

While many people from ethnic minority backgrounds have excellent skills in spoken and written English, a significant minority regard their first language as being other than English and have significant difficulty in comprehending written and/or spoken English. Information for employees must be comprehensible and employers should take account of difficulties where employees have a limited command of English. Verbal communication may often be adequate to comply especially where changing conditions require quick reaction to verbal communication. In some circumstances failure to understand basic verbal instructions can have serious consequences, for example a failure to communicate effectively with colleagues. This is particularly so in workplaces where conditions change rapidly, such as construction sites and agricultural activities. However, there will be circumstances where written information will be essential.

The information to be supplied under *Regulation 10* of the *MHSWR 1999* should link with the risk assessment and the measures to be taken for prevention, protection, in emergencies or as a consequence of the work conducted by other employers in the same workplace. The assessment under *Regulation 3* should identify any group of employees (and others not in the employer's employment) who are especially at risk and employers should ensure employees in such groups fully understand what they must do. Similar standards should also be applied to temporary workers and contractor's employees (*Regulation 5*). The action to be taken by employers should include:

- assessing the risks associated with the fact that the individual does not speak and/or understand English;

- considering reasonable means of reducing the risk;

- translating safety notices and training manuals into relevant languages or replacing written notices with clearly understood symbols;

- using internationally recognised safety signs which offer a means of communication that should be clear to all regardless of literacy or language.

- providing safety training sessions in relevant alternative languages to English;

- providing appropriate English language training ranging from key words only to oral and written fluency in English for longer term workers; and

- using bilingual employees to interpret/translate information to their non-English-speaking colleagues. The employer must satisfy themselves that the interpreter/translator has sufficient command of English to understand what is being communicated and is given sufficient authority to discharge the responsibility placed upon them.

There is no evidence to suggest that immigrant workers are more prone to accidents than any other group of employees, although since immigrants tend to be employed in those industries where there are greater dangers, obviously they may have a higher than average accident rate. The problem must be tackled by means of adequate training, and language and cultural factors must be taken into account. Safety instructions will have to be prepared in the language of the worker concerned, and signs and posters which need little translation should be used to indicate the hazards and the precautions to be taken. The *MHSWR 1999* require employers to provide employees with 'comprehensible' information, which implies that account should be taken of language difficulties. The HSE publishes several of its guidance notes in a wide range of languages.

Inducting immigrant workers   5.6

An example of inducting immigrant workers into the workplace is provided through Watton Produce Ltd, one of the country's largest growers and packers of root crops for leading supermarkets and currently employs some 250 staff. Roy Hart, the factory manager, was faced with a major problem in that although the factory's output had increased the income had declined in real terms which meant that because of low pay he could not recruit and retain a local workforce. To keep the factory in business he had to look for a workforce that formed the economic migration from Eastern Europe and south Mediterranean. This of course added to his problems in that the workers had to be legally allowed to work in the country and be able to understand the requirements of the company, including health and safety. Mr Hart had to address the issues of recruiting, housing, inducting, training and assimilating the immigrant workforce. The employment aspect was overcome by utilising one trusted labour provider who would recruit and provide the agency workforce. Once the workforce came under the control of the company, they had to be inducted and trained in the work they were required to undertake and equally important they had to be integrated with the existing workforce. A key aspect of the whole process was the corporate culture of health, safety and welfare of all staff, whether employed directly or through the agency, but with different languages and cultural considerations there needed to be a robust system developed and established in place.

There is a comprehensive introduction to the company's Health, Safety and Environment Policy which is undertaken using an interpreter. The company has an in-house Portuguese trainer in health and safety and basic hygiene. There is an introduction to the systems and nature of the work, as well as the workforce's responsibilities to meet the corporate objectives. It is further explained about the company's responsibilities to its customers. The local workforce were involved in the process and potential prejudices were dealt with through an explanation of the management's principles to overcome the difficulties of staff retention and work commitment from a local labour force. The management developed a strategy to meet staff requirements and involved local employees through the PAL system, where a local member of staff becomes a mentor for an immigrant worker. This not only helps integration, but also provides a watchful eye on matters of health, safety and welfare. All staff receive training in health and safety and basic hygiene and all workplace signs and notices are dual language all of which are monitored by trained staff who speak the language.

The company recognises that it is in their interest to maintain a constant workforce having invested in training and integration into the factory workforce. Mr Hart has taken the process a step further and provided English language lessons for all immigrant workers, but has adopted a unique concept and offered Spanish and Portuguese language lessons for the local staff, all of which is undertaken in work time. They also sponsor their staff to act as external interpreters and assist social services, police and emergency services.

Because the staff involved in this operation are for the most part either Spanish or Portuguese the language and signage can be controlled. However, with the influences of the future workforce when the EEC enlarges into Eastern European countries there would be additional challenges of language and culture to be overcome. The company philosophy is to recruit, train and retain staff from a wide range of backgrounds and cultures, enabling an efficient, proactive and skilled workforce all employed in a corporate culture of good health, safety and welfare.

114

Lone working   5.7

As mentioned in **CHAPTER 1**, a growing number of workers fall into the category of lone workers including the following.

Council employees   5.8

A Council serving around 160,000 people in rural and urban areas and employing approximately 8,000 staff may include between 700–1,000 lone workers, mainly classed as mobile workers. Council employees carry out a wide range of jobs and may be required to work alone. They include social workers, personal care staff, housing officers, environmental health officers (EHOs), building control officers (BCOs), special school teachers, joiners, plumbers, refuse workers and gardeners.

The focus is mainly on the Council's social workers, personal care employees, and environmental health officers who undertake a range of tasks which includes various lone working duties. There are a large number of personal care staff whose main activities include visiting the homes of people to help them wash and dress. Their working hours range between 7.30 am and 10.30 pm. Social workers' activities include talking to people who feel unable to cope and more difficult tasks such as removing children from homes where they may be in danger, or where care is inadequate. Social workers often carry out these tasks at the person's home. EHOs visit restaurants to check standards of hygiene and buildings, and to investigate complaints of noise disturbances. This often means working late in the evening.

Working late means that the normal office support is not available, there may be the need to close a business with the resulting loss of revenue for the owner and there are actions where children are involved. All are emotive situations and the employer has to have effective procedures to ensure the health and safety of personnel involved. The risk factors include employees being required to work at all hours, including late at night. EHOs may have to close down a restaurant because of poor hygiene standards. This may mean that a business loses money and it can lead to aggressive and abusive behaviour towards the EHO. Social workers may have to take children away from their home. This is often a highly intense and emotional experience for parents, children and social workers. Personal care staff are often on foot and have regular patterns of visits and this may make them more vulnerable targets for assault. They may experience verbal abuse, including sexual harassment, and may be mistaken for health visitors carrying drugs and be attacked.

Bus drivers   5.9

Bus drivers take fares and this means that the cash they carry increases the risks of theft, which could be violent. As the roads become more busy, tempers become frayed and there are risks from road rage incidents. Delays through traffic congestion often means timetables cannot be met and so there is the threat from angry passengers. The risks are higher in the afternoon and early evening when passengers are returning from work, particularly if they have had a long wait for a bus. There is an increased threat of violence from youths and anti-social behaviour, as well as passengers who are drunk or are drug users. Such violations are not restricted to the buses, because in certain locations bus termini are particularly at risk from vandals.

Taxi drivers   5.10

Taxi drivers, whether in London or any part of the UK, are at risk because they carry money in the taxi and because the public know that the driver carries money they are targets for robbery. In every part of the country there are higher risk geographical areas or trouble spots which place the drivers at greater risk to violence. Drivers working late at night or early in the morning are at risk and the late night shift increases the need to contend with drunk and aggressive customers. A taxi driver may have to leave the cab in the case of non-payment of a fare and is then exposed to a violent confrontational situation. Taxi drivers should carry mobile phones and where possible have radios so that they have immediate communication with a control room.

Police   5.11

Most uniformed officers, plain-clothes detectives and some civilian support staff often work on their own and the majority of police officers carry out lone working duties for more than 50 per cent of their time and these officers in uniform patrol on their own, in vehicles or on foot and are classed as mobile workers. Civilian staff occasionally work alone in enquiry offices but do have the support of officers and staff in the event of an incident.

Prison officers and other staff   5.12

Violence to staff within the prison service is a major problem and assaults comprised almost 26 per cent of all injuries reported under the *Reporting of Injuries, Diseases and Dangerous Occurrences Regulations 1995 (RIDDOR 1995) (SI 1995/3163)* to prison staff in England, Scotland and Wales in 1998/99. The prison services put a lot of effort into reducing the risks arising from this problem and whilst policies exist within the prison services and the prisons themselves, they are not usually as a distinct safety policy document on violence to staff. The policies and procedures are instead to be found in a number of areas, such as levels of staffing and supervision, control of prisoner privileges, separation and movement of prisoners and contingency plans. Young Offenders Institutes and secure units have had a particularly bad 'press'. Risk assessments are frequently poor or non-existent, with little central guidance from Her Majesty's Prison Service. Risks are usually from inmates, but may also come from others, such as visitors. Risk assessment should include non-uniformed staff, as well as prison officers.

Security staff 5.13

The critical factor for this type of work is that often the staff operate alone, mainly when they have to leave buildings during the night. There are a number of key risks that they face, whether static in one building or patrolling a number of buildings, and they include the possibility that intruders may be present when staff are sent to investigate a security incident. Staff may be patrolling different buildings in different areas of a city or town and there will be some areas where violent incidents are more likely to occur. Often security staff are key-holders whose duties are to check and lock up buildings for the night and in the event of a 'call out' are often sent alone to deal with potential incidents. It is acknowledged that on Friday evenings and weekends the risks are higher because of increased alcohol consumption in town centres.

Window cleaners 5.14

Conflict can arise because window cleaning is a competitive business and some cleaners try to undercut one another, which can lead to violence and abuse. They must acknowledge that the risk of violence or abuse is higher in some areas than others and aggressive customers can be influenced by alcohol, drugs, having a 'bad day' or shift workers who are woken up. They can also have problems with collecting money when there are disputes over payments or customers refuse to pay. They also have to be aware of animals where they be attacked or bitten.

The above list is by no means definitive, there are literally hundreds of different occupations where employees may find themselves diverse because of their lone worker status.

It is essential that managers ensure that the risks associated with lone working are taken into account when risk assessments are carried out. If risk assessments show that it is not possible for the work to be done safely by a lone worker, then other arrangements must be put in place. Those working alone can face hazards, such as accidents or emergencies arising out of the work and lack of close support, first aid equipment, fire fighting equipment, hygiene and welfare facilities. Some employees will face possible violence from members of the public.

The legal position for people to work alone 5.15

A risk assessment is required under the *MHSWR 1999*, which will look closely at how the job is done and identify the work hazards, assess the risks involved and ensure that adequate measures are put in place to avoid the person carrying out the work being harmed. Once risks have been addressed, a safe working procedure should be developed. This should contain as much relevant information as possible, both for the worker and their supervisors. Where staff work alone there are additional requirements to identify specific hazards.

Safe working procedures for lone workers 5.16

Checks should be carried out by regular visits by a manager or supervisor to employees when working alone. The system by which workers are required to check in at regular intervals must be audited. Where personal checks are used, the duration between checks should be based on the estimated hazard of the job. It may be that periodic telephone contacts are adequate for low risk working alone situations, while a more stringent contact procedure is required for a high risk activity.

Managers' responsibilities for health and safety 5.17

Managers are responsible for the safety of their employees in their care. This is particularly appropriate in the case of lone working and managers need to consider the hazards and risk associated with employees working alone. The following checklist provides an example of management actions to consider.

No	Managers Workplace Considerations
1	Carry out informal inspections of the workplace and equipment on a regular basis.
2	Ensure that the workplace is safe and that people are working safely.
3	Identify if as a manager you would feel safe undertaking the activity.
4	Make sure risk assessments of all processes and activities are available for workers to refer to and that Safe Working Procedures are available.
5	Make sure employees know that managers do not want them to put themselves at risk and enquire if the job could be made safer.
6	Periodically speak to those who work alone informally to find out if they have any concerns that can be dealt with.
7	Make sure you have a reliable system for contacting the lone worker through a call-in system, with a mobile phone or a tracking device.
8	Ensure that all employees are fully aware of the company's policies and procedures.
9	Check to make sure equipment is being maintained properly and records are kept.
10	Make sure Materials Safety Data Sheets are available for all materials used and stored by the company.
11	Consider what emergency situations could arise and make sure procedures are in place to cover them.

Workplace safety considerations 5.18

Employees who work alone have a duty of care under *section 7* of the *HSWA 1974* to ensure the health and safety of themselves and others who could be affected by their actions. There is also a moral aspect for individuals not to place others at risk and to look after themselves. To achieve workplace health and safety there are a number of considerations that individuals need to address. The list is not exhaustive.

No	Workplace Safety Considerations
1	Lone workers should ensure that someone knows where they are and establish a contact system to advise someone when they're at work and when they're leaving.
2	Lone workers should not do anything which they consider might put them in danger. They should report any dangerous incident or situation to their line manager and when in doubt, they should ask for advice.
3	Loneworkers should know and follow their company's relevant safe working procedures and guidelines for operating equipment and handling and using substances.
4	If a lone worker doesn't know how to do something, they should not do it and leave it until someone is available to assist them,.
5	If a lone worker is injured they should stay calm and if they need assistance they should contact the emergency services giving clear details of their location, a lone worker should always know exactly where they are.

Home visits and meeting the public 5.19

Employees who are required to undertake home visits or deal face to face with members of the public have to consider risks to their health and safety. Managers need to ensure that there are robust procedures in place and that employees understand them. The list is not exhaustive.

Personal safety training should include being aware of body language, eg signs of anger, tension, stress or nervousness and people adopting a hostile or aggressive stance. The employee should also bear in mind that they may be sending out body language messages.

Women 5.20

The evidence has shown that women are presented with different hazards or the same hazards in different circumstances. This can be quantified in that men might

No	External Workplace Safety Considerations
1	Have employees been fully briefed about the areas where they work, or will work?
2	Do employees understand the importance of previewing cases?
3	Have staff been provided with all available information about the client?
4	Have employees been fully trained in strategies for the prevention of violence?
5	Have employees been made aware of attitudes, traits or mannerisms that can annoy clients?
6	Do employees understand the organisation's preventative strategy?
7	When working away from the main workplace do employees leave an itinerary?
8	Is there a system to keep in contact with colleagues?
9	Are there procedures for contacting managers even when the main workplace is unattended and do employees have managers' numbers for emergencies?
10	Is there a system to arrange an accompanied visit, security escort or use of a taxi?
11	Do employees understand the provisions for support by the organisation?
12	Do employees appreciate their responsibility for their own safety?
13	Do employees carry forms for reporting incidents, including violence or threats of violence?
14	Do employees know how to control and defuse potentially violent situations?
15	Employees need to avoid invading other people's personal space or touching them.
16	Employees need to greet customers politely and with eye contact.
17	Employees must trust their intuition and if the situation feels unsafe or makes them uneasy they should use a plausible excuse and get out.
18	Employees must have a mobile phone for emergencies but should keep it secure and out of sight with a number pre-programmed for emergency use.
19	When employees are using car parks in busy areas they should use ones which are well-lit at night.
20	Employees must not leave a brief case or lap top visible in the car and must ensure that the car is locked.
21	Employees should consider meeting clients in public places, eg hotels.

lift heavy weights on construction sites, whilst women lift equally heavy and often awkward weights in hospitals and care settings. This can be further qualified where men employed in the manufacturing context might move one heavy object a minute, while women will move dozens of smaller objects over a supermarket scanner in the same time period. It has been identified that certain types of especially demanding emotional jobs are almost entirely the preserve of women, where they are required to manage their feelings to produce a publicly observable facial or bodily display of control. An example may be women airline attendants who are employed to manage their own and the passengers' emotions with the objective of preventing fear and developing a customer loyalty. Another major factor is that women's workplace health problems are frequently compounded by getting more of the same at home, where they encounter domestic work and a second shift of lifting, responsibility and chemicals added to those encountered during the working day.

The design of work activities, the organisation and equipment are often based on the model of the 'average man', although the principle of matching work to workers is enshrined in EU legislation. The culture of the prevention of ill health and promotion of well-being at work are equally important for the quality of work of both women and men. It follows that making jobs easier for women will make them easier for men too.

Employers with female staff must carry out a proper risk assessment to identify potential hazards to pregnant workers and those who could become pregnant. Advice can be found in *New and Expectant Mothers at Work, A Guide for Employers*, which explains what to do and how to do it, with detailed advice on the possible chemical, physical and biological risks to new and expectant mothers. The guide and its advice is supported by the Equal Opportunities Commission (EOC).

Evidence shows that more than one in four pregnant women experience a miscarriage, one in 200 babies are stillborn and 100 premature babies are born every day. It is imperative that new and expectant mothers should avoid:

- lifting heavy loads;
- working in confined spaces;
- working at unsuitable workstations;
- working in stressful or violent environments;
- working at night; and
- working with lead.

The Head of the HSE's Health Management Unit has identified that pregnancy is not an illness and that pregnant women should not be signed off sick for work-related ill health problems. Employers have a legal and moral duty to protect women of childbearing age from hazards and risks in the workplace and should understand that new and expectant mothers are entitled to a change in working conditions. This means that they should be offered suitable alternative work or, if that's not possible, be suspended from work at the same rate of pay if risks to her or her child's health and safety have been identified. It is important that women employees inform their employers that they are pregnant or breastfeeding as early as possible, because employers are not required to take any specific action until they have received written notification.

Senior management needs to set up a maternity policy based upon the guidance which will give greater benefits to employers and employees. If employers fail in their duties to take account of the employment of pregnant members of staff they could be found to be in breach of health and safety legislation and be prosecuted by the HSE. In addition, the member of staff could take the company to an industrial tribunal where they could face substantial compensation payouts. It is very important that health professionals should, where ill health is detected, investigate to identify whether the employee's work is a contributing factor and provide advice to her employer on how to solve the problem, rather than signing her off sick. It is emphasised that being pregnant or being a new mother does not prevent women from working and developing their career. Every year around 350,000 women continue to work during their pregnancy and of these 69% return to work soon after giving birth.

There are certain industries and processes that are of particular risk to women. One such activity falls under the *Control of Lead at Work Regulations 1998 (SI 1998/543)*, which defines that a woman of reproductive capacity is prohibited from being employed in certain processes and activities involving lead and lead products.

Other industry processes that affect women fall under the *Ionising Radiations Regulations 1999 (SI 1999/3232)* which sets lower dose limits for exposure to ionising radiation for women who are still of reproductive capacity and for pregnant women than the limit set for men. There are also restrictions on the employment of pregnant women as aircraft flight crew, air traffic controllers and on merchant ships while at sea (Air Navigation (No 2) Order 1995 (SI 1995/1970) and the *Merchant Shipping (Medical Examination) Regulations 1983 (SI 1983/808)*). However, according to the *Employment Act 1989, s 4*, it is lawful to discriminate against a woman insofar as it is necessary to comply with the above restrictions.

The *Suspension from Work (on Maternity Grounds) Order 1994* (as amended) *(SI 1994/2930)* specifies *Regulations 16 to 18* of the *MHSWR 1999* to be the relevant statutory provision for the purpose of *s 66*. There are thus two grounds for maternity suspension:

- If the risk assessment of a woman of child-bearing age reveals a risk which cannot be avoided, the employer shall, if it is reasonable to do so, and would avoid such risks, alter her working conditions or hours of work. If it is not reasonable to do so (or if doing so would not avoid the risk) the employer shall suspend her from work for as long as is necessary to avoid such risk (*Regulation 16* of the *MHSWR 1999*). However, the employer is not required to take any such action unless the woman informs him, in writing, that she is pregnant, or has given birth within the previous six months or that she is breastfeeding (*Regulation 18*).

- Where a new or expectant mother works at night and a certificate from a registered general practitioner or midwife shows that it is necessary for her health or safety that she should not be at work for any period of such work, the employer shall suspend her for as long as is necessary (*Regulation 17*).

A case example involves the consideration by an employment tribunal in *Hickey v Lucas Services (ET 1997)*, where, following a finding of dissatisfaction with the applicant's performance, she was told that she had to transfer to work as a store's assistant in a warehouse. She discovered that she was pregnant and because the new work would have involved her lifting heavy objects, she was advised by her doctor that this could constitute a risk to her health and to the health of her unborn child. Consequently, she went off work sick and was paid statutory sick pay. She complained to an employment tribunal that she should have received her full pay, as she had been effectively suspended from work on maternity grounds, and was thus entitled to her usual remuneration under *s 68* of the *Employment Rights Act 1996 (ERA 1996)*. Her claim was upheld because the employers had not carried out a risk assessment, as required by the *MHSW 1999*. If they had done so, they would have realised that the risks to her health could not be avoided by preventative or protective measures. Thus, they should have altered her working conditions or suspended her on full pay under *ss 66 to 67* of the *ERA 1996*.

Before suspending a woman from work under the above provisions, the employer, where he or she has suitable alternative work for her, must offer her such work. The work must be suitable for her and appropriate in the circumstances, and the terms and conditions, if they differ from those which normally pertain to her work, must not be substantially less favourable than those which previously applied (*ERA 1996, s 67*). Otherwise, she is entitled to be paid her normal remuneration, unless she is offered suitable alternative employment which she unreasonably refuses (*ERA 1996, s 68*).

Under the *MHSWR 1999* suitable rest facilities for pregnant and breast-feeding workers shall be provided. The HSE has also issued guidance documents, *HSG122: New and Expectant Mothers at Work: A Guide for Employers* and *Infection Risks to New* and *Expectant Mothers: A Guide for Employers*.

Bullying at work   5.21

A pro-active personnel policy is needed to deal with the problem of bullying at work. Frequently, the bully will be unaware of the effect of his or her actions, and while it may be difficult to change a person's personality, training in man-management may be indicated. A complaint's procedure may be set up, complaints investigated and appropriate action taken. Counselling can be provided for those affected and monitoring procedures put in place. As pressures increase for more output and greater efficiency in working practices, the consequences of bullying at work should be faced up to and should not be dismissed as mere incidents of over-sensitivity on the part of alleged neurotic employees.

There is a focus on bullying in the school environment, and it can be found both amongst the pupils and the staff. The role of the head teacher, as manager of the school, is to ensure *as far as is reasonably practicable*, structures and procedures embedded in school behaviour policies prevent bullying. Ultimately, it is the responsibility of the whole school community to eradicate bullying by ensuring the development of a caring and supportive ethos.

Bullying can be:

- physical: pushing, kicking, hitting, pinching, any form of violence and threats;
- verbal: name-calling, sarcasm, spreading rumours and persistent teasing;
- emotional: tormenting, threatening ridicule, humiliation and exclusion from groups or activities;
- racist: racial taunts, graffiti and gestures; and
- sexual: unwanted physical contact and abusive comments.

The headteacher is responsible for promoting good behaviour and discipline inline with the governing body's statement of general principles. A written policy should be drawn up, which will include procedures for making and enforcing school rules. There are four major elements to those disciplinary rules:

- to promote self discipline and proper regard for authority among pupils;
- to encourage good behaviour and respect for others and to ensure as far as is reasonably practicable the prevention of all forms of bullying among pupils;
- to ensure pupils' standards of behaviour are acceptable; and
- to regulate pupils' conduct.

The school discipline policy may include the anti-bullying policy and should be publicised annually to pupils, staff and parents. It should also be regularly reviewed. It is good practice to indicate in the school prospectus the main tenets of the policy, which should be given to the parents on admission of their child. If the school bullying policy is maintained as a separate document, this should be treated in a similar way and reviewed on a regular basis. The employer also has duties under the *HSWA 1974* to ensure the health, safety and welfare of all those using their premises. This includes pupils, parents and visitors. Headteachers have a legal duty to take measures to prevent all forms of bullying among pupils.

Professional relationships between members of staff are best conducted with respect and in a non-threatening manner, but there is also a legal requirement, under the *HSWA 1974*, for the employer to provide a safe place of work for employees and all others that use the establishment. The Local Education Authority (LEA) or the governing body, as the employer, has the responsibility to ensure this legal responsibility is fulfilled. That responsibility cannot be delegated. However, the headteacher will be required to ensure the enactment of that responsibility within the school. The headteacher, therefore, has a duty to do all that is reasonably practicable to ensure the health, safety and welfare of employees. As bullying can irrevocably damage the mental health of an individual, it is clear that responsibility extends to the eradication of bullying in the workplace.

Children who are being bullied at school will not always be prepared to tell those in authority. However, when a disclosure is made, it should always be treated seriously. While others may not feel that certain actions or words are of a bullying nature, if the recipient feels they are being bullied that is sufficient evidence to treat the case as *prima facie* bullying. For those pupils who are unable to inform staff about their problem, observations regarding specific behaviour patterns can be routinely established within the school.

Signs of bullying might include:

- unwillingness to come to school;

- withdrawn, isolated behaviour;

- complaining about missing possessions;

- refusal to talk about the problem;

- being easily distressed; and

- damaged or incomplete work.

Where these difficulties are associated with a special need's pupil, a pupil from a minority racial or cultural background or where there are indications of sexual harassment, these indicators may well confirm bullying is occurring. Investigation should be undertaken, checking with colleagues and maintaining rigorous vigilance.

Staff will be able to use their knowledge of the pupils to identify changes in their behaviour that might indicate bullying. The school policy should identify the process to be pursued when staff have concern with regard to a particular pupil. Pupils should be encouraged to be open with their parents, who can then pass on concerns to the school.

Bullies are often in positions of power or authority over their victims. They may behave as they do to hide their own inadequacies or their personal envy of another colleague. Bullying may occur between professional teaching staff, support staff and voluntary workers. Overwork can also lead to bullying with the bully inflicting their frustration and anger on their colleagues. Tell-tale signs in victims are indicated in the following list, that is neither inclusive nor exclusive:

- general low morale;

- increased level of staff turnover;

- high rates of absenteeism;

- frequent disputes, complaints and grievances;

- isolated members of staff; and

- inefficient team working.

Firm management style can often be given as an excuse for what is seen by others as bullying.

Victims of bullying, both pupils and staff, may end up believing that they deserve to be bullied. They feel powerless and vulnerable. Self esteem can be badly damaged and self confidence needs to be re-established. The school should declare that bullying will not be tolerated and that all incidents will be taken very seriously. Investigations into bullying incidents should be thorough and involve both the bully and the bullied. The bully should be helped to recognise their unsociable behaviour and offered support to modify that behaviour. Bullying will not be eradicated if the behaviour of the bullies is not modified. Efforts should be made to identify why a pupil has bullied; support can then be offered to the bully to prevent reoccurrence. Ways of reporting bullying must be clearly established for both pupils and staff. Parents must be clear as to how they can ensure their concerns for their child are taken seriously. Consideration should be given to appropriate 'assertiveness' training for the bullied and other vulnerable groups.

The school policy dealing with bullying may be part of another policy (eg the general discipline policy) or it may stand alone as a separate policy. Whatever its status, there are elements that all schools should consider including in the policy, for example:

- all bullying problems should be taken seriously, both of pupils and adults;

- all incidents should be investigated thoroughly;

- bullies and victims should be interviewed separately;

- witness information should be obtained;

- a written record of the incident, investigation and outcomes should be kept;

- staff should be informed about the incident where a pupil is involved;

- appropriate staff should be informed where a member of staff is involved;

- action should be taken to prevent further incidents. Such action may include:

    o   imposition of sanctions;

    o   obtaining an apology;

    o   informing parents of both bully and bullied;

    o   providing appropriate training; and

    o   providing mentor support for both victim and bully.

Parents should be made aware of the school complaint's procedure and be assured that, should they make a complaint through that procedure, the matter would be taken seriously and dealt with accordingly.

Responsibilities of the health and safety manager   5.22

To manage the health and safety of diverse workers effectively, it is necessary to integrate equality and diversity by making it central to business strategy planning and decision-making.

Managers will need to:

- keep up with best practice in the management of diversity;
- understand the importance of developing organisational ethics and values that embrace and value diversity;
- invest in awareness training for staff and managers;
- ensure that everyone in the organisation behaves in a way that complies with equality legislation and with the company's policies;
- monitor and evaluate the impact of policy and business decision on equality and diversity; and
- review practice and policies on a regular basis.

Employers should recognise and value individual difference and allow everyone to contribute to their full potential. To achieve the right equality standards, the employer will need to identify key resources, systems and procedures. Employees also have a key role in working closely with their employer to promote a positive organisational culture for diverse employees. Employees can advise, support and monitor progress in implementing diversity across the workplace.

Like all occupational health and safety, the diversity strategy of the organisation must be part of the core business activities and not a 'bolt on', with adequate resources devoted to the strategy. To establish good practice all organisational processes and systems must include the positive management of diversity. Also all business projects must be developed and audited to ensure that they do not discriminate and that they actively promote positive diversity. Bringing together people's diversity will produce an environment where everyone feels valued and part of the team. This, in turn, will lead to the talents of all workers being fully utilised and the organisation's goals being met.

Human factors are the cause of approximately 80% of all accidents, therefore, the management of health and safety must review the types and causes of human failures and develop ways of reducing them. There is a need to develop better design of tasks, equipment and procedures. Critical issues for many organisations are operational issues that, for example, include shift work and the potential implications with employees working unnatural time frames. Outside of the core workplace hours communications with shift workers becomes a vital element. Without proactive management, an employee's perception of risk and their behavior can fall short of the organisation's standards. Lone workers can fall into this category where they work outside of the confines and direct control of those employed in a closed environment, such as a factory or workshop. This also extends to employees who have an impediment where management must know the limitations and capabilities of their employees in a way that does not focus on an individual in a negative way.

Managers should ensure employees are provided with the following information:

- guidelines to promote safer working practices in the community, ie prevention and management of aggression;

- clear reporting procedures;

- the lone working policy; and

- procedures for care of individuals who are violent or abusive.

Management will need to examine:

- the job, which encompasses what people are being asked to do, such as workload, task, environment, controls and procedures. It is important to evaluate the capabilities required by an individual to carry it out and identify any changes that could effectively be undertaken that would make the job easier;

- the individual, the person doing the job, their competence, skills, personality and attitudes. It is important to evaluate the capabilities of an individual to carry out a particular work task; and

- the organisation, the health and safety resources, the corporate culture, works systems and communications needs to be robust in that it can accommodate the needs of all employees.

Duty of care   5.23

So far as acts committed by others are concerned, the general test of the conduct of the reasonable employer has to be applied and the question posed, has the employer taken reasonable care to see that his or her employees are not exposed to the risk of injury? The employer must take precautions against risks which he or she knows of or which he or she ought to know. Thus in *Houghton v Hackney Borough Council (1961) 3 KIR 615* a rent collector, employed by the defendants, was attacked while collecting rents on a housing estate. He alleged that the council had been negligent in failing to take proper precautions to protect him from injury. On the facts of the case, his claim for damages failed. The council had taken a number of precautionary steps, such as arranging for an estate porter to be around when rents were being collected, inviting the police to keep a watchful eye on the estate and arranging for the claimant to be collected by car in order to take all the monies to the bank. In the circumstances, it was not negligent.

There are some occupations where the risk of being assaulted is not a negligible one, for example, when dealing with violent offenders or mentally disturbed people. This does not mean that the employee voluntarily accepts the risk of being injured and the employer must still exercise reasonable care to ensure appropriate protection and assistance (see *Michie v Shenley and Napsbury General Hospital Committee [1952] CLY 2411*).

It should be noted that if the employer fails to institute the necessary precautions to protect an employee from violence, the employee may resign from employment and claim constructive dismissal.

Although there are no statutory provisions specifically for diverse employees, reference may be made to *s 2(1)* of the *HSWA 1974*, a duty of care towards employees, and the *MHSWR 1999*, which require an employer to make an assessment of the risks to the health and safety of employees to which they are exposed whilst at work. Arrangements for dealing with that risk must be put into effect.

Once the risk has been determined, appropriate measures can be taken for protective measures. The working environment can be changed as appropriate, systems of work can be monitored and made safe, security measures can be introduced and appropriate training given.

Employers also have a responsibility for buildings and premises in that anyone controlling non-domestic premises must take reasonable steps to provide employees and volunteers with equipment and premises that are safe, including safe routes of exit. This means that the employer who controls or is responsible for the premises, has a duty to make sure that the building is safe to use and complies with all the relevant health and safety regulations (for example, ensuring signs meet the *Health and Safety (Safety Signs and Signals) Regulations 1996 (SI 1996/341)*). This duty applies to places such as offices, warehouses, shops, factories, etc, as well as premises where volunteers may undertake their tasks, such as community centres or scout huts, and also to attached carparks or playgrounds. A recent case highlights the need to take these responsibilities seriously. A young child was hospitalised after daubing himself with a paintbrush left in a toilet of a cricket club. The executive members of the club were fined £8,000 between them for breaching health and safety regulations.

Developing a diversity policy   5.24

Diversity policies should be developed in partnership with employees and their representatives and should include genuine and transparent consultation. Equal opportunities and diversity policies should be written as an integrated policy and show:

- the name of the board or senior management member with overall accountability for policy implementation;

- a definition of diversity that covers age, sex, race, disability, sexual orientation, ethnicity, religion and belief, health status and those who do not fit into the stereotype of 'normal', etc;

- a commitment to identify and remove barriers to equal opportunities;

- a strategic plan encompassing outputs and accountabilities;

- an outline of commitment and responsibility;

- education and training requirements;

- details of the procedures for dealing with complaints of discrimination (this may be part of the overall health and safety policy which includes bullying and harassment, application for special leave, etc); and

- details of the processes and structure for implementing the policy.

The policy will also identify how the implementation and impact of the policy will be monitored, audited and reviewed.

Employers will need to ensure that employees, contractors, customers/clients and the public are aware of the relevant policies. Furthermore, employees should be encouraged to discuss any concerns about equality and diversity issues. This can be communicated through:

- the staff handbook;

- use of leaflets/posters;

- staff newsletters;

- managers operating an open-door policy;

- feedback to staff on progress made on equality and diversity issues;

- encouragement to regularly talk about equality and diversity issues at team meetings and health and safety meetings;

- appraisal and development reviews;

- employee surveys; and

- in induction training for new employees.

Action plans that link with the monitoring, audit, review and budgeting processes need to be implemented. Action plans may cover a variety of activities, such as the development of training programmes, tailored recruitment approaches, development of mentoring schemes, publication of action plans, regular progress reports to the board and reviews of staff attitudes/experiences via a staff attitude survey.

Carrying the diversity policy forward   5.25

If the policy is to be successful the manager responsible for carrying it forward must have strong leadership qualities, be a good people manager and lead by example. Commitment to change and the ability to communicate well with all levels of the workforce is essential. If the policy is to be taken seriously it must also have the full commitment of the whole board, as with the health and safety policy. Any expectations within the policy must be understandable and achievable. The policy must be a living document, which can change to identify all areas of diversity within the workforce, any future workforce and 'others', ie contractors and customers who may come into contact with the undertaking.

Benefiting from diversity   5.26

Improved employee relations can be one of the benefits of managing diverse employees effectively. This will lead to a healthier, safer, more productive working atmosphere with fewer disputes. As a result, improved morale will lead to better staff retention with greater ability to attract quality staff and improved management systems. This in turn will provide better services to customers. A more diverse workforce that is encouraged to use its talents to the full can better understand the needs of its customers and adapt services accordingly. The legal costs of discrimination will be avoided along with the associated negative publicity and damage to employee relations.

For the diversity policy to be a success, dedicated resources for training, promotion and monitoring are needed. Details of the budget and expenditure should be contained in the annual report to the board.

Training   5.27

Training should include:

- identifying the meaning of diversity and the meaning and impact of discrimination and institutional racism in the workplace;
- the difference between acceptable and unacceptable behaviour; and
- the employee's role in making the management of diversity a reality.

It should be emphasised that personal attitudes and values can affect behaviour and can have a serious effect on the success or otherwise of a successful diversity culture.

Monitoring, audit and review   5.28

Monitoring, audit and review will need to take place in the same way as that described in the HSE publication *HSG65 Successful Health and Safety Management*.

The purpose of a monitoring, audit and review exercise will be to identify:

- the effects of past discrimination;
- any existing barriers to the promotion of diversity and equality; and
- the impact of current policy – both anticipated and unanticipated.

The information gathered should be used to identify priorities and to create an action plan that identifies the necessary resources. The process should lead to continuous improvement that strives to overcome past inequalities and to prevent new forms of discrimination and inequalities.

The process of monitoring will gather information, analyse data, define the actions needed to overcome any inequalities and to promote positive diversity. The audit activities will include:

- interviews with stakeholders, ie employees, supervisors, managers and customers;

- the review of policies and procedures;

- written questionnaires; and

- observation of current practices, etc.

An audit should give a comprehensive picture of what is actually happening in the organisation and activity can be prioritised to effect change.

Organisations should analyse information on its workforce profile and job applicants according to sex, race and disability. There may also be a need for further analysis, for example, on contractual status, age, number of dependents and marital status.

Records that can be used to provide useful information in the monitoring process are:

- job applications;

- number of applications compared with appointments;

- training since appointment;

- promotions and transfers;

- resignations, redundancies and dismissals;

- occupational groups;

- grievances;

- disciplinaries;

- implementation of specific policies, for example requests/refusals for special leave arrangements;

- complaints of bullying and harassment;

- personal injuries;

- ill-health; and

- employment tribunals, etc.

It is better that active monitoring takes place, in that it is carried out before a problem exists, rather than waiting for reactive monitoring after an incident.

A 'Personal Safety at Work' policy with guidance notes setting out the procedures that staff must abide by will also need to be part of the diversity policy.

6
Management Systems/Tools

Introduction 6.1

As can be seen from earlier chapters, violence is one of the most likely risks to a growing number of diverse employees, along with the more highly publicised discrimination cases in terms of racial, sexual and disability discrimination. In recent years, violence at, or due to, work has increased and it is a problem that is spreading to more types of business and industry. Violence is not always physical, it can also be psychological in the form of bullying or harassment and quite often leads to stress. What were once accepted as low risk safe occupations have changed and a growing number of employees face the threat of violence. The Health and Safety Executive (HSE) has been very proactive in promoting the health and safety message to a diverse range of occupations, on a wide range of subjects. One such promotion has identified violence to workers, and in particular lone workers, and looked at the type and degree of violence and the lessons to be learned from organisations that have been proactive and have developed measures to counter confrontation. Many organisations have adopted measures to select, train and support staff who can, as a result of their work, be placed in risk situations and cover a diverse range of businesses. Some workplace activities that are reviewed require staff to be placed in confrontational situations and, therefore, their needs differ from staff who, for example, are in the caring profession who should not encounter violent situations. The valuable lesson for managers is to identify the problems that staff face and decide if special training is required, then review what approaches worked and what did not. As is repeatedly stated, every organisation has its own particular problems and concerns. It is accepted that the problems encountered in an inner city will differ to those of a country location. However, there are many examples where what applies to a city applies equally to a market town.

Acts of violence against employees 6.2

The fact that acts of violence against employees, whilst carrying out their employment duties, are on the increase is clearly becoming a factor that must be addressed in health and safety policies. Such acts may be committed by fellow employees, customers or third parties. So far as acts perpetrated by employees are concerned, these should be dealt with within the confines of the disciplinary procedures and generally an employee would be left to pursue his or her own legal remedies, either criminal or civil, for assault.

The possibility of an employee suffering an act of violence whilst at work should be included in the risk assessment. There may be organisations where there is no history of such acts, but if it can be shown that the risk is not negligible, either in that particular type of industry or because of special features of the organisation, ways of avoiding or mitigating against such acts should be considered. Employees particularly at risk include those who handle cash in isolation (eg all-night petrol station assistants and rent collectors in certain housing estates) and those who come into contact with violent people who are affected by drink or drugs (eg social workers, A & E hospital staff and carers). There are also employees who have to deal with dissatisfied customers or complainants (eg administrators in Benefits Agency offices and those who handle or transport cash or valuables).

Risk assessment   6.3

Due to the importance of risk assessments in all organisations, the HSE has produced a guidance leaflet, *5 Steps to Risk Assessment*, that contains information designed to help management in understanding what is required and how to set about undertaking risk assessments. The leaflet contains a blank risk assessment form that can be adapted by most businesses and organisations, focusing on topics of hazards, who might be harmed, is the risk adequately controlled and what further action is necessary to control the risks. The requirement for risk assessments in an organisation employing less than five persons is that the findings do not have to be recorded and where there are five or more employees only significant findings need to be recorded. This is a very important point because if there is an accident the evidence to show that risks have been assessed can only come from risk assessments that have been recorded and held on file. It is strongly recommended, therefore, that risk assessments are carried out and that they are recorded regardless of the size and type of business. An important part of the risk assessment process is that employers have to identify the capabilities and competencies of its employees and provide training, where necessary, with the emphasis on health and safety. This can be achieved by providing adequate health and safety training when employees are recruited and when they are exposed to new or increased workplace risks.

Risk assessment in respect of new or expectant
mothers   6.4

The *Management of Health and Safety at Work Regulations 1999 (SI 1992/3242)* requires specific risk assessment in respect of new or expectant mothers where the workforce includes women of childbearing age and the work is of a kind which could involve risk, by reason of her condition, to the health and safety of a new or expectant mother or to that of her baby from any processes or working conditions, the assessment needs to include an assessment of such risk. Where the risk cannot be avoided by preventive and protective measures taken by an employer, the employer will need to alter her working conditions or hours of work, if it is reasonable to do so, to avoid the risks. If these conditions cannot be met, the employer will need to identify and offer her suitable alternative work that is available. If that is not feasible the employer will have to suspend her from work. The *Employment Rights Act 1996 (ERA 1996)* (which is the responsibility of the Department of Trade and Industry) requires that this suspension should be on full pay for so long as is necessary to avoid such risk. Employment rights are enforced through the employment tribunals.

Where a new or expectant mother works at night and a certificate from a registered medical practitioner or a registered midwife shows that it is necessary for her health and safety that she should not be at work for any period of such work identified in the certificate, the hours of work must be altered or the woman must be suspended on full pay.

The additional steps of altering working conditions or hours of work and offering suitable alternative work or suspension, as outlined above, may be taken once an employee has given her employer notice in writing that she is pregnant, has given birth within the last six months or is breastfeeding. The employer may request confirmation of the pregnancy by means of a certificate from a registered medical practitioner or a registered midwife in writing. If this certificate has not been produced within a reasonable period of time, the employer is not bound to maintain changes to working hours or conditions or to maintain paid leave. A reasonable period of time will allow for all necessary medical examinations and tests to be completed.

If the employee continues to breastfeed for more than six months after the birth, she should ensure the employer is informed of this, so that appropriate measures can continue to be taken. Employers need to ensure that those workers who are breastfeeding are not exposed to risks that could damage their health and safety as long as they breastfeed. If the employee informs her employer that she is pregnant for the purpose of any other statutory requirements, such as statutory maternity pay, this will be sufficient for the purpose of the *ERA 1996*.

Risk assessment for young persons   6.5

The *Management of Health and Safety at Work Regulations 1999* also requires specific risk assessment in respect of young persons the employer must manage the risk of accidents, which it may reasonably be assumed cannot be recognised or avoided by young persons owing to their insufficient attention to safety or lack of experience or training or in which there is a risk to health from extreme cold or heat, noise or vibration. The determining of whether work will involve harm or risks for the purposes should be identified in the risk assessment.

It is important that employers should not employ a young person for work which is beyond their physical or psychological capacity. Nor should employers employ a young person if it involves harmful exposure to agents which are toxic or carcinogenic or involve harmful exposure to radiation.

The employer needs to carry out the risk assessment before young workers start work to see where risk remains, taking account of control measures in place. For young workers, the risk assessment needs to pay attention to areas of risk. For several of these areas the employer will need to assess the risks with the control measures in place under other statutory requirements. When control measures have been taken against these risks and if a significant risk still remains no child (young worker under the compulsory school age) can be employed to do this work. A young worker above the minimum school leaving age cannot do this work unless it is necessary for his or her training, he or she is supervised by a competent person and the risk will be reduced to the lowest level reasonably practicable.

Consideration must be given to the fitting-out and layout of the workplace and the workstation with regard to young persons. Full consideration must be given to the nature, degree and duration of exposure to physical, biological and chemical agents, which because of a young person's inexperience could leave them vulnerable to harm. The organisation of processes and activities need to be clearly identified to determine the extent of the health and safety training provided, or to be provided, to young persons. Where work equipment is used, the instruction and supervision must be sufficient and effective. Consideration should be given to the risks from agent's processes and work listed in the Annex to Council Directive 94/33/EC on the protection of young people at work.

Risk assessment for lone workers

Council social workers, personal care staff 6.6

Many council employees and personal care staff generate key risks which are generic in nature and the predominant key is the necessity to take some form of action in a confrontational face to face situation.

As part of the risk assessment process the development of successful measures for each of their employee groups is necessary. The key elements are that information relating to the risk assessment is passed to all personnel that may be affected and the need for training which can be identified by managers or employees. The main focus for management and for staff development is to avoid potentially violent situations through knowledge and evolving confidence so that they use care and common sense. Members of staff will cope with confrontation and violence in different ways and so there must be an effective system to maintain staff confidence and moral.

The training of a large number of staff will provide feedback of experiences, both of trainers and staff, and that in turn highlights some principles that apply to all situations and these are identified, but not limited to, being aware of their surroundings, not to sit down, not to spread any belongings or papers out and if they feel at risk to make an excuse to leave.

Many organisations put control measures in place as part of the risk assessment process and management just accepts that everything is working. However, the appropriate follow up action is to monitor and review. The information gathered is reviewed against the measures used to ensure they are working effectively. If they are not or there are concerns identified then further controls may be necessary to improve the risks. Managers must accept responsibility for their risk assessments and consult with employees in carrying out this responsibility.

Systems must be in place to encourage employees to report incidents, so as to establish what the problems are and allow management to develop and introduce appropriate prevention measures. It also raises the profile of violence prevention. To encourage reporting, the system should be user friendly and easy to use. This will address the problem of under-reporting. A simple flow chart will help people know what to do and how to report different types of incidents. The problem that organisations face is that staff can become conditioned to violence and what was reported suddenly becomes acceptable with the resulting under reporting. Employers will need to establish a benchmark level of violent incidents and encourage the increase of reporting so that management can evaluate safety measures and monitor incident trends.

Safe guards for employees when they are out of the office carrying out their work tasks is important. Further control measures include the use of mobile phones, lone worker systems can be adopted which means that employees can leave a message with a central point detailing a visit and the time it will take. If the employee has not called in to cancel the system after the stated time, someone tries to contact the employee, then the line manager and eventually the police, if there is no response. The phone can also have a panic button for emergency use. This can link directly to reception and allows the receptionist to listen into a conversation. The employee uses code words in the conversation to alert reception to organise assistance if needed.

Personal alarms can be issued, but information should be given on when and how to use the alarm, for example if attacked from behind it can be used in someone's ear to disorientate the attacker and give the employee a few extra seconds to get away. Personal alarms should be kept where they are easily accessible and not in handbags or brief cases.

Systems need to be in place for social workers visiting potentially violent people, enabling them to recommend who should or should not visit those people. This would identify risks to females, males or lone workers, it would also recommend when there is a requirement for two social workers.

In situations where a high risk of violence is faced by staff, such as environmental health officers, police officers can accompany them when attending potentially violent locations and, in particular, where repeated and extreme threats have been made to them. It may be appropriate to use alternative staff to visit where employees have been previously threatened. All of the potential risk situations can be identified through joint risk assessments with input from management, employees and the trade unions. The police can be consulted where they need to assess their involvement in a potentially violent situation.

Home care   6.7

Guidance for home care service providers is available from the HSE, entitled *Handling Home Care: Achieving Safe, Efficient and Positive Outcomes for Care Workers and Clients*. The guidance is aimed primarily at care service managers and those responsible for assessing mobility assistance risk in home care situations.

Not only are care workers subject to acts of violence, but they are also highly likely to suffer back injury as a result of manual handling operations. The social and health care sector is one of the highest risk areas for back injury, with around 50% of all accidents reported in the sector attributed to helping people whose mobility is reduced by disability and chronic illness. Each year an estimated 642,000 people in Great Britain suffer from a musculoskeletal disorder which affects their back and is caused by work. Disorders affecting the back may cost Britain up to £3 billion per year.

Head of HSE's Services Sector, John Cullen, said:

> 'The problem for home care service providers is in getting the correct balance between ensuring the safety of care workers performing the manual lifting and handling and meeting the individual needs of the client. HSE supports that client personal wishes on mobility assistance are respected wherever possible, but we do not want to create back problems for those doing the lifting. We are confident that if the guidance is implemented, this will go a long way towards improving the health and safety of both care workers and clients.

> 'The HSE recognises that this is a difficult area and we have consulted with organisations representing disabled people to provide practical advice. I hope that service providers, care workers and clients will find the guidance useful.'

Frances Hasler, Director, National Centre for Independent Living (NCIL), which suggested a number of amendments to the guidance, said:

> 'We are happy to see that HSE's Guidance includes a reminder that "no lift" policies should be avoided. We look forward to being involved in future work to develop comprehensive guidance on safe ways of supporting independent living in a range of settings.'

Handling Home Care: Achieving Safe, Efficient and Positive Outcomes for Care Workers and Clients gives practical advice on how to safely assist clients' mobility. The guidance not only focuses on the physical risks to workers and clients, but also takes into account the wider risks to the client if they are not suitably assisted, for example loss of independence. The guidance contains case studies, highlighting poor practice that is detrimental to care workers and their clients. Each case study explains the problem and identifies solutions that minimise the risks involved.

The guidance encourages service providers to find solutions to manual handling risks, which include taking the views of the client and their family into account. It recommends that service providers develop, in consultation with services users and their representatives, clear policies and management procedures to achieve these aims successfully.

Community midwives   6.8

For community midwives, many risks are not a direct result of being with the clients they are visiting. Some examples of incidents that have been known to occur, and that management needs to be aware of and address, include the following:

- During a parenting class, a drunken male became very disruptive and sarcastic. This made the midwife feel nervous and at risk.

- A client became abusive when asked to turn off a mobile telephone during a parenting class.

- During a home birth a midwife had to call for assistance because the client's partner started to fight with a neighbour who was complaining about the noise of the birth.

- On one occasion a midwife was held hostage, but this kind of incident is very rare.

Management needs to have effective feedback from staff on the realities of the risks and the actual confrontational experiences they face, both with the clients and outside of the client's direct environment, again it is important to have user friendly systems for reporting incidents so that employees feel confident about reporting.

Staff should be provided with incident report forms and are encouraged to report incidents, no matter how small. Even telephone abuse should be identified. This helps to establish what the problems are and to develop appropriate prevention/management measures. Potential problem areas or problem clients need to be identified and recorded so that midwives visiting them receive early warnings, allowing joint visits to be arranged if necessary.

Midwives can use a mobile phone central message system. Where they log on to the system when they leave home in the morning and send text messages during the day, detailing where they are going and how long they will be. This process continues until the end of the day. If a midwife takes longer than anticipated at a job and does not check in at the expected time, an alert is sent to the midwife's mobile phone. The midwife then has to send a text to confirm that they are OK. If this does not happen an escalation procedure is put into place whereby the midwife is called every few minutes. Eventually, if the midwife cannot be located the police may be contacted. In addition, staff may be provided with personal alarms if they need one.

Management should design the job to pre-empt potential incidents and safeguard the staff. All staff and management need to be encouraged to carry out risk assessments of their jobs and the situations they encounter. Effective measures include doubling up with two midwives being sent to night-time calls, depending on the location and proximity of midwives. Another effective measure could be adapting the time of parent craft classes so that the caretaker of the health centre is around and can help a midwife should an incident arise.

Council housing services   6.9

A council serving a diverse area in a town and country environment which includes a Housing Services Division may employ several hundred people, including housing officers, surveyors, clerical staff, maintenance staff, cashiers, project managers, rent arrears collectors, caretakers and sheltered housing wardens. They may manage 10–15,000 council properties and deal with requests and complaints from council tenants, which means that the type of work varies with, for example, housing officers interviewing tenants and dealing with complaints, while surveyors inspect occupied and empty properties. So that this work can be carried out, the majority of staff spend their time working alone. Some staff are required to be on call 24 hours or live on the site itself to help manage the property. Other members of staff may be considered lone workers, even though they work in the council building, and about two-thirds of the employees are mobile workers.

The management has to undertake risk assessments to identify potential high risk situations and has to have proactive systems in place to ensure the safety of staff and, most importantly, have control of the staffs' whereabouts. Having carried out an evaluation, the key risks for the council include:

- interviewing tenants in their homes and in offices;

- having to give bad news, for example telling tenants that it is not the council's responsibility to fix a particular problem;

- being unable to complete particular jobs to the tenant's satisfaction;

- evicting people from their home; and

- having to leave a job because the tenant is not at home or because the job is different to that reported.

There are certain geographical areas or trouble spots that are high risk and so there needs to be a focus on working late at night. Other factors that have to be considered include psychological abuse caused, for example, by customer complaints of 'improper' conduct by employees and exposure to potentially violent or aggressive members of the public, for example drug users or dealers and large groups of youths.

Managers responsible for lone workers need to undertake risk assessments and have systems to deal with potential conflict. The evidence of violence against staff includes:

- threats of violence, including use of offensive weapons and other implements;
- verbal and physical threats and assaults;
- staff being held hostage;
- intimidating behaviour from tenants;
- vehicle break-ins;
- theft and road rage incidents;
- attacks by dogs; and
- allegations made by a client of 'improper' acts by a member of staff.

The work of the council has to continue and so potential conflict cannot be removed from the agenda, even where risk assessments produce a high value. It is important to have a training package for all employees for dealing with aggression. A 'walk away' policy is necessary, so that if employees feel uncomfortable or threatened they can walk away from the situation. This is considered to be the most successful form of violence prevention.

The key elements of the training package include:

- employers' and employees' responsibilities for risk assessment;
- procedures and safe working practices;
- understanding sources of aggression and violence, for example leaving someone waiting;
- how to respond to aggression and violence; and
- body language, personal space and methods of communication.

It is also important to be aware of signs of aggression, such as the tone of voice and how to handle a conversation in order to reduce aggression, for example, listen and maintain a calm tone of voice, but be firm in response. Staff need to be in control and avoid confrontation, as well as assertiveness versus aggression and equally important know when to terminate the interview or job and leave if necessary.

Violent incidents will need to be included in accident reports and information about health and safety issues, including violence, communicated to staff. This helps to increase and update knowledge and to encourage reporting of incidents. A proactive approach can include:

- promoting a good relationship with the police;
- forming health and safety working groups; and
- creating forums and tenant groups.

Prosecution in serious cases will help to convey the message that violence is unacceptable and serves as a deterrent to others. Counselling should be available to employees following a violent incident. Managers should be encouraged to look for signs of potential cases where staff have suffered so as to ensure support.

Further control can take place through the use of CCTV in key areas. An effective system means that staff can contact the CCTV control centre to direct the cameras on them if a potentially violent situation is developing. In addition to cameras, good lighting is essential in areas of potential concern. A 24-hour call centre needs to be available when employees work late at night so they can then contact the call centre to tell the duty staff where they are and to give regular updates on progress.

A system needs to be developed to ascertain the need for doubling up for high-risk areas or jobs to be undertaken, which means that two people attend a job if they know there have been problems in the past. If it is late at night or during a weekend, employees on stand-by have an informal arrangement whereby an employee can call another if they feel uncomfortable.

Police officers 6.10

Unlike other staff who can operate a 'walk away' policy when a situation becomes confrontational and potentially violent, the police officer has to remain and deal with the situation. The police do have an effective system of rapid back up in the event of a call for assistance, however that does take time and an incident can deteriorate rapidly with a real and serious threat to the officer. The immediate option available to senior officers is to deploy two officers on patrol, but that does reduce the available resources. The police, through experience, are able to identify critical aspects of the work, which include late evening work between 8pm and 2.30am where it has been identified that more assaults occur between these hours when there tends to be fewer witnesses/members of the public around. In addition, licensed premises at the above times are subject to sudden tensions that arise when large groups gather in localised areas. The major factor is alcohol consumption and drug abuse by members of the public can lead to anti-social behaviour. Another area identified is football matches involving large crowds of troublesome and potentially aggressive fans. In the wider context there is a resentment of police authority and aggression can arise when the police tell people what to do. The geographical area makes a difference and certain industrial, urban and rural areas pose particular risks to officers working alone, particularly where resource support may be some distance away in rural areas.

For groups of workers who face violent confrontation every time they go on duty it is not feasible to provide a list of the types of incidents that have been encountered and so a small sample has been provided which shows that when an officer responds to assist a member of the public or stop crime the violence can be severe. In one case an officer was speaking to a car driver he was about to arrest when the driver drove off dragging the officer half a mile down the road. The officer was seriously injured and unable to return to work. In another situation an officer attended an incident concerning a reported assault on a woman. The officer was struck with an axe and badly injured. An officer was pursuing suspects down a narrow alleyway when he was cornered and severely beaten up. This type of attack occurs and officers have been 'jumped from behind' and assaulted at night. Even police stations are not excluded from violent confrontation and groups of angry people have gathered at enquiry offices where only a lone worker was present.

While certain violence prevention measures are mandatory in the whole Police Service, individual Police Forces can adopt other measures, with advice from the Home Office. All officers undertake initial personal safety training and attend refresher courses every two years. This training, with the provision of radios and personal safety equipment, is considered the best way of reducing and tackling violent incidents. The training follows a format that meets the police requirements and is modified to reflect changes. The key messages include non-verbal communication skills, where officers are taught to look for signs that aggression is building up, using eye contact if appropriate. They are taught the use of the conflict resolution model, which is intended to help officers make the most appropriate response. It sets out a number of issues which officers should consider when making decisions so that officers assess the threat before taking action. The standard procedure taught is to focus first on verbal conflict resolution and if this fails they can resort to use physical conflict resolution, such as CS spray, batons and other restraints. A critical factor is that an officer has to make an on the spot assessment of the situation and if deemed appropriate await back-up. Modern UK society requires officers to be aware of, and to respect the diversity of, the public with whom they work.

Police officers report incidents because failure to report an assault may have implications for an officer in terms of his or her pension, a prosecution case or entitlement to compensation. This is an effective driving force to encourage officers to report all assaults which result in bodily injury. This effective system enables the Force to keep accurate data on levels of physical violence against officers, although it is likely that actual levels of violence or attempted aggression are considerably higher than the data indicates. Verbal abuse is not recorded, as it is now accepted as a normal part of the job.

Police use local intelligence and knowledge of the area to establish any concerns or problems which might give rise to tensions or potential violence. A vital part of modern policing are the communication devices, such as radios and telephones, and all officers have radios which they pass through a system to sign in, notifying the control room they are on duty. A radio alarm button can warn the control centre to alert other officers to assist a lone worker and officers also use code words to alert the control room of danger. Police on patrol are provided with physical conflict resolution tools, which include CS spray, batons and handcuffs.

Police officers and civilian staff at police stations are not immune from violence and some support staff work behind desks which are designed to prevent a physical attempt to grab them. They also have an escape route to another part of the building which is secure and separate from the reception area. Depending on the location of the police station, some enquiry desks have screens made from toughened glass, which means that staff can still be seen but are physically protected from potential aggressors. In addition, panic alarms are installed in enquiry offices and interview rooms. For officers working alone outside of the police station, dynamic risk assessments are carried out and supervisors constantly reassess risks as circumstances change. The assessments help to reduce risks for lone working officers and separate risk assessments can be undertaken for city centre officers, where it may identify that officers do not work alone in some higher risk areas and situations.

Prison officers and other staff   6.11

The Prison Service is held to be part of the Crown and, therefore, subject to Crown administrative enforcement procedures.

Sentenced adult male prisoners are divided into four security categories that determine the type of prisons in which they can be held:

- Category A – prisoners whose escape would be highly dangerous to the public or the police or the security of the state, no matter how unlikely that escape might be, and for whom the aim must be to make escape impossible;

- Category B – prisoners for whom the very highest conditions of security are not necessary, but for who escape must be made very difficult;

- Category C – prisoners who cannot be trusted in open conditions, but who do not have the resources and will to make a determined escape attempt; and

- Category D – prisoners who can be reasonably trusted in open conditions.

The Prison Service Headquarters produces large numbers of overall policies on a wide range of issues, such as:

- security;
- fire precautions; and
- contingency plans to cover, for example:
  - emergencies involving prisoner disruptions;
  - outbreaks of contagious diseases; and
  - evacuation procedures.

Each prison is responsible for producing its own safety policy, with some arrangements set down in the centrally produced policies.

Some specific factors that a prison risk assessment should consider are:

- induction training (including breakaway training);
- availability of prison officers to assist others;

- safe means of escape;

- emergency alarms (availability of and training in the use of); and

- are teachers/volunteers required to escort inmates from cells to classrooms?

For prison staff, there are internal systems for reporting violent incidents (collated nationally), recording noteworthy events or behaviour on each wing and communicating these to each new shift or the control room. Further measures include control and restraint training (C&R), provision of alarms throughout the wings, personal alarms and radios, and anger reduction classes/therapy. Levels of C&R competence are a very important part of the prison services' approach to controlling violence from inmates. Two levels of C&R training/competence exist:

- basic training – breakaway techniques, application of simple restraint techniques, 3-officer teams for cell rescue/intervention; and

- advanced training – public order techniques for riot control.

All newly-trained prison officers will have had basic training. Officers with longer service will usually have had training in similar techniques in the past. Each prison is also expected to maintain a cadre of officers trained to advanced level. These make up part of a geographical or regional resource that can be called on by other prisons in times of crisis. Advanced-trained officers are equipped in the same way as police support units, for example a Nato helmet, fire resistant overalls, boots, shin pads and full length or half length polycarbonate riot shields. These officers will have periodic training sessions which can be very realistic, though in the interests of safety, wooden blocks are used instead of bricks and real fire extinguishers are no longer thrown.

Because prisons have large numbers of staff who are not prison officers, some of whom will have regular contact with inmates, there should be procedures in place governing their access to wings and other areas when inmates are present and arrangements for escorts if necessary. They will have been trained in prison security procedures, such as the use of alarms and keys and breakaway techniques. All staff are usually offered training in dealing with hostage taking situations and there are set procedures to be followed in such situations until a trained negotiator can attend. Equally, there should be set procedures for non-prison service visitors. Some will need to be escorted, such as Citizens Advice Bureau and official prison visitors. Some, who visit regularly, such as clergy and teachers, may need little assistance. The procedures and precautions required will ultimately depend on the individual, the area to be visited and the profile of the inmate(s). They should be the subject of appropriate risk assessments.

Because of the inherent risks, the prison services have extensive policies on both HIV and Hepatitis B and have produced the Prison Service Order *Blood Borne and Related Communicable Diseases*, which provides information on how to deal with infected prisoners. While prisoners who are HIV or Hepatitis B positive pose a higher risk of infection, all prisoners are regarded as potentially infected and, therefore, as posing a high risk. The prison service requires universal precautions to be used when handling any blood or body fluid/product spill, and an effective measure is for prison officers to carry a pouch on their belts with gloves and resusci-aid. Spill packs should be kept on wings to soak up and sterilise blood/fluid spills. It is recommended that prison staff are vaccinated against Hepatitis A and B. Tuberculosis (TB) is a matter of concern in prisons, not least because of the emergence of antibiotic resistant strains and the susceptibility of prisoners already infected with HIV. Tuberculosis is usually spread by inhalation of water droplets contaminated with the bacteria. Prisoners who are known to be infected with TB must be isolated until the infectious stage of the disease has passed. There is also a potential risk of legionella arising from the hot and cold water systems and there should be a stated policy for the water systems to be tested regularly.

Prison officers are at risk when cells are searched for drugs, other contrabands and weapons. This requires set policies on how and when such searches are to be conducted. Carrying out cell searches can give rise to a number of risks, in particular potentially infectious needles/sharps used in drug taking (referred to as 'works') and unsafe electrical equipment or wiring.

There have been considerable problems in the past with the 'illegal abstraction' of electricity (a potential breach of prison disciplinary rules) by prisoners in their cells. This basically involves the prisoner breaking in to the mains electrical supply within the cell via the light fitting or switch. This can be done for a number of reasons, for example to run radios and other equipment, stills or to electrify the door or another part of the cell so as to cause injury. There have been cases when a prison officer searching the cells received an electric shock.

The extent of the problem varies greatly between prisons and various programmes have been put into place to attempt to control/reduce it, including the provision of protected 240 V supplies to cells, 12 V supplies and the provision of rechargeable batteries. The implementation of these programmes has sometimes been compromised by the cost of the necessary modifications, so a variety of systems may be found in practice.

Security staff   6.12

An important aspect for employers of security staff is the recruitment and selection process where prospective employees have more than one in-depth interview and there is a vet of their previous ten years' work record. It is important to explore all avenues as part of the selection process, including police checks, to ensure that they have no previous criminal record. This helps to ensure that the company recruits suitable security staff.

Companies who employ security guards direct or companies who deploy their guards to client premises have to have a system that encompasses sound staff selection and training. One company has new-starter training where both internal staff and external contractors receive on the job training for three months and one month respectively. This includes health and safety and security training and dealing with members of the public. The employees receive a flowchart outlining standard procedures to follow when working alone or leaving the site. The procedures include telephoning the security control room during the lone working period and maintaining the logbook with details about staff location. One company has adopted the 'regulation round-up' test, which means that after completing the initial training all internal staff complete a test which includes several questions on health, safety and security before they start the job.

It is generally accepted that security guards adopt the 'do not put yourself at risk' policy and a company policy should reflect that. If staff feel uncomfortable in a situation they should withdraw and not put themselves at any unnecessary risk. Management must be seen to support this policy and a failure to do so could result in a confrontational situation with a resulting loss of trust in management. They must not approach buildings alone if in doubt or if they feel unsure or at risk, but should wait until the police arrive.

Many organisations employ a 24-hour security control room which should be manned by two people who monitor the different areas of the buildings and provide back-up if an employee needs it. Out of normal hours they would call the police for support in dealing with intruders. Mobile security staff should inform their control room when they are on duty and contact the control room regularly (every 30 minutes) to confirm that they are okay.

There has been a dramatic use of CCTV cameras. They enable security to monitor staff safety constantly. For example, when a member of staff informs the control room that they are to patrol a building, the CCTV camera can indicate whether the area is safe and monitors the member of staff during patrol. When security staff are on patrol they should carry mobile telephones to maintain contact and inform the control room when they leave and return. If they fail to report back, a controller phones to check their whereabouts. If there is no response and there is cause for concern, a key-holder and the police are called to the site.

Many organisations have adopted a 'dress down' uniform where security staff wear a normal suit-style uniform with blazer and trousers. This is less confrontational than a security uniform and helps to reduce friction between security staff and other people. In some locations it may be more appropriate to have security staff in uniform so that they can be readily identified, for example in a large store or shopping mall.

Nightclub stewards   6.13

The nightclub management must set clear guidelines of what is acceptable and what is not. The club must publicise its rules about immediate removal for fighting, causing annoyance, being drunk or being found in possession of drugs. Staff should then be trained to enforce strict control of customers entering the club based upon the guidelines. The guidelines should identify that admission is restricted to those who are sober and not under the influence of drink or drugs.

The policy should extend to the searching of people on admission, including use of a metal detector to identify weapons, such as knives or guns. All staff must be trained to be non-provocative and to let the stewards handle difficult customers. It follows that stewards must be trained in customer service and how to remove or restrain with minimal force. The use of excessive force could find the steward prosecuted for assault. Management must play an active part in the nightly briefings for stewards to exchange information on troublemakers and those banned from the premises.

There are a number of actions that clubs can put in place so as to reduce the potential of incidents, such as uniformed stewards being deployed in high profile at key points and kept in contact visually and by radio. Money should be kept out of sight and large amounts removed from the public areas at regular intervals and tills should be kept out of reach from customers. The use of low lighting to provide intimacy must still allow sufficient visibility, coupled with emergency back-up lighting and tamper-proof switches installed. Some areas of the club may need to be kept closed until the number of customers requires more supervised space, all of which can be monitored by visible CCTV cameras. All of these actions are dependent upon sufficient staff who are always available to serve and control the customers and that empty glasses are collected promptly so they cannot be used as weapons.

Bus drivers   6.14

The level of threat will vary from people refusing to pay their fare to robberies, where drivers have been threatened with knives, air guns and samurai swords. One incident involved a driver who was getting into his cab when a firework was thrown onto the bus. The driver managed to get out of the cab in time but the force of the explosion damaged the cab, shattering both front windscreens and damaging the assault screen. In another incident a shotgun was fired at the windscreen of the bus. Equally vile behaviour occurred when youths urinated down the periscope through which the driver sees the top deck of the bus. The driver left his cab to talk to the youths and was attacked by them.

The consequences for the bus operating company and individuals of such incidences of violence means that there is physical injury, stress and fear which have a cumulative effect on health, lost time and production because of sickness absence, demoralisation and staff losses. The media report such incidents and that in turn has a negative effect on recruitment, because people are put off when they hear about the problems. There is also financial loss through compensation claims.

Bus drivers must receive health and safety training as part of their induction where some of the course modules deal specifically with violence and aggression, so drivers learn key techniques and they also develop their interpersonal skills. They need to understand the importance of self-control and display non-aggression attitudes and mannerisms towards customers. They need to adopt assertive communication skills, as well as being able to acknowledge customer concerns. It may be possible to use humour to defuse a situation.

Drivers must not carry cash in an obvious cash bag. While driving, they must not tell others how much they have taken because people might be listening. If they do have to deposit money, they should use well-lit areas and known safe locations. There should be good liaison with the police and the management should encourage and support drivers who have to resort to calling the police in difficult circumstances, particularly in violent situations.

All incidents must be reported and should be categorised by type. Categories include:

- assaults due to robbery or fare dispute;

- assaults involving motorists; and

- assaults involving spitting, vandalism and missile throwing.

It is a matter for the company to determine if it will record incidents of verbal abuse. However, it is worth considering that if verbal abuse becomes the norm how long will it be before minor assault becomes part of the job? In any event, the data gathered will help the management to detect patterns in assaults and implement safety measures.

There are safeguards that can be adopted to aid the safety of not only the driver but also the passengers and this can include having attack alarms fitted on buses. This means that the driver presses a button in the driver's cab which activates an alarm and a synthesised voice says: 'This vehicle is under attack: dial 999'. The loud speaker in the cab points towards the door, so it is loud and frightening to a potential assailant. Assault screens are fitted in all new buses to separate the driver from the public. The screens are see-through barriers which normally cover the area from the left of the driver to the ticket machine. They prevent 'random' punches from the public and are effective if the driver sits back as far as possible in the cab. Assailants are at the limit of their reach when trying to hit the driver and are forced to use their left hand, normally the weaker. Both these factors reduce the power of a punch. Drivers should be equipped with a mobile phone for use in case of emergency but the operating company should consider fitting a radio in every vehicle which will contact to a central point at the depot and communication can be maintained with all drivers. Another option is to install digital CCTV, which consists of very small digital cameras and can constantly record on a 24-hour cycle. The tapes from such cameras are useful in the event of prosecution. Other safeguards for the driver include the possible use of a laminate adhesive high-security safety film on driver cab windows to prevent missiles or shattered glass harming the driver. Some types of film are ineffective so it needs to be evaluated before it is adopted.

Taxi drivers   6.15

Driving a taxi can be hazardous, as drivers face armed robberies. They also have drunken passengers who can become aggressive and verbally abusive over fare disputes. In some areas there can be racial and verbal abuse from customers and, in an extreme case, an older driver was found beaten to death, lying in the gutter at the side of his cab and it is understood that the assailant has not yet been found. The message here is that drivers must not put themselves in a situation where they might be at risk.

Proactive action by taxi drivers may help, they must be polite and maintain a good customer service. It helps to maintain eye contact in a non-confrontational manner and they should not try to fight back if threatened. Drivers should not leave the taxi cab as they are safer in their own space, where they can call for assistance if an incident occurs. It is important that drivers do not volunteer personal information to passengers and should not mention that they are finishing a shift or going home. All drivers should have the right to refuse a job if they feel unsafe or consider that they could enter a conflict situation.

Taxi companies, while competing for business, should consider sharing advice about known trouble spots, unsafe areas and safe rest places. This information can also be disseminated through trade magazines, newsletters and websites. Although most drivers are self-employed, a culture of open communication should be maintained between them. It helps if they share information and advice about violence issues and help one another if an incident occurs or if a taxi breaks down. There can be valuable liaison with police who can provide information to drivers and alert them of known potentially violent people and locations.

Taxis can be modified to reduce hazards, such as modifying door handles so they only open from the inside, activating deadlocks only in known violent areas and installing CCTV in the cab along with visible signs to act as a deterrent. Other options include the use of safety film to cover glass windows and having a decoy money bag, with the real money kept hidden. Inside the taxi lockable sliding screens can be fitted between the customer and driver. With this option it is important to ensure that openings in screens used for paying fares are not in a direct line with the driver's head so as to prevent attacks.

Drivers can use an emergency fuel-stop button to simulate problems with the taxi, which makes it easier to get aggressive or troublesome passengers to leave the cab.

Taxis should be fitted with a radio which allows the drivers to maintain contact with other drivers and the control room and to request advice or assistance. Taxis can be fitted with panic alarms to alert other taxi drivers and computers can be installed which display 'regular' messages from the control room about new jobs, as well as information from police about potential troublemakers or incidents in the area; and sound an alert if there is an emergency call. The drivers should avoid certain geographical locations and driving to or through known trouble spots. Drivers are advised before dropping off a passenger to stop in a way that they can make a 'quick getaway' if needed. Some may advocate drivers undertaking martial art training but drivers can develop a false sense of security and act more aggressively. It has been shown that non-confrontational techniques are more effective, posing less risk to personal safety.

Window cleaners   6.16

Examples of incidents of violence towards window cleaners include a window cleaner who had been doing a particular job for a while and had priced it at £10. Another cleaner, later discovered to be on the dole, quoted £8 for the job which resulted in an argument and a fight. One window cleaner's van was smashed up while parked outside a job and another was followed one evening while collecting money, causing him some anxiety.

There is no right solution to keeping safe but the window cleaner, as with many others serving the public, must always try to be polite to customers. They should apologise if something goes wrong and put it right straightaway, for example offering a free clean. This on the spot action can defuse a potential confrontation and is probably the most successful measure. Self-employed window cleaners, who rely on the good will of the customer, may need to deal calmly and tactfully with verbal abuse or customers refusing to pay. They should leave an aggressive or potentially violent situation and if a customer refuses to pay, the window cleaner should walk away and should not return, remembering that the experience must not adversely affect the rest of their working day or week.

Window cleaners should have phones for emergency use and to let friends or family know where they are throughout the day and when they expect to be back. At premises where mobile phones are not allowed, they should give somebody the telephone number of the premises where they are working. Many window cleaners work in pairs, however, two people working on the same job in a large office building may actually be working 'alone' at opposite ends of a building. In this situation they should keep in regular contact with each other throughout the day. If the window cleaner feels that an area is not safe then they should not do the job.

Shop workers   6.17

All staff should receive training to provide appropriate responses to theft, the threat of violence and handling complaints. Such training should focus on being non-confrontational and to be diplomatic when dealing with customers. There is a need for staff to be vigilant and anticipate potential confrontational situations so that positive action will reduce the risk of violence and form the best defence against customer threats. Staff should be taught to observe body language that spells potential trouble, such as red faces, glaring eyes, swift and agitated movements, loud voices and standing very close, because all of these can signal that a customer is unhappy. An unhappy customer may wait until a shop is full before raising a complaint because they see this as the best way to get the result they want. Good intelligence and observation should make staff aware if customers have had previous problems with certain goods or services so that a proactive approach can be made which makes the customer feel looked after and noticed.

Information about potentially difficult or abusive customers should be shared and an accident book kept with a record of any incidents entered. CCTV is commonplace and it allows staff to observe the shop and detect any problems or potential incidents. If an incident occurs then there may be a visual record. Shops need to have good lighting and visibility of activities which combine to help deter potential troublemakers. A discreet emergency panic alarm can be installed to be activated in an emergency and they can ring until turned off and so is very effective in alerting the need for assistance. Staff in shops without a panic alarm could have a speed dial function on their telephones so that if used it connects directly to the police station. Employers need to ensure that staff are well trained in customer service skills, as this will help to minimise incidents involving angry and frustrated customers. It should be a policy of the business to ensure that customer problems are dealt with quickly, calmly and positively to avoid the problem escalating.

Service engineers 6.18

There must be a system in place that provides managers and office staff with a reasonable idea of where service engineers are during the day. Management must give support to staff where there is an incident of violence or abuse occurs. The response must be for managers to write to clients making it clear that this behaviour is unacceptable and advising of any action the company is considering. Engineers are out doing the job and it is important that they are encouraged to offer suggestions and raise problems or concerns during meetings in the office and meetings with supervisors on different sites.

The use of mobile phones is generally considered to be a successful safety measure and all employees carry mobile phones so they can contact the office quickly. It may not be a good idea to have a formal system for telephoning the office at given times, as it may be considered that staff may feel that management are 'keeping tabs' on them. However, there is regular contact as engineers often telephone the office for materials and parts orders so that if an engineer does not call the situation can be highlighted. This will be most important where a job is at a location considered a potential risk so that measures can be put in place to reduce the risk.

Each job requires a health and safety plan which sets out all the risks involved. All job tenders also include a method statement which will highlight any health and safety risks. Co-operation between management, the engineer and the client can add to the method statement until it is satisfied that all risks, including violence, have been sufficiently highlighted.

Sales and field representatives 6.19

Training and information for sales and field representatives is paramount and should include customer service skills, such as being polite at all times. Field representatives are encouraged to present a friendly and caring approach and not to act aggressively. Staff should apologise if appropriate, as an apology often defuses a difficult situation. Staff must walk away if they feel threatened and tell the customer they will return at a more convenient time. Sales staff must be advised that 'no sale is worth your safety' and management must support this approach.

It is the responsibility of individual employees to assess the risks continuously while out on visits and they must be trained on how to do that. Staff must learn that if a customer is violent or abusive they should not take it personally and they must ensure they have an easy and quick means of escape. Staff must be encouraged to report all incidents of violence, including verbal abuse, and there must be a formal procedure for doing so.

It may be possible to develop 'stock answers' so that the sales team in particular have some stock answers which they can use if they want to get out of a situation. For example, 'I am sorry, but we are not allowed to enter the client's house'. This is not likely to offend customers and allows the employee to leave quickly and without incident. Personal alarms should be available to all staff if they want them and lone working staff should be provided with a company mobile phone or be able to use their own. Clip-on ties and identity badges, that can be easily released, help to prevent injury if the tie or badge is grabbed and enables the member of staff to get away quickly. High visibility vests are worn on warrant visits and help to identify that the field representatives are legally entering a house. Staff must stop work if they feel threatened, but if the job must be done, for example debt collections, they must call for help from colleagues or the police.

The company need to have a policy so as to make sure the correct people are recruited for the type of work and that no one is forced to work in an area in which they feel uncomfortable. Certain staff may not be sent to particular areas, for example, if a locality has a history of racially motivated attacks on particular ethnic minorities, care is taken not to send staff of the same ethnicity to that area. Company uniforms or vehicles are not recommended to be used in some areas and if staff need to determine if there is a dog at a property, for example, before a staff member enters a house they should rattle the gate or whistle.

Health and safety of volunteers   6.20

Despite the increasing importance of volunteering (22 million people volunteer each year), the legal obligations of organisations towards their volunteers with regard to health and safety are less clear than they are for employees. Nevertheless, organisations do have legal obligations towards their volunteers and it is clearly good practice to treat volunteers with equal consideration when it comes to health and safety. A 'volunteer' is defined as someone who commits time and energy for the benefit of others, and who does so freely, through personal choice, and without expectation of financial reward, except for the payment of actual out-of-pocket expenses.

The duty of care is a general legal duty on all individuals and organisations to avoid carelessly causing injury to persons. It has been developed by the courts over many years. The duty is regardless of the size of the organisation, its income or whether the organisation has paid staff. If the organisation asks a volunteer to do a task which results in them injuring themselves or anyone else, the members of the governing body may be liable. No matter what activities the organisation is involved in, from running a major hospital trust to organising day trips to the seaside, they will have to consider the duty of care owed to their volunteers. Liability depends on establishing that the organisation failed to take reasonable care.

A duty of care can arise in many ways which may not always be obvious, for example:

- collecting charity appeal money;
- a victim support volunteer;
- loaning equipment to others;
- charity walks and sponsored runs;
- running fetes or fairs;
- organising day trips;
- selling food at a charity stall; and
- selling goods in a charity shop.

Organisations also have a responsibility to carry out a risk assessment, which may require volunteers to be provided with information and training.

There are some areas of health and safety law which every organisation should examine and whilst not all of the duties are legally binding on organisations that do not employ staff, organisations that have paid staff and also involve volunteers should implement the same health and safety requirements for volunteers as are demanded by law for paid employees. Most organisations now support equal opportunities and it would be difficult for any organisation that claimed to have an equal opportunity policy to justify offering a lower standard of health and safety protection to volunteers. If an organisation has no employees, it may not be able to achieve the same standards of health and safety as required for employees in the short term. These organisations should set a timetable to aim to accomplish this, which will demonstrate to the volunteers and the outside world the value the organisation places on them and their efforts to support the organisation.

Any organisation that involves volunteers should always include them in the health and safety policy as a matter of good practice. If an organisation has no employees there is no obligation to have a health and safety policy, but any such organisation is strongly advised to produce one which will be a positive step and will help clarify the organisation's procedures and responsibilities. It is further recommended that volunteers are involved in the process, as it will make them much more aware of health and safety issues.

All public and community buildings are obliged under various pieces of legislation to specify minimum levels of standards so that the risk of fire is reduced and there should be consultation with the local fire brigade for advice.

Any organisation employing staff, regardless of size or location, must register its existence with the HSE or the local Environmental Health Department. However, organisations with volunteers only do not normally have to register their activities with the enforcement authorities unless they are involved in dangerous activities, such as putting on a fireworks display. However, groups that control, or are responsible for, premises and buildings have to register with the local Fire Authority. If food is prepared, stored, supplied or sold on five or more days in any five-week period, they must register with the local Environmental Health Department. If there is any doubt, organisations should check with the authorities about the need for registering activities.

All employers have a duty under law to make a first aid assessment. The need for first aid will depend on the organisation's activities. For instance, an outward bound centre will have very different needs from a morning coffee club. Again, an assessment of the workplace is the key to deciding what first aid provision is required. There are, however, minimum standards for organisations with employees. There must be at least one first aid box and a notice displayed in the workplace that tells staff the location of the first aid box, the name of the first aider, or appointed person, and where the first aider or appointed person can be found. An appointed person is someone who has basic first aid knowledge, is available whenever people are at work, can take charge in an emergency and are responsible for calling the emergency services. Voluntary groups with no employees are not bound to do a first aid assessment, although it is clearly good practice. However, in certain circumstances, such as a large public fireworks display, there may be a legal duty to provide first aid facilities. For example, if an organisation holds a public exhibition without first aid facilities and someone is injured, they may have broken their duty of care. If a manager has any doubts whatsoever they should always contact the local HSE office for advice.

Lone worker risk assessment   6.21

Hazards that lone workers can encounter include:

- accidents or emergencies arising out of the work, including inadequate provision of first aid;

- sudden illnesses;

- inadequate provision of hygiene and welfare facilities; and

- violence from members of the public.

The key to maximising safety wherever lone work is under consideration is the performance of a satisfactory risk assessment which should address two main features:

- whether the work can be done safely by a single person; and

- what arrangements are required to ensure the lone worker is at no more risk than employees working together.

The risk assessment should prescribe arrangements for systematic monitoring of the hazards of lone working by competent supervisors/managers.

Employers have to determine whether the job can be done safely by a single person and should demonstrate that a lone worker is not exposed to extra risk compared to a group of employees working together. Where the job involves a significant risk of violence from the public, doubling of staffing levels will almost always substantially improve safety.

To ensure safety for lone workers, employers have to consider a number of key issues including:

- How long should the work take and how frequently should the worker report in?

- Has the worker a safe means of travel to and from the location, especially out of normal hours?

- Is there access to adequate rest, hygiene, refreshment, welfare and first aid facilities?

- Can emergency services approach the location without hindrance? Procedures for responding to emergencies should be in place.

- Can all equipment, especially powered tools and access equipment such as ladders, be used safely?

- Can lifting operations be performed safely by one person? and

- Are fire precautions sufficient for the job?

Special caution should be identified where home visits, especially for the provision of personal care, involve exposure to infectious diseases in addition to other hazards. The condition of premises should be assessed by qualified staff before visits commence.

Lone worker communications   6.22

It is imperative that effective communication is maintained with the lone worker, especially when continuing supervision is required. The lone worker should be equipped with a means of two-way communication in the form of a mobile phone, a pager or a personal alarm. The system should enable the worker to raise an instant alarm or be located accurately if assistance is required. In situations where staff conduct confidential interviews, the rooms should be equipped with a hidden alarm and a system to provide immediate support.

Preventing violence   6.23

In addition to the provision of mobile phones, pagers or personal alarms, procedures should be devised to minimise the risk of violence from the public, such as elimination of handling cash, constant changes of route when transporting valuables and adequate building security for out of hours working. Consideration should be given to the fact that women working alone are particularly at risk.

There needs to be a system that will monitor staff who work alone to ensure that they remain safe. These can include regular contact with the lone worker; warning devices that operate manually or automatically by the absence of activities and checks that the worker has returned to their base or home at the end of their shift/session. Additional procedures will be needed if the work of staff includes extended visits to clients away from their main work base.

Employers have to take positive action to tackle violence and aggression in the workplace where the incidents often result in physical injuries or anxiety and stress for the people affected. They also have serious consequences for their employers who have to deal with the resulting poor staff morale, high absenteeism, recruitment and staff turnover problems and poor business image.

Medical considerations will need to be determined, including:

- Does the job impose any extra demands on the lone worker's physical or mental stamina?

- Does the lone worker suffer from any illness that might increase the risks of the job?

Information and training   6.24

Suitable and sufficient training and information must be provided to the lone workers to enable them to identify hazards and carry out risk assessments so as to take appropriate action to avoid them. It is important that lone workers are entitled to leave the workplace if there is serious and imminent danger and there must be a reporting system that identifies the problem.

Written instructions   6.25

The employer must provide detailed written instructions for carrying out hazardous activities, such as entry into confined spaces or electrical testing.

The instructions should include:

- suitability and testing of communications equipment;
- length of the work period;
- provision and use of suitable first-aid equipment;
- equipment, tools and electrical safety checks;
- suitable personal protective equipment;

- systems for manual handling;

- arrangements for working in bad weather; and

- emergency procedures.

Participation of the workforce   6.26

Safety representatives, employee's representatives or nominated persons should participate with management about safe working practices for lone working.

Their participation would focus on:

- consulting/negotiating on the necessity of lone working in the first instance;

- representing any suggestions and complaints from the lone workers to the employer;

- obtaining support from the trade union if unsafe working practices become established and/or referring these to the enforcement authorities;

- ensuring that a proper risk assessment is carried out, including the provision of training, information and suitable supervision;

- having an input into the details of safe systems of work;

- making sure that work practices are not introduced unless specified in the risk assessment;

- advising staff of safe working practices; and

- checking that all accidents, near misses and dangerous occurrences go into the accident book and are properly investigated.

Lone worker in the workplace checklist   6.27

The table overleaf can be used as a loneworker checklist.

Workplace Bullying   6.28

As has already been shown in **5.21** it is very often difficult to identify when someone is being bullied as very often employees will not face up to the problem and report the fact for fear of being seen as over-reacting. Although in **5.21** we discussed the problems of bullying in schools the same problems can be encountered in any workplace.

A pro-active personnel policy is needed to deal with bullying at work. Frequently, the bully will be unaware of the effect of his or her actions, and while it may be difficult to change a person's personality, training in man-management may be indicated. A complaint's procedure may be set up, complaints investigated and appropriate action taken. Counselling can be provided for those affected and

No	Workplace Hazard Considerations	Y/N
1	Is the worker competent to undertake the task?	
2	Has the worker been trained to carry out the work safely?	
3	Has the worker been provided with the appropriate PPE and are they trained in its use?	
4	Will the worker obtain assistance when they reach the limit of their knowledge or experience?	
5	What is the appropriate level of supervision for the activity?	
6	What arrangements are in place to communicate with the staff to ensure their well being?	
7	Is the worker medically fit to undertake the work activities?	
8	Is the access to, or exit from, the workplace safe?	
9	Is the lighting and ventilation safe and appropriate?	
10	Will other adjacent work activities present a risk?	
11	Has the worker been provided with sufficient information about the job, equipment or substances?	
12	Can substances and goods be handled safely?	
13	Has the worker been trained in manual handling?	
14	What risks will the worker be exposed to in the event of equipment failure?	
15	Is the workplace equipment safe and regularly maintained with records kept?	
16	Are there arrangements for the worker in the event of an emergency?	
17	Is first aid provision provided and are workers trained in first aid?	
18	Are there specific lone worker risks such as cash being handled?	
19	Is there a risk of violence?	

monitoring procedures put in place. As pressures increase for more output and greater efficiency in working practices, the consequences of bullying at work should be faced up to and should not be dismissed as mere incidents of over-sensitivity on the part of alleged neurotic employees.

The role of senior managers, is to ensure *so far as is reasonably practicable*, structures and procedures embedded in behaviour policies prevent bullying. Ultimately, it is the responsibility of the whole workforce to eradicate bullying by ensuring the development of a caring and supportive ethos.

A written disciplinary policy should be drawn up which will include procedures for enforcing all health, safety and welfare policies. The discipline policy may include the anti-bullying policy and should be publicised annually toall employees. It should also be regularly reviewed. As bullying can irrevocably damage the mental health of an individual, it is clear that responsibility extends to the eradication of bullying in the workplace.

Employees who are being bullied at work will not always be prepared to tell those in authority. However, when a disclosure is made, it should always be treated seriously. While others may not feel that certain actions or words are of a bullying nature, if the recipient feels they are being bullied that is sufficient evidence to treat the case as prima facie bullying. For those employees who are unable to inform colleagues or managers about their problem, observations regarding specific behaviour patterns can be routinely established within the workplace.

Signs of bullying might include:

- unwillingness to come to work;
- withdrawn, isolated behaviour;
- complaining about missing possessions;
- refusal to talk about the problem;
- being easily distressed; and
- incomplete work.

Where these difficulties are associated with an employee from a minority racial or cultural background or where there are indications of sexual harassment, these indicators may well confirm bullying is occurring. Investigation should be undertaken, checking with colleagues and maintaining rigorous vigilance.

Managers will be able to use their knowledge of employees to identify changes in their behaviour that might indicate bullying. The company policy should identify the process to be pursued when managers or colleagues have concerns with regard to a particular employee. Bullies are often in positions of power or authority over their victims. They may behave as they do to hide their own inadequacies or their personal envy of another colleague. Bullying may occur between professional staff, manual workers, support staff and voluntary workers. Overwork can also lead to bullying with the bully inflicting their frustration and anger on their colleagues. Tell-tale signs of bullying are indicated in the following list, that is neither inclusive nor exclusive:

- general low morale;
- increased level of staff turnover;

- high rates of absenteeism;

- frequent disputes, complaints and grievances;

- isolated members of staff; and

- inefficient team working.

Firm management style can often be given as an excuse for what is seen by others as bullying.

Victims of bullying may end up believing that they deserve to be bullied. They feel powerless and vulnerable. Self esteem can be badly damaged and self confidence needs to be re-established. The school/company should declare that bullying will not be tolerated and that all incidents will be taken very seriously. Investigations into bullying incidents should be thorough and involve both the bully and the bullied. The bully should be helped to recognise their unsociable behaviour and offered support to modify that behaviour. Bullying will not be eradicated if the behaviour of the bullies is not modified. Ways of reporting bullying must be clearly established. Consideration should be given to appropriate 'assertiveness' training for the bullied and other vulnerable groups.

Manual handling   6.29

A number of diverse workers may be exposed to the possibility of manual handling operations. Manual handling operations that involve risk of injury should, where possible, be avoided. Risk of injury relating to any remaining manual handling operations should be reduced to the lowest level reasonably practicable. It is identified that injuries sustained while handling, lifting or carrying are expected to be the most common kind of over three-day injuries to employees.

There must be a Manual Handling Policy and Guidance for employees. The employer must ensure risk assessments are undertaken and an ergonomic approach to manual handling is of prime importance. Audits of all risk assessments need to be carried out on at least a six monthly basis and actions both proactive and reactive be undertaken.

Training is a fundamental aspect of a manual handling safe system of work. The organisation must be able to demonstrate that they have carried out this training, who to, when, where and what was taught. This can be achieved through a list of attendees supported by certificates for course completion providing details of what was taught, what equipment was used, when the training took place and who taught it.

The organisation's health and safety committee needs to monitor training and workplace activity. On a quarterly basis they should send a report to the occupational health and safety manager and the HR director providing details of the training provided.

As part of the audit and review process, the organisation should have a system that every two years requires a training survey to be carried out which is in the form of a staff survey and asks whether staff have received training, whether they learned anything new, whether they feel training is effective and how they think it can be improved.

There should be a Fast Track Physiotherapy Referral and a managed return to work for all staff who encounter physical problems due to lifting. Once a member of staff has seen an occupational health practitioner, if appropriate, they should be referred for physiotherapy ideally within five working days. In addition, the occupational health advisors should work closely with managers to promote staff rehabilitation and a managed return to work. There may be a number of problems encountered by the injured party and so there should be a facilitator who can offer support for those staff who have a disability or have returned to work and require adaptations in their workplace.

Training 6.30

The provision of training is often a key part of an organisation's strategy for tackling workplace violence. Suitable training and equipment must be put in place to allow any policy to be effective. Research has shown that training alone will have no significant impact on an adverse manual handling culture within an organisation and that it must be accompanied by risk assessments, provision of necessary equipment, and monitoring and auditing of the interventions put in place. Successful physical skills training for the protection of healthcare professionals facing violence at work needs to be effective, task-related, lawful, ethical and as safe as possible with minimum-injury potential to both parties. Skills that are taught should be proven to be useful, relevant, simple and instantly available when required. They need to be easy to teach and easy for staff to maintain competency in their use. The employer should assess the employee's capabilities and provide appropriate training. The employer should also ensure that appropriate systems of work are in place, including appropriate policies, procedures and suitable staffing to undertake the identified techniques. Independent healthcare establishments also need to meet separate standards imposed by the *Care Standards Act 2000*.

There is little evaluation evidence to indicate which techniques are most effective for preventing and managing violence and the types of control and restraint/physical interventions used. The extent to which the use of such interventions is used is a controversial issue in health and social care. The question as to whether the use of such interventions is justified in particular circumstances is often a balance between clinical judgment, common law duties and the duty to protect the safety of staff and others. However, restraint should usually be a last resort for managing violence to staff. Current medical opinion is that mechanical restraint should not be used within mental health services. If restraint is deemed necessary it should be used with consideration for the self-respect, dignity, privacy, cultural values and any special needs, for example physical illness or disability, of the service user. Methods of restraint to be used for particular service users should be recorded in care plans.

Effective training and information need to be given to include violence and aggression training.

The main themes being:

- how to defuse violence and aggression before an incident occurs, for example by persuading clients that the employee is there to help them;

- good customer care; and

- what to do if employees feel uncomfortable in a client's house, for example, they:

  o should keep their wits about them;

  o should not sit down;

  o should not spread belongings out;

  o should make excuses to get out if they feel at risk, for example say they need to get something from the car; and

  o should keep escape routes clear to ensure they can get to the door quickly.

Managers will need to be seen as leaders and not as bosses in playing a key role to influencing the culture of an organisation. They will also need additional training to ensure that they have the necessary skills to manage staff. The importance of this cannot be underestimated. Some key issues to include in a management training programme are:

- recruitment and selection;

- conflict resolution skills, such as conciliation and mediation;

- performance appraisal;

- how to conduct a review of own decision-making and staff management;

- conducting interviews for grievances and disciplinary investigation;

- leadership skills that include self-examination of own behaviour styles, attitudes, beliefs, acting as a role model; and

- change management.

Employers should ensure that staff training covers all aspects of the company's occupational health and safety policies, part of which will be the diversity policy, including the organisation's aims and objectives.

Employee training programmes will need to establish all the issues that need to be addressed.

An important area of training will be the recognition of, and tactics for, dealing with different types of behaviour, eg aggressive, manipulative, passive and assertive. This will include ideas for calming a situation before the possible aggression gets to the physical stage. Training in 'personal safety' will include these techniques as an important part of the course.

Regulation 13 of the *Management of Health and Safety at Work Regulations 1999 (SI 1999/3242) (MHSWR 1999)* requires employers to provide adequate health and safety training when they are recruited, on being exposed to new or increased risks, when given new responsibilities or when new technologies, equipment or systems of work are introduced. The training will need to take account of new or changed risks and take place during working hours, should it be necessary to carry out training outside of normal working hours then the employee should be compensated for the extra hours. A record of all employees' training will need to be kept, this will identify any deficiencies and will also monitor when additional or refresher training is needed.

The information provided in this publication is not exhaustive and every organisation will have differing needs. It does provide a foundation on which to develop specific systems to meet the hazards and associated risks of a diverse workforce. Large organisations will have a range of suitable staff to manage employees, while a small organisation may be hard pressed to provide back up out of hours. However, no matter the size of the organisation, the complexity and hazardous nature of the work, management has to ensure the health, safety and welfare of its employees so far as is reasonably practicable. This is achieved through risk assessment, work task analysis and training to ensure staff are suitable and competent.

Discussion of HR management tools   6.31

As discussed in **6.30**, the key to identifying which diverse employees have health and safety vulnerabilities is to complete a risk assessment on individuals whose particular diversity may put them more at risk. This would most likely be personal and specific to that employee, but sometimes it could also be looking at activities in general if, for example, there is a large group of similarly diverse employees, eg a group of work placement candidates who will all be completing similar tasks. This will highlight any hazards specific to that individual or grouping and give a framework around which their particular health and safety can be managed.

Once this is completed, there are a variety of tools with which one can ensure that any risks to the individual are minimised, most of which revolve around checking or monitoring that certain tasks are completed or refrained from, that individuals receive the correct protection and that pro-active steps are taken to ensure that potential problems are highlighted early on.

The main causes of ill health or potential threats to health and safety in the workplace are:

- hazardous substances – inadequate controls in the use of chemicals;
- manual handling operations – lack of training in the use of physical effort to move an object whether by lifting, carrying, pulling or pushing;

- noise – failure to provide correct personal protective equipment/health surveillance;

- ergonomics – when machinery, equipment or environment is ill suited to the job role;

- stress – excessive pressure within employees' working lives;

- violence at work – both within the workplace and from customers/the public; and

- general hazards – physical aspects in the workplace not made safe for use/training or supervision not provided.

Unfortunately, while all of these can be managed using various methods of control, there is often a variety of reasons why there is a failure to ensure that all the above risks to health are minimised. These include:

- resources:
  - low priority given to health and safety in budgeting;
  - inadequate staffing levels for safe achievement of tasks; and
  - high number of untrained/inexperienced staff.
- staff attitudes:
  - managers' not setting good health and safety examples;
  - breaches in health and safety procedures ignored; and
  - poor standards tolerated by management in tidiness and housekeeping.
- communications:
  - only from management levels downwards; and
  - no consultation with staff.
- training:
  - ignored or done inadequately.
- conflicting priorities:
  - pressure to achieve job, ignoring safe working practices; and
  - being advised by senior staff to ignore rules and procedures.

It is these types of attitudes that the *MHSWR 1999* aimed to help eliminate, by encouraging employers to become more pro-active and to develop a 'safety culture'. To achieve this within the realm of HR, the focus on health and safety needs to be reflected in every policy and decision made and certain systems of work established and maintained with regular monitoring to ensure completion. These systems are discussed in more depth in **6.32** to **6.36**.

Systems of work   6.32

In most organisations and fields of work certain systems and ways of working are established. Sometimes they can simply be the most productive way to complete a task, but also they can provide a valuable means of preventing possible risk to the health and safety of employees. Systems of work tend to be used either to complement existing safety measures or where the actual method of completing a task is the key to ensuring it is done safely, needless to say, this may not always eliminate the risk completely.

An example of this is for lone workers who may have to visit people in their homes. Dependent on the nature of the role, this can sometimes pose a very high risk. A system of work might include:

• leaving a list of addresses with appointment times and expected finish times;

• ensuring a mobile phone is carried, with adequately charged batteries;

• carrying an attack alarm of some sort; and

• where a known risk exists, perhaps arranging to meet at a public venue.

This is just a general list and for a particular job role, specifics could be added to tailor it to suit. However, the important point is to stress to employees using it that it is vital that they carry it out on every occasion and then monitor and review it to ensure that it is complied with. To not do so could be as injurious to health as something much more obvious, such as failing to use machinery guarding.

Restricting the completion of certain tasks   6.33

There are occasions where the completion of certain tasks by certain people can be considered a risk either to their own personal safety or to that of others. For example, the cleaning or servicing of certain pieces of machinery should not be undertaken by young workers under the age of 18. Equally, there may be certain articles of clothing, or jewellery or particular hairstyles which certain religions or cultures may deem important and must be worn to show respect. However, for tasks which require no jewellery or loose clothing to be worn and hair to be tied back to avoid entanglement with machinery, it may be a necessity to restrict an individual role so that they do not perform that task, as it may pose a safety risk to them. Some disabilities may also require restrictions to be put in place. If an employee suffers from a mental impairment it may be necessary to limit their responsibilities for their own and potentially other's safety. However, it is crucial that if this should need to be done, then a full investigation into exactly what should be limited must be carried out, stating explicit, clearly justifiable reasons, otherwise it is highly possible that such action could be considered discriminatory. Some cases may be much more straightforward, for example an employee who has just been diagnosed with epilepsy and had their driving license revoked should have all driving responsibilities suspended and a review completed on their ability to operate dangerous machinery.

Additional supervision and/or training   6.34

This is very similar to the point made in **6.33**, with the key difference being that the tasks can be completed by diverse groupings, but they simply need to be specifically supervised or have additional training before they can undertake the activity. For example, the *MHSWR 1999* states that young workers should not be employed for work which:

- is beyond their physical or psychological capability;

- involves a risk of accidents which they reasonably may not be able to avoid due to insufficient attention to safety or lack of experience; and

- involves a risk to health from extremes of temperature, noise or vibration.

However, there is the stipulation that they can be employed for such work provided it is necessary for their training, the risks are reduced to the lowest practicable level and they are supervised by a competent person.

Often ensuring that training or supervision is carried out is far more difficult than simply preventing the completion of certain tasks, as it is more difficult to determine simply by observing someone completing an activity whether they have received adequate training. Therefore, it is best practice to increase the frequency with which the completion of training is monitored for those individuals considered to be in high risk groupings

Monitoring of working time   6.35

The *Working Time Regulations 1998 (SI 1998/1833)* set out specific requirements for the management of working time and rest breaks. These Regulations include:

- a limit on the average length of a working week to no more than 48 hours;

- a limit on the average working shift for night workers to 8 hours;

- minimum rest breaks and rest periods – particularly a rest period of a minimum of 11 hours (12 for young workers) between shifts;

- minimum requirements for paid annual leave; and

- health surveillance for night workers.

With young workers, the appropriate length of rest breaks is also increased – half an hour for shifts over 4.5 hours.

While naturally these recommendations should be adhered to, there is the facility for employees to 'opt out' where specific requirements do not fit with their working life. However, great care should be given when deciding to allow these opt outs, as the intentions of the Regulations are to protect the health and safety of workers by decreasing the chance of fatigue from overwork and lack of breaks. However, if an employee was to attempt to make a claim over not receiving their full entitlement of rest breaks/periods or being asked to work longer hours, it must first be proven that they had previously highlighted that this was something that they were unhappy with. This follows similar lines to the requirement that grievance procedures must be instigated before a claim is brought – allowing adequate opportunity for the employer to correct the problem. (See also CHAPTER 4)

Health surveillance   6.36

As we have already seen in **6.35**, health surveillance for night workers was stipulated as a requirement under the *Working Time Regulations 1998*. However, there are many occupations where aspects of working life may be deemed to be hazardous and, therefore, the benefits of introducing health surveillance to these roles would also be numerous.

To introduce such a scheme, care must be taken to ensure that it is administered sensitively, with employers mindful of data protection and aware that employees have rights to the data collected on them. Unfortunately, such schemes are sometimes viewed with mistrust by employees, who may feel that an employer is attempting to prove them unfit for work. It is important for the employer to explain that the scheme is there for the employee's benefit and protection and to encourage them to participate where possible.

Other health information, which may be of benefit to employees, is the disclosure of any serious medical condition to company first aiders or medical representatives. Again, this would be voluntary (except in particular occupations where medical assessments are compulsory), but would be of benefit to the employee if they required medical assistance of a particular type.

The management of the points discussed in **6.32** to **6.36** and other health and safety requirements within an organisation can be included in a checklist of activities which should be completed periodically – the frequency of which may vary, depending on the size of the company or on the type of activity or point being monitored. For example, a large organisation may wish to include a check on the completion of training on a weekly basis, however, a small company with few employees may find this is not necessary as training is easily implemented for new staff or when new procedures are introduced. Certain checks may be required by law, such as controls on substances hazardous to health (COSHH), records on equipment inspections and accident reporting.

To give an example of a possible list of points for inclusion on a checklist for a larger organisation, the following might apply:

- Frequent checks – eg daily
  - for any hazards in the workplace which need immediate attention; and
  - check off fire precautions, eg escape routes, extinguishers, hose reels.

- Regular checks – eg weekly;
  - o all accidents have been reported and dealt with correctly;
  - o all risk assessments and medical questionnaires have been completed;
  - o any training required has been completed;
  - o integral fire protection, eg alarm system and emergency lights tested;
  - o general check of frequently used machinery and equipment, eg lifts and packing equipment;
  - o the security of restricted access areas, eg electrical switch rooms/cupboards;
  - o progress on unresolved issues; and
  - o hygiene and cleaning schedules are adhered to.
- Periodic checks – eg monthly:
  - o all electrical equipment is safe, ie no loose wires and has had an annual inspection;
  - o whether any personal protective equipment needs replacing;
  - o any chemicals are stored safely and correctly in their own containers;
  - o fire evacuation procedures – conduct a drill;
  - o more detailed check of machinery/equipment – perhaps specify different section or area each month for thorough review;
  - o first aid provisions – basic equipment and first aider coverage;
  - o workstations – ergonomics;
  - o working practices – correct handling methods being used and equipment being used for correct purposes, supervision being carried out appropriately; and
  - o general structure – building or workplace is structurally sound.

Within the checking document there should be provision for noting any issues highlighted and also for carrying forward issues from previous documents which have not been resolved. When a problem is resolved it should be noted. Equally important is that the checks should be completed by a competent person, who has had training in what to look for and how to deal with issues should they arise.

Obviously, this is just an example, some checks may not be relevant to certain organisations, others may have many more that they need to include due to the nature of their business. However the checklist is laid out, it is important that completion is kept up to date to provide adequate protection in case of claims of negligence or breaches in health and safety.

7
Managing Changing Relationships

Introduction 7.1

Change is inevitable in all aspects of life and, therefore, how we manage the changes that affect us is key in determining how well we will adapt to new circumstances. Businesses too must be aware of and plan for changes that occur, whether they happen gradually or are much more immediate. Industries evolve and it is those companies that recognise how they need to adapt which respond most effectively and take competitive advantage in that evolution.

Embracing diversity has come gradually, emerging from the earlier equal opportunities policies and being underlined by the legislation to support this. Companies have seen the benefits of this by being able to take advantage of the broader skill base and wider perspective that a diverse workforce can bring. However, as with all change, there are natural periods of adjustment and difficulties to be overcome – by its very definition, diversity brings not only broader skills and perspectives to a workplace, but also more cultures, beliefs, languages, religions, age ranges and general differences. Companies must ensure that the potential conflict that could arise from these is minimised in all circumstances.

Unfortunately, this is not always achieved and, sadly, stress, bullying and harassment are still very much part of our workplaces. The Health and Safety Executive (HSE) website (www.hse.gov.uk April 2004) states that 'up to 5 million people in the UK feel "very" or "extremely" stressed by their work'. As discussed in **CHAPTER 4**, the employer's duty of care is to ensure that they provide a safe working environment for their employees and they must take all practicable precautions to ensure that an individual's working life is not detrimental to their health – including minimising the potential for stress. Equally, bullying and harassment, while not necessarily more prevalent, is certainly seen now as unacceptable behaviour and, therefore, particularly with the protection afforded by new legislation, more individuals are feeling able to come forward to address these issues when they occur.

In this chapter, diversity will be discussed in more depth to examine how diversity has broadened out from the original equal opportunities' policies and the specific impact that this has had on relationships within the workplace – both employee to employee and employee to employer. Problems that can be caused by this increasing diversity, such as stress and harassment and best practice guidelines on creating a culture where these kinds of problems are minimised, will also be examined, along with how to recognise signs that there may be a problem either within a workforce in general or between individuals specifically. The chapter will conclude by discussing the best ways to manage such problems when they do occur.

What impact does diversity have on causing shifts in working relationships?   7.2

If an examination is made of early equal opportunities policies, several key points can be noted. Firstly, the emphasis is placed around discrimination that can take place under the three key Acts – the *Sex Discrimination Act 1975 (SDA 1975)*, the *Race Relations Act 1976 (RRA 1976)* and the *Disability Discrimination Act 1995 (DDA 1995)*. Secondly, the focus is on avoidance of the negative impact that failing to comply with this legislation can cause. Finally, there is little acknowledgement of the great benefits that employing a broader base of employees can bring to an organisation.

As these policies have widened out to include the concept of diversity, the above points have been addressed. Diversity policies do not limit where discrimination must be avoided and although this shift has been backed up by increasing legislation, many companies have gone further and are already covering areas such as age, where official regulations have still not yet been passed. Attitudes have become far more pro-active, and, as discussed in **CHAPTER 4**, companies are actively seeking to recruit a broad cross section of the population in order to benefit from the experiences they bring.

A key point to emphasise is that diversity affects a far wider range of people than equal opportunities' policies cover and people can range in and out of diverse groupings throughout their working lives. For example, a 17-year-old male worker would need to be given special consideration with regard to length of hours worked, how heavy and difficult the tasks he has to undertake are and the amount of supervision and health and safety training provided. Unless he also fell into another category of diverse grouping, on his 18th birthday he would be considered less vulnerable and more capable of self management and, therefore, only receive the same consideration as any other 'ordinary' member of the workforce. Equally, individuals can move into the category of diverse worker in their lives. An employee may adopt a religion that requires them to pray at certain times or eat particular foods. The employer would have to ensure that no discrimination takes place with regard to refusing any such reasonable request.

Other examples where individuals may range in or out of one or more categories of diverse grouping might include the following.

- New parents, who would receive the right to maternity, paternity and parental leave and the option to request flexible working.

- Parents whose children had reached the age of five and were, therefore, no longer entitled to parental leave.

- A worker in a petrol fuelling station who suddenly becomes a lone worker after changes in trade patterns and staffing levels mean that they are now required to work on their own. The worker would need additional risk assessments and safety measures in place to ensure their continued safety.

- A worker over the age of 65 will soon be afforded new protection to ensure that whilst physically and mentally able, they cannot be forced to give up work upon reaching automatic retirement age.

As seen in the above examples, the changes in where individuals fit with regard to their diversity status can either depend on their own circumstances or on legislation that may be brought in to protect their rights. Either way, a workforce can be in constant flux and it is important that there is a monitoring system in place to ensure that should further training, risk assessments or even a change in the facilities provided, be required, then it is dealt with promptly in order that no discrimination should take place.

Monitoring who in the workplace is affected by diversity   7.3

A company can only monitor changes that it is aware of and, therefore, an individual who, for example, decided to adopt a particular religion, but refrain from mentioning this to their employer cannot logically expect to have accommodations made with regard to this. If, however, they approached their employer and requested, eg, the provision of a quiet place for prayer, then the organisation would be required to make reasonable adjustments to comply with the request.

A monitoring system need not be complex. With regard to ethnicity and gender, which would change only in exceptional circumstances, the monitoring system used in recruitment (as mentioned in **CHAPTER 4**) would be adequate in determining any specific needs. Pregnancy in its early stages and non–obvious disability can only be monitored once the employee has made their employer aware of their circumstances and while with regard to the former, there should be encouragement to inform an employer as soon as possible in order that they can be afforded maximum protection, with regard to the latter, some individuals may simply feel that what may be legally classed as a disability as irrelevant in relation to their working life and choose not to disclose the information. The only concern in the latter case may be if an individual is suffering from a disabling condition that may endanger other workers if an employer was unaware of it and could not limit activities appropriately. In extreme cases, particularly where long term absence is involved, or the individual's capability is in question, it may be appropriate to ask for a medical report, however, if an employee is performing well in their role and gives an employer no cause for concerns, then there would be no reason to attempt to investigate suspicions of a disability without the individual themselves instigating a disclosure of information.

Young and older workers can be monitored by a simple check on dates of births, with risk assessments to determine what additional help or supervision may be required. With regard to young workers, there are limitations set by legislation on what hours can be worked and rest periods required, and while we are still awaiting the regulations applying to older members of the workforce, it is important to be guided by what the individual feels their limitations are and whether or not there are activities they cannot carry out. Remember, however, as with all legislation, while it is important not to discriminate against these groupings while a company can provide reasonable adjustment in order that they can fulfill their duties, it must not be forgotten that the capability rules still apply. If an individual cannot complete a substantial part of the role's requirements, then consideration must be given to whether there is another, more suitable, role or whether that particular employee is actually not capable of employment in any capacity, regardless of accommodations made. As with disability, health and safety legislation overrides other regulations. If an individual poses a risk to themselves or others, a company has an obligation to remove that risk. (See **CHAPTER 4** for more information on capability and dismissals and **CHAPTER 6** for information on the completion of risk assessments.)

Sexual orientation and religious groupings can be viewed together, as they are often as difficult to monitor as disability, with sexual or religious preferences being difficult to determine, unless the individual is quite open about their choices. They also have in common the fact that, at the time of writing, they are the most recent pieces of legislation passed (2003) and as such, companies may not yet have policies and practices in place to deal with any issues that could arise. Although generally, it is obviously key to have a workplace environment that promotes equality and encourages diversity, it is important to reiterate that it is only possible to protect individuals specifically from discrimination if an employer is aware of their particular circumstances. As such, an employee in a same sex relationship who claimed that their partner had been denied benefits afforded to married couples, could only do so if they had made their employer aware that that person was indeed their partner and, therefore, should be awarded equal benefits. Similarly, a person with particular religious beliefs could not claim discrimination if their place of work did not, for example, serve or prepare appropriate refreshments, unless they had specifically informed their employer that this was required due to the nature of their religion. Once an employer is aware of an individual's circumstances, then the appropriate action can be taken for each and any monitoring should simply ensure that this is consistent throughout the working relationship.

Unfortunately, while embracing diversity is seen generally as a good thing for industries, there will always be a number of individuals who feel that legislation designed to protect a minority can be exploited for their own personal gain. The rest of this chapter is designed to look at ways to recognise, minimise and deal with the problems that stress, bullying and harassment can cause in the workplace. Sadly, there will always be some individuals who will instigate grievances or claims on false grounds, but the important thing to remember is that having proof of consistent monitoring and management of diversity in all its forms will provide a good defence against any individuals that attempt to utilise legislation inappropriately.

What issues are caused by these changes in working relationships? 7.4

The key change to a workplace that embraces diversity is that there will literally be far more differences amongst its members. Differences are often misunderstood and can cause conflict, so it is vital to mange the workforce in order to promote harmony and understanding wherever possible.

Everyone has at least one peer grouping and share similarities, be they behavioural or cultural, with that group, this is regardless of how often they make contact with each group. So, for example, a working mother in her twenties may come into contact with:

- a family grouping;

- a workforce grouping;

- a group of friends from school or college;

- a group related to their child or children's activities in some way; and

- a grouping related to a hobby or activity.

In each of these groups the woman may encounter individuals to whom she feels more drawn and those to whom she cannot relate so well. Again, in each of these groups there is an element of choice regarding the amount of contact that the woman can have with particular individuals – this is with the exception of the working environment.

Obviously, there are exceptions to this generalised example, for example an individual worked on their own or ran their own business and were in complete control of their workforce. However, for the majority of workers, that level of control simply does not exist and they must nurture working relationships with those designated to be employed alongside them, regardless of whether their cultural beliefs, values and behaviours share any matches at all.

Herein lies the main reason for diversity training – while individuals can pick and choose friends and acquaintances outside of the world of work, within a workplace people who would not necessarily come together may be thrust into close contact. This is not necessarily to say that when people of different backgrounds work together there will immediately be conflict, however, it would be naïve to assume that there would never be any issues that need addressing.

Frequently, the reaction to difference is fear and misunderstanding, often manifesting itself in bullying, victimisation or harassment. Examples of this may range from name-calling, jokes spread about a particular person and their background, malicious rumours or a whisper campaign initiated against a person, up to physical assault or regular abuse either with or without the tacit consent of line managers. While we all hope that this would not be the case within our workplaces, it is important to acknowledge the reactions that may occur in order to proactively manage to avoid them.

Where a company has a significant external customer base with whom the workforce comes into frequent contact, then it is also vital that management policies are extended to cover the protection which may be necessary to minimise bullying, harassment and violence perpetrated by individuals external to that organisation. The National Health Service is one organisation that has taken this issue particularly seriously recently with its 'zero tolerance' campaign designed to express to those that come into contact with their staff that violent and abusive behaviour will simply not be tolerated.

Stress 7.5

Following the leading cases of *Hatton v Sutherland; Barber v Somerset County Council; Jones v Sandwell Metropolitan Borough Council; Bishop v Baker Refactories Ltd [2002] IRLR 263* the Court of Appeal laid down 16 legal principles which apply to claims for work-related stress, with the primary principle or 'threshold question' being whether the employer was aware, or ought reasonably to have been aware of the possibility of the particular employee suffering from stress. Other key principles are:

- that an employer should be able to assume that an employee can cope with the normal pressures of their job provided no particular vulnerability has been highlighted;

- that an employer can generally accept what he or she is told by an employee and does not need to make investigative enquiries regarding their health;

- if an employer offers a confidential advice and, where appropriate, counselling service, then it is unlikely that they will be found at fault; and

- no occupation should be viewed as intrinsically injurious to mental health.

So, from the above points, it is clear that the onus is on the employee to clearly indicate to their employer that they feel at risk from stress in order that the employer can then take steps to minimise this likelihood. In *Pratley v Surrey County Council [2003] EWCA Civ 1067* this primary point highlighted. The High Court held that the employee had failed to make her employer fully aware of the risk to her health and, therefore, the employer had not been negligent in its duty of care.

This said, if an employee showed considerable signs of stress at work, such as becoming withdrawn or being visibly upset, and yet was not approached to discuss whether they were experiencing any particular difficulties or problems, then it could be deemed that the employer may be at fault. This is because although the individual had not actually informed their employer of their condition, with the symptoms that were manifest it would only be fair for the employer to initiate a discussion to ensure that stress was not a factor in their behaviour. If it were found to be an issue, then the employer would be under the same obligation to take reasonable steps to remove the risk of further stress to the individual as if it had simply been originally highlighted by the employee.

When looking at steps that can be taken to minimise the risk of stress to a specific individual, it is important to look at all the practicable ways that this can be done, and to listen to the concerns of the particular employee. In *Thanet District Council v Websper, [2003] All ER (D) 246 (Jan)* the employee had stated very specifically that on return from long-term sick leave for work-related stress he should be found work in an alternative department. This had also been the advice of the Council's occupational health officer. When he was informed that an alternative post would be found, but within the same department, the employee resigned and claimed unfair constructive dismissal. The Council was found, even after appeal, to be negligent in its actions, with the key points being its failure to fully investigate the exact problems relating to the employee's health and importantly its insistence on returning him to work in the same department with no consideration for other alternatives. Had there been clear alternatives within other departments offered or a clarification that this was the first role suggested but alternatives could be considered and were up for negotiation, then the employee's claim would have been much harder to uphold.

Bullying and harassment 7.6

While case law can be dated as far back as 1986 stating that harassment of a sexual and racial nature can constitute direct discrimination under the *SDA 1975* and the *RRA 1976* and more recent legislation has broadened the definition, the term bullying has no legal concept in its own right – it is only the consequences arising from a situation where an individual has been bullied which may have legal implications.

So, for example, where a manager frequently used foul and abusive language, threatened and generally adopted a bullying attitude towards their employees, it could be claimed that this destroyed the relationship of trust and confidence between employer and employee and a case for constructive dismissal could be brought. Equally, where bullying takes a more aggressive form and comments and threats may be backed with physical abuse, then an employer may be found negligent in its duty to provide a safe working environment for its employees.

Harassment is much more clearly recognised within the law in its own right, although not actually mentioned within any of the three key discrimination Acts, numerous case studies can be quoted to provide examples of where harassment has been cited as direct discrimination by causing less favourable treatment for the individual concerned. For an employer to be liable for this discrimination, it must either fall into one or more of the categories of recruitment, dismissal or denial of benefits, or show some other kind of detriment. This last point is often where grey areas are caused, as while an individual may take offence at unwanted conduct, it is difficult to determine whether the behaviour actually caused a detriment to that individual.

This should soon be made clearer however, as in October 2002 the government published draft regulations outlining how it plans to implement the EC workplace directives on equality and provide some clarity on the understanding of detriment. Importantly, the emphasis moves away from direct and indirect discrimination and defines unlawful harassment as when:

> 'A person ...engages in unwanted conduct which has the purpose or effect of
>
> (a) violating that other's dignity, or
> (b) creating an intimidating, hostile, degrading, humiliating or offensive environment for that other.'

The regulations continue that:

> 'conduct shall be regarded as having the effect specified in paragraphs (a) and (b) ...only if having regard to all the circumstances, including in particular, the perception of that other, it should reasonably be considered as having that effect.'

In summary, the new regulations provide protection where an individual's dignity or working environment is violated or made hostile by the conduct of one or many others. However, the inclusion of 'should reasonably be considered' gives the opportunity to discount claims that may have been brought by an overly sensitive complainant – although the emphasis is still on the perception of the victim. As well as the original discrimination laws, the above regulations also now include sexual orientation and religious belief.

An employer becomes responsible for harassment as stated above, when it occurs in the course of employment, when the circumstances giving rise to the harassment remain under the control of the employer and there is evidence that good employment practices would have prevented or reduced the harassment. It is important to remember that it is not just the usual place of work that is considered when looking at potential harassment claims. We can see from *Chief Constable of Lincolnshire Police v Stubbs [1999] IRLR* 81 that although the harassment took place outside of the actual workplace, it was during two workplace functions and was, therefore, found to be in the course of employment. Equally, when the harassment is perpetrated by a third party, such as a customer, the employer is still responsible, as the circumstances remain in their control – it is due to their employment that the employee is in the situation and it is the responsibility of the employer to remove either the employee or the third party to ensure that the harassment does not continue.

Violence 7.7

Violence within the workplace is, unfortunately, on the increase and the last British Crime Survey estimates that every year in England and Wales there are 1.3 million incidents perpetrated by members of the public against employees (*IDS Brief* 735, June 2003). The highest risk industries are:

- the security sector;
- care professions;

- service industries;
- public transport; and
- education workers

This is mainly because of the customer facing aspect of their roles. Obviously, there is also a risk of violence within the workplace from worker to worker and there are occasions where this does occur, quite often though this is linked to bullying and harassment and is treated within these contexts.

Similarly to stress, if an employer fails to provide a workplace free from violence, then it is failing fundamentally in their duty of care to their employees. In addition to this, failing to provide a safe workplace can also be considered a breach of duty under health and safety legislation, which may be considered a criminal offence. Although an employee does not have to be diverse to become the victim of a violent or abusive attack, there are many situations where diversity may exacerbate the problem. For example, for a member of the public wishing to make a complaint, a younger worker or a woman may seem to be more vulnerable and, therefore, more of a target for an aggressive outburst with the intention of gaining as much from complaining as possible. A lone worker is immediately more likely to be at risk, purely by the definition of their role, particularly if this is exacerbated by, eg, cash handling requirements. Ethnic minorities are another target for abuse, particularly when there is conflict between ethnic groups in the wider community.

Employers must take whatever reasonable steps they can to avoid placing their employees in danger, however, again the emphasis is on the word reasonable and cannot apply if the danger could not have been foreseen. In *Dutton & Clark Ltd v Daley [1985] IRLR 363* a building society employee resigned and claimed constructive dismissal after the second of two armed robberies, the claim was not upheld as the EAT felt that the provision of floor to counter steel plating, above counter glass screening, clearly visible surveillance camera and panic buttons at every cashier desk provided adequate protection. Even though the building society had chosen not to install bullet proof glass, due to low level of effectiveness and high cost involved, this was felt to have been a reasonable decision, given the other safety measures in place.

Naturally, however, should a risk to safety be identified and no steps had been taken to reduce that risk, an employer would be considered to be liable. If an employee believes they are in 'serious and imminent' danger and cannot reasonably avert that danger, they may leave work and not return until after the danger has been removed. Should they be dismissed in such a case and their claim of unsafe working conditions be upheld, their dismissal would automatically be deemed as unfair.

Although most employers discourage their employees from involving themselves in violent incidents, there may be occasions or particular professions where this avoidance is simply not practical. It is vital in such cases that the employees required to deal with potentially violent situations are given full training with regard to what their level of participation should be and when it would be appropriate to back down or call for assistance. Security staff, in particular, are in a difficult position, as they have none of the special privileges granted to members of the police force and yet are often required to perform similar tasks. It is important to remember here that not only can employees be victims of attack from the general public, but also that there may be occasions where an employee is guilty of attacking a member of the public while in the working environment. It is then important to clarify whether the employee was acting totally outside of their recognised role or whether the attack constituted an over-zealous attempt to fulfill part of a job requirement. If it is deemed that the employee was acting within their recognised role, then it may be that the employer is liable for the attack, as the employee's actions were intended to benefit their employer.

Best practice methods to avoid negative issues diversity can create   7.8

The next step is to look at ways that issues such as stress, harassment, bullying and violence can be minimised by good management practices within the workplace.

As with the management of any key issue, the primary starting point is to develop, use, support and maintain a clear policy regarding what a company has decided will be their commitment to that particular agenda. With a subject such as stress, there may not be an individual policy to cover a drive towards the reduction of this, but it may easily be incorporated into the general health and safety policy, with regard to the provision of a safe workplace. Bullying and harassment do not easily fall under the umbrella of any other policy, unless they are covered by a very broad and comprehensive diversity or equal opportunities' policy. The importance is so great, however, for an employer to have clear guidelines on what is and is not acceptable in the workplace and the courses of action and consequences that may arise from inappropriate behaviour, that it is good practice to implement a separate policy on bullying and harassment if they are not already covered comprehensively elsewhere. This could also easily be extended to include clear guidelines on violence within the workplace, whether from fellow workers or from the public or customer base pertaining to that organisation.

The Advisory Conciliation and Arbitration Service (ACAS) gives guidelines on what is advisable to include within such a policy, and these include:

- a statement of commitment from senior management;

- acknowledgement that bullying and harassment are problems for the organisation;

- a clear statement that bullying and harassment will not be tolerated;

- examples of unacceptable behaviour;

- a statement that bullying and harassment may be treated as disciplinary offences;

- the steps the organisation takes to prevent bullying and harassment;

- responsibilities of supervisors and managers;

- confidentiality of any complaint;

- reference to grievance procedures (formal and informal), including timescales for action;

- training for managers;

- protection from victimisation; and

- how the policy is to be implemented, reviewed and monitored.

Inclusion of all the above points should ensure that the policy is practical and workable within the context of the organisation.

Case study – Managing bullying and harassment in the workplace   7.9

A good example of a company that has taken a pro-active step towards managing bullying, violence and harassment is Lloyds TSB. This is an example of a company which had to combine two sets of policies and procedures following the merger of Lloyds bank and the TSB in 1995. Immediately following the procedure, it was the responsibility of a certain group of trained HR managers to investigate and deal with claims of bullying and harassment and they could find themselves having either large case loads of work and excessive travelling or very little responsibility at all. This could mean that sometimes cases were not dealt with as soon as they ideally should have been, causing further grievances regarding lack of response to complaints.

In 2000 the method of dealing with complaints of bullying and harassment was reviewed to enable initial investigations to begin more promptly and while the company did consider outsourcing this responsibility, it was eventually decided that an internal team of investigators would be developed. Consultation with employee and union groups gave guidelines on what was required and a team was established which would not only provide an immediate response to any claims that may arise, but would also be able to train and coach managers and staff in ways to minimise and deal with these types of issues in the workplace.

The benefits that Lloyds TSB has gained from this new strategy are many, not least of which is the confidence that their employees have avenues down which to seek resolution should they feel ill-treated. Also complaints are far more likely to be resolved satisfactorily, resulting in less cases reaching tribunal and causing bad publicity and detriment to the company.

This case study was taken from *IRS Employment Review*, 780, July 2003, Attendance and Absence by Debbie Sanders.

Case study – Managing violence in the workplace   7.10

Another good example of an organisation that has seen the benefits from taking an active stance against anti-social behaviour in the workplace is that of the NHS. In 2000 the Department of Health launched the National Taskforce on Violence Against Social Care Staff. This combined several aspects, with reports and research generating an action plan which provided both a checklist for employees on action they should take in certain circumstances and a self-audit tool for the various health service trusts and organisations to ensure that they were complying with the minimum requirements.

The employee checklist includes a statement of both the employer's responsibilities and the employees' responsibilities, which includes the use of risk assessment tools to determine how likely it is that a violent incident will occur, planning and being prepared in case of attack, ways to reduce risk and action to be taken after an incident. The self-audit tool is primarily a list of questions to determine whether the employer is using all appropriate methods to ensure that risk is reduced wherever possible.

The benefits to the NHS have been not only a reduction in the number of violent incidents perpetrated against their employees, but also greater confidence by individuals on how to minmise the risks to themselves and a greater understanding of the appropriate action to take should an attack occur.

Case study – Managing stress in the workplace   7.11

A recent example of where a company has taken specific steps to minimise stress in the workplace is that of BP's Grangemouth petrochemicals manufacturing complex. In 2001 there was to be an extension to the section which dealt with the demonstration of new chemical process technology, the Applied Technology (AT) Group. Aware that this type of extension can be difficult and demanding for all concerned and having already addressed the potential physical hazards and improved the safety culture, the AT team decided that it would be beneficial to tackle work-related stress.

It was decided to outsource the stress management to an external chartered psychologist who formed part of a team, including a cross section of workers from the plant. This team looked at all possible causes of stress within their particular working environment and added these to a list of generic causes of stress. They then assessed how much impact each stress factor had and assembled a list of the top five stressors. The team then worked together on how these stress factors could be minimised, presenting findings to the whole of the AT team at a later meeting.

The benefits that were derived from this were not only that stress was minimised in the working environment and a safety culture enhanced, but also that the initial discussions by the original team facilitated an open and honest culture where discussions on stress could be held freely. The team was commended by the chartered psychologist commissioned for the project in their pro-active approach at tackling the issues of stress before a problem arose.

How to recognise signs of stress and harassment in the workplace 7.12

One of the key points within a policy for managing harassment is to accept that such a problem exists within one's own workplace. To not do so would not only be naïve, but it would also mean that there would be less awareness of issues when they do arise and, therefore, less capacity to deal with them effectively. Therefore, it is key to have an understanding of how to recognise signs and symptoms of problems, such as stress, harassment, bullying and violence.

Signs of stress 7.13

The HSE defines stress as:

> 'the reaction people have to excessive pressures or other types of demand placed upon them. It arises when they worry that they can't cope.'

Stress at Work: A Guide for Employers, HSE Publications, 1997.

Signs that someone may be suffering from stress may include:

- reduced levels of productivity or an inability to make effective decisions;

- loss of interest in work projects and/or social interactions – the person may become withdrawn when previously they enjoyed actively participating;

- increased levels of absence;

- physiologically they may have problems sleeping and appear fatigued and may experience lack of appetite and, thus, weight loss; and

- they may be prone to emotional outbursts, either crying or anger directed at others.

While these signs are good indicators that an individual is suffering from stress, the causative factors can sometimes be more difficult to determine. This is particularly the case when the majority of them may be external to the workplace, and although the employer is not under a legal obligation to prevent stress due to non work difficulties, it is often of benefit to employers if they can provide services, such as counselling or helplines, which can assist with non work-related issues. This could potentially reduce the likelihood of the general pressure of work becoming a contributing factor in the employee's difficulties. For smaller organisations that do not have the infrastructure or resources to do this, it is good practice to have a list of local contacts who can provide free confidential advice on a range of topics, such as the local Citizens Advice Bureau or Relate. Most unions also provide a helpline for use by its members and some give free legal advice sessions.

Where the reasons for stress are solely work-related, they may be caused by factors over which the employer has total control or they may be caused by external factors which an employer cannot change, they can only seek to minimise the effects that they may have on their workforce. Either way, the employer is under a legal obligation to limit the damaging effects that stress can have.

Factors that may cause stress and over which employers have considerable control include:

- individuals being expected to do a job without the provision of adequate tools, training or resources;

- where there is a lack of clarity over targets to be met – an individual may be unsure of expectations of them;

- where management styles may be over aggressive or bullying in nature;

- where there is a general culture of harassment or bullying in the workplace; and

- where working environments are intrinsically stressful, eg extremes of temperature or dangerous machinery, and proper rest breaks or adequate safety equipment are not provided.

External factors over which an employer has considerably less control may include:

- economic decline causing the possibility of business closures;

- changes in a particular industry, eg the introduction of new technology potentially resulting in redundancies; and

- the merger, or takeover of a company

Signs of Bullying and Harassment   7.14

ACAS (www.ACAS.gov.uk) gives a definition of both bullying and harassment in their guide for managers and employers. It states that:

> 'Bullying may be characterised as offensive, intimidating, malicious or insulting behaviour, an abuse or misuse of power through means intended to undermine, humiliate, denigrate or injure the recipient.'

Harassment is defined as:

> 'unwanted conduct affecting the dignity of men and women in the workplace and may be related to age, sex, race, disability, religion, nationality or any other personal characteristic of the individual and may be persistent or an isolated incident.'

While it is certainly valuable to have definitions of both of the above terms, the difficulty comes when attempting to apply these definitions to actual workplace events. Some incidents will naturally be very clear cut versions of the above, but more often there will be difficulty in deciding exactly how serious an incident was, as it will be perceived differently by all those involved, including those called in to investigate it. It is, therefore, useful to have examples of what constitutes behaviour which may be defined as bullying and harassment in order that it can be recognised more easily by employees and managers alike.

As bullying and/or harassment are by their nature likely to cause an individual to feel stress, then the outward indicators that an individual may be suffering from this kind of abuse would be similar to those listed as possible signs of stress. It also may be possible to determine the behaviour that is causing this effect, although naturally some bullying and harassment is perpetrated in secret or witnessed only by those who are fearful that they may also become victims if they were to speak out.

How best to manage incidences of stress, bullying, harassment and violence

Example situation: employee exhibiting signs of stress   7.15

To best illustrate the steps that should be taken to deal with managing incidences of stress, bullying, harassment and violence a hypothetical situation involving an employee who works in the administration department of a large branch of a national organisation shall be examined. Their line manager has recently noticed that an employee is failing to meet deadlines and no longer goes to lunch with other colleagues, instead choosing to eat at their desk and trying to complete additional work. Several days ago the employee was witnessed having an argument with a colleague and walking away, visibly upset.

The line manager decides to talk to the employee to try and determine why they are failing to meet deadlines that would have previously been achieved and will also include concerns over the confrontation with another colleague. During the discussion, the employee is reluctant to disclose any particular problems that they are having and when pressed and, in particular, reminded of the importance of achieving their particular targets, they insist that they are not having any difficulties currently with their work. Unable to get the employee to open up any further, the manager concludes by reiterating the importance of achieving the work loads and that should things not improve then they may have to meet again to discuss the situation further, also that should they think of anything that may be causing them problems and wish to talk about it then to come back to discuss them anytime.

Some days later, the employee requests a meeting with their line manager and explains that there have been problems, which they were reluctant to even admit to themselves. These relate to a new system of work that had been introduced some months earlier and although the employee had received training, this had been at a 'mop up' session, as they had been on holiday for the original roll out. This was compounded by the fact that they were also experiencing problems at home with their partner and subsequently coming in to work more tired than they would normally. The problems with the new system and increased fatigue meant that they were trying to catch up with things in their lunch hour and subsequently were losing the support network of colleagues who may have been able to assist in showing them better ways to use the system. They were also missing out on meals because of this.

The line manager's response was to designate some of the employee's current workload to another individual and arrange for some immediate refresher training on the new system. They advised the employee of the importance of taking proper rest breaks, which the employee felt able to do now that the workload had been reduced and while there was nothing that the manager could impact directly on regarding the difficulties at home, they supplied the employee with telephone numbers of a counselling service and Relate.

The line manager then diaried review dates to ensure that the employee was progressing well and symptoms of stress were alleviating.

The key points for managers to note from this example are as follows:

- be aware of employees exhibiting symptoms of stress;

- instigate a discussion with them at the earliest opportunity – it is usually easier to solve a problem in the early stages;

- during the discussion, managers should express their concerns and their wish to help where possible, but should do not be afraid to reiterate the standards expected of that employee and offer to assist them to achieve if they are struggling with something in particular;

- if the employee provides the manager with reasons as to why they may be struggling, then it is important for the manager to provide support and perhaps retraining where necessary (Also see **CAPABILITY CHAPTER 4.**)

- if the employee is unwilling to discuss any particular problems, the manager should explain that it may be necessary to meet again, particularly if one of the symptoms is failing to achieve work targets. However, an open door policy should be operated, so the employee can feel able to come back when they may feel more ready to talk, but perhaps before a formal review is due;

- if the employee mentions difficulties which are not work related, it is beneficial to be able to offer some form of guidance either in-house or external; and

- importantly, the manager should continue to monitor the situation and ensure that planned training or support sessions actually take place.

Example situation: employee suffering harassment

This example looks at a hypothetical example of an employee who makes a formal complaint to their line manager regarding the behaviour of one of their colleagues. The employee was a member of a religious grouping that was a minority within the workplace and required special provisions for prayer at certain times of the day. The particular colleague that was alleged to have harassed the employee was said to have made derogatory comments regarding the time taken to make these religious observances and how no work would ever be achieved if all employees had to take the time to do such things. Such comments had been addressed directly to the employee and they had also heard reports that the views had been expressed in to the workforce in general in the staff restroom. The employee expressed in their letter of complaint that they felt demeaned by the comments and that it was implied that they only made the religious observances to avoid working.

The line manager commenced the investigation immediately by interviewing the alleged harasser and explaining that a complaint had been made against them, asking for their version of events. It was likely that there would be one of three responses. Either:

(a)   the colleague could deny having made the comments, in which case further investigation involving witness statements may have been necessary;

(b)   the colleague may admit to making the comments, but be genuinely surprised that they were taken as offensive, as they had expressed them jokingly and not realised the seriousness of what had been said; or

(c)   the colleague may admit to making the comments and then go on to counter claim that due to time allowed for prayer the other employee was being treated more favourably and they were at detriment.

The investigating manager's next steps would obviously depend on which of the three scenarios occurred. With the first, (a), if reliable witnesses could be found, then it would likely be necessary to take disciplinary action against the colleague for the deliberate harassment of another employee and an apology made to that effect. If no witnesses were available then it would be necessary for some kind of mediation to be established between the complainant and their colleague to establish the chain of events and what was intended. It must not be forgotten, however, that the emphasis must be on how the complainant perceived the comments rather than on how they were intended and this must be made clear to the colleague with some form of reconciliation as the ideal outcome. There is also the possibility that the complaint had been a malicious invention on the part of the employee and should this be proven to be the case then it may be necessary to discipline the complainant for attempting to damage another's reputation. Many companies actually include this in their policy.

The second scenario, (b), is perhaps the most simple for the investigating manager to resolve. If the colleague was genuinely unaware of the effect their comments were having on the other employee, then it is most likely that they would wish to apologise and reconcile the situation with no encouragement, but some assistance from the manager.

The third scenario, (c), is again more difficult, as while the colleague has made the admission that they did indeed make the comments, they do not perceive why this should be viewed wrong. This is most likely to occur where a policy on bullying and harassment has not been made clear to all levels of an organisation and highlights the importance of why clear, comprehensively understood policies are key in avoiding such issues. In such a case, the investigating manager would have to spend some time going back over the policies of that company designed to promote equality and diversity and discourage conflict with the colleague, emphasising the reasons behind such policies and stating the company's refusal to tolerate such behaviour. Again, ideally, reconciliation would be the preferred outcome from the meeting.

The decision on whether to take disciplinary action against the individual is a difficult one, as no form of harassment should be tolerated. However, as stated in **CHAPTER 4** when covering disciplinaries, the penalty should be appropriate to the wrongdoing and consideration should be given to the intent to cause distress – if there genuinely was no intention of causing offence and the colleague is oblivious to the fact that their actions may be felt to be injurious to another, then counselling may be more appropriate, particularly where a lack of obvious training in the bullying and harassment policy is evident. In all cases, the ideal outcome is for the two parties to be reconciled and the unacceptable behaviour stopped.

Whatever decision is made by the investigating manager, they must be sure that it is fair and based only on the facts that can be ascertained and does not include any assumptions made or prejudices about one employee or another. As the complaint and subsequent investigation form is part of the formal grievance proceedings, it is vital that all points are documented accurately. Should the complaint be taken further and reach a tribunal, the recording of the chain of evidence upon which a decision was based is vital in providing a defence for the company that all procedures were followed correctly.

So, in summary:

- act immediately once a complaint has been received – delays may cause breach in grievance procedures;

- interview the person about whom the complaint has been made – it may be that they were unaware their behaviour constituted harassment and may wish to reconcile as soon as possible;

- obtain witness statements where possible and make as thorough an investigation as possible – this is the oragnisation's defence should a complaint reach the courts;

- document all evidence collated;

- make a decision based only on the evidence available, do not rely on assumptions – if the case cannot be proven, action cannot be taken;

- aim for reconciliation between the parties in order to promote workplace harmony; and

- finally, look at why the incident occurred – is it a failing on the communication of the company's policy? Is there a need for re-training on key points?

Example situation: bullying   7.17

The key difference with bullying is that it is not covered by legislation in its own right, but when perpetrated can be the cause of unfair constructive dismissal, as it leads to a breach in the implied duty of the employer to maintain trust and confidence.

The example used here involves an employee who has recently joined a company straight after taking their GCSEs. It is their first experience of working life and they find the role to their liking and initially achieve well. After some months, however, they begin to find some of the work more difficult and have occasionally got into trouble for not achieving a target or even for not completing a task they were unaware of. Some of their colleagues make over critical remarks about their performance and the only way to win approval is to participate in the practical jokes instigated by this group. After several informal warnings the employee approaches their line manager to discuss their concerns that they are being encouraged to participate in activities designed to get them into trouble and deliberately being misinformed of targets or tasks required of them.

The line manager initiates an investigation and after interviewing several of the employee's colleagues finds that the initial success of the young employee was found to be irritating to some of the longer serving members of the workforce who began a campaign to ensure that they would no longer be shown up as being less productive. They ensured that the employee received incorrect information about deadlines and tasks that were required – effectively setting them up to fall and then highlighted the underachievement. They also encouraged the employee to participate in inappropriate activities, knowing that they would comply due to their lack of experience as to what is acceptable workplace behaviour.

The manager had no choice but to take disciplinary action against the key workers responsible for the bullying and reiterated the company's policy regarding this. The action taken previously against the young worker was dropped due to the mitigating circumstances. The company policy on bullying and harassment was given greater focus and trained back out to ensure that all employees were aware of it and the consequences of breaching this.

- remember that bullying can take many forms – not all are obvious, so be aware;

- a colleague may not always be confident enough to make a complaint formally, it is important to be receptive to hints given, but not to over react;

- there may have been threats made as to the possible consequences of making a complaint – ensure the employee knows that they have the full protection of the company;

- when investigating, try to gain as much information as possible, not only does this provide a clearer picture, but again provides defence that the conclusions reached were the correct ones;

- again, should such incidents occur, review the effectiveness of the bullying and harassment policy – does retraining need to be carried out?

Example situation: violent incidents 7.18

Violence is difficult to catagorise. It can sometimes form part of a bullying campaign, it can sometimes be in the form of anticipated attacks from members of the public or customers that come in the line of duty for some professions, it can be one off incidents between employees, sparked by a single argument, but for whatever reason it may occur, it is still the employer's responsibility to ensure that the risks are minimised and action against perpetrators is swift and appropriate.

A very general example that can be used is where two employees are having an argument and rather than taking the matter to senior management for resolution, either or both of them initiate a violent act against the other. Not only will the aggressor be subject to disciplinary action from their employer, but also there is the likelihood that the victim may press criminal charges.

As with the examples in **7.15** to **7.17**, a timely response is essential and the most senior person in charge at the time of the incident must take immediate action. It may well be necessary to suspend either or both of the employees to secure the safety and well being of all colleagues, but both should be interviewed immediately after the incident to gain as much information before memories of what occurred begin to fade. Witness statements from those present should also be taken to try and gain an accurate picture of what occurred.

Action taken must be considered in light of all the evidence collected, again, the disciplining manager must be confident that it is the evidence for that particular set of circumstances which has led them to conclude on a particular course of action.

Violence perpetrated by a member of the public against an employee is in a sense much more clear-cut and criminal proceedings would be instigated. It is however important for a full investigation to take place into whether the risks of the violence occurring can be minimised and whether the employer was in any way responsible for not ensuring the safety of their employee.

Violence from an employee directed towards a member of the public is again quite clear-cut and usually criminal proceedings will follow. The exceptions are however when a certain amount of force may be necessary to fulfill a role, for example, bouncers or security staff, although if excessive force is used, prosecution may result.

So in summary, there are three main types of violent incident involving the workplace and different employer responsibilities for each:

- Firstly – employee to employee, the HR manager should:
  - ensure full, immediate investigation takes place;
  - suspend to ensure safety of other workers;
  - collate as much evidence as possible – witness statements, CCTV evidence etc;
  - ensure that action taken is appropriate to evidence and facts and that mitigating circumstances are taken into account; and
  - review workplace to ascertain whether isolated incident or an emerging pattern due to escalating problems.
- Secondly – public to employee, the HR manager should:
  - remove member of public to where no further harm can be caused;
  - ensure full immediate investigation takes place;
  - report to police where appropriate;
  - ensure the employee receives support and counselling as appropriate; and
  - review workplace to minimise risk of a repeat incident, if necessary, safety measures may need to be introduced, as long as the cost is reasonable to the benefits provided to the employees.
- Thirdly – employee to member of the public, the HR manager should:
  - ensure full, immediate investigation takes place;
  - report to police unless exceptional circumstances;
  - if physical contact is likely due to employee's job function, attempt to determine level of force used – was it excessive?
  - if physical contact is a requirement of the job function, complete retraining to ensure no repeat incident; and
  - if the employee suffered provocation, implement training in how to deal more effectively with potentially inflammatory situations.

Conclusion 7.19

So in conclusion, while conflict does occur generally in the workplace, the growing diversity encountered within industries, while beneficial in many aspects, can also serve to exacerbate potential problems which may occur. Stress, harassment, bullying and violence play an increasing part in the day to day management of workers and it is vital to ensure that these are handled effectively to avoid possible tribunal cases being brought against organisations.

The case studies and checklists above give clear guidelines on what action is essential to take and how best to minimise any further incidents. Underpinning all of this is the commitment to a clear policy on bullying and harassment, the use of which should be continuous. The policy should be updated to ensure all employees are protected from any kind of detriment.

8
The Future of Diverse Employees

Introduction

This Chapter is intended to highlight the impact on diversity in both society and the workplace, as well as show how the changes in diversity will affect HR. The likely changes in legislation will also be considered, together with the more immediate changes due in October 2004.

The influx of new legislation, to many employers and in particular small employers, will be seen as a further move to give employees more protection than the employer. Although on the surface this is certainly how it appears, particularly with the implementation of the *Employment Act 2002*, it is not, however, all one-way traffic.

Other Regulations allow for the employer to monitor their employees' activities particularly with the increased use of email and the Internet. Those employees who misuse company time and property can now be located quicker and dealt with properly and effectively. This in itself will save organisations both money and man hours. After all, it has been said that the most common and largest theft from employers is time. Therefore, although the issues that protect the employer do not necessarily get front-page coverage, they do enter the employment remit, even if only by the back door. They also provide effective ways of ensuring that a good working relationship can be maintained and those employees who wish to break the rules can be dealt with fairly, efficiently and, in many cases, to the employer's advantage.

The new regulations also provide the employer with additional protection through the use of procedures and creating paper trails. By following the grievance and disciplinary policies properly and ensuring that there are clear and concise notes an employer is protecting itself (provided the ultimate decision is fair and reasonable) from a claim being brought in the tribunal; or at the very least, ensuring that there is a clear and obvious defence to the employee's claim.

Impact of diversity

This section will look to the effect of the growing number of diverse employees and workers in the British workforce. Due to legislation defining more areas as diverse, the number of employees who fall into these categories can only increase.

But this change is reflected throughout society. With the increase of the number of people immigrating to the United Kingdom, together with the impact of asylum seekers, the section of the population looking for work will become more and more diverse. There will be no guarantee that an employee base will have English as its first language. Immediately, therefore, policies will need to be translated into other languages (or at least the main language of any non-English speaking employees).

As a country we are becoming more multi-cultural, from the small cities and towns in the fens and East Anglia, to the Midlands, the North, Scotland and Wales and, of course, the south of England. Therefore, as society increases its awareness of others, including different and 'new' religions, different value systems and work ethics; so must the general employer.

It is very likely that in the next five to ten years diverse employees will become the norm. Most employees will fall into one of the groups set out in **CHAPTER 1** at some time or other. These categories will also increase in number, in particular to include old workers in regard to age discrimination. As men's rights increase in relation to their roles as fathers, a new category will be introduced setting out the man's rights when on paternity leave and adoption leave. It is highly likely that their rights will become the same as the mother's. It has been suggested that paternity leave should be increased to mirror ordinary maternity leave. However, whether this will occur is yet undecided. It would certainly encourage employers not to employ married or cohabiting couples if both employees can take six months off when a child is born. Although should this situation occur, caution should be used as this could then give rise to claims for indirect and direct discrimination, much in the same way as not employing a woman of childbearing age and not employing people because they are married.

Hopefully with the changes that have taken place and with those being implemented in October 2004 there will be an increase in the number of people being employed with both physical and mental disabilities. With more awareness of these disabilities and the fact that the 'token' disabled employee is to be discouraged, the workforce should start to reflect what is happening in society.

With rose tinted glasses it could be suggested that the rise in diversity could stop prejudices. Unfortunately this is not likely to occur. However, by the use of careful organisational policies, discrimination (of whatever type) in the workforce should reduce.

Knowledge of others needs and beliefs can only help to ensure that a workforce is happy and fully integrated. The greatest impact, therefore, is one of vigilance in identifying and dealing with issues of diversity followed closely by the need to keep abreast of changes in legislation.

Impact of demographics – the changing face of HR 8.3

Human Resources has become the new name for Personnel in recent years. This will not be the only change that has occurred.

With the increase in legislation, HR managers and officers need to become conversant in all matters of employment and health and safety law. HR is the front line of the employer's protection machine. As mentioned in **CHAPTER 4**, the HR manager must act in the best interests of the company, while ensuring that the needs of the employee are also met. From a cynic's point of view, it could be suggested that the only role of HR is to protect the employer. By dealing carefully and properly with the needs of the employee the HR manager is protecting the employer against claims in the tribunal or, at the very least, from losing claims in the tribunal. The fact that this also involves an element of protection for the employee is an addition rather than the original purpose. The HR manager is, after all, an employee him or herself.

No longer is the role one where the officer shuffles paperwork and ensures that all appraisals are done on time and are placed in the right file, or that payroll is completed and changes to salary and personal details are noted and made. A good HR manager will ensure that they regularly review the employer's policies on equal opportunities and diversity, disability, race and sex discrimination, health and safety and risk assessments, and of course ensure that contracts are reviewed and kept up to date with changes in regulations including the minimum wage, maternity pay, etc. All this must be done together with dealing with recruitment, training, grievance and disciplinaries.

The role, therefore, has expanded and the HR manager has become the equivalent of a mini-lawyer. They will be the first port of call when other managers have problems with employees. They will be expected to know how to deal with these problems and provide the answers. The HR manager is by their very nature a man-manager.

Unfortunately many managers, whether they be company directors, partners in a partnership or shift managers, do not, on the whole, hold skills in man-management. Many do not know how to deal with an employee who is upset or on long term sick leave due to stress, or even how to deal with an employee who is merely under performing. However, the HR manager must know how to deal with them and do so properly.

It is for the HR manager to ensure that although they may be the first port of call for guidance (and not just for the employer), they must also be able to train and advise on how to deal with issues that may arise without making matters formal by invoking disciplinary or grievance procedures.

The HR manager must ensure that they have a full and careful training plan for their colleagues and general workforce. However, particular attention should be given to those colleagues who work in a supervisory capacity. This training must ensure that these managers have at least the basic knowledge of how to deal with problems with their workforce. This may merely involve in-house training in grievance and disciplinary procedures. However, where a manager has an employee with a disability in their supervisory group, it is important to ensure that at least one member of the group (be it the manager or otherwise) is aware of how to deal with any problems that the disabled employee may have. For example, if they are diabetic, how to assess the signs of a hypoglycaemic attack and what to do should it occur.

HR managers should also ensure that there are trained first aiders and fire wardens in enough numbers throughout the organisation. The first aiders should have basic knowledge of treatments and practices necessary for dealing with the specific health problems of the workforce, as well as the more general first aid skills. This should include how to deal with an epileptic fit, angina attack, falls from wheelchairs, etc. Where an employee uses a wheelchair or crutches due to their disability it is important to ensure that they should have at least one designated person trained in how to assist them should they fall. This person should be trained in how to lift and in basic first aid.

As can be seen from the basic roles and duties set out above, the face of HR is continually moving between social worker and employment lawyer. To enable existing HR departments to cope and to encourage the use of a designated HR manager in firms where they currently do not exist, the biggest change to HR will be the increase in numbers throughout the workplace. Every employer should have someone they can use for HR. Whatever the size of the organisation, it is important that there is one designated person who is responsible for keeping the organisation's policies up to date and in practice.

The larger the organisation the greater the number of HR officers. This may well mean that the hands-on approach lessens, but the managers are still responsible for ensuring that training is up to date, not only within the workforce for which they are responsible, but also within their team.

The HR manager will also be responsible for ensuring compliance with the *Data Protection Act 1998 (DPA 1998)*, ensuring that there is very little access to personnel records. There is no need for 'shop floor managers', whether they be directors or otherwise, to have access to personnel records. HR managers also need to ensure that the records are up to date and that where information has expired it is removed, for example spent disciplinary warnings.

The hardest thing for the new HR manager to deal with will be the increase in paperwork. The legislation which has come into force in recent years, together with that which is due in the future, will involve devising and using checklists to ensure compliance. This will involve ensuring that there are paper trails in respect of recruitment, as discussed in **CHAPTER 4**, together with clear notes and decisions relating to grievances and dismissals. There needs to be clear evidence of decisions relating to the reasons for promoting or not promoting an individual, together with justifiable evidence for why one person was allowed flexible working rights and another not.

If the processes required are dealt with properly, the fear that HR will disappear in a pile of paperwork should not occur. Once the correct procedures are in place to deal with issues arising within the organisation and training is undertaken to ensure that these policies and procedures are used and used properly, the amount of paperwork will reduce. It should only be possible at this stage to use managers outside of the HR unit to undertake disciplinary and grievance procedures and meetings. A workforce that is fully trained and has good policies to rely on is less likely to raise complaints or grievances.

Forthcoming legislation and regulations   8.4

There are a number of changes that have occurred in recent years and many are set out in **CHAPTERS 2** and **3**. However, there are further changes due over the next few years in respect of employment legislation.

Initial changes will occur in October 2004 with regard to disability discrimination and dispute resolution. There are also likely to be changes relating to case law in respect to post-termination discrimination. 2006 brings with it the long awaited *Age Discrimination Act*, the impact of which is not yet known, but which could have strong repercussions throughout the workplace. These issues are discussed below together with changes to grievance procedures, minimum wage and asylum seekers.

Minimum wage   8.5

After a number of years of the minimum wage being in place, 16 and 17 year olds will, from 1 October 2004, be afforded some protection against wage exploitation. An initial minimum wage has been set of £3.00 per hour. As with the main minimum wage, there are no justifiable reasons for paying a lower hourly rate. Where an employer is found to be paying their employees less than the minimum wage they will be investigated and in some cases penalised by the Minimum Wage Office. Should this occur, any wages, which have been paid at a rate lower than the minimum wage, will have to be uplifted and the accrued difference paid to the employee.

The minimum wage for 18 to 21 year olds also increases to £4.10 per hour, with over 22s increasing to £4.85 per hour.

The exemption in relation to apprentices under the age of 19 will remain in place. This is to encourage the provision of a high level of training. It is also thought that 16 and 17 year olds on pre-apprentice programmes will also be exempt.

Asylum seekers   8.6

From 1 May 2004 new Regulations will be in place in regard to asylum seekers and illegal immigrants generally. These Regulations, (the *Nationality, Immigration and Asylum Act 2002*) are likely to be tightened further in the future. The idea is to make companies and organisations easier to prosecute for employing illegal workers. On occasions it can be difficult to assess who has the right to work and who does not. Therefore, it is important to ensure that every applicant and existing employee provide a work permit to prove that they are entitled to be employed within the UK. Even if the documents are forged, there is a defence to show that everything possible was done to ensure the employee had the right to work. It is also important to ensure that a National Insurance Number is taken and checked, as this is another way of ensuring the right to work.

If every employee must provide a work permit or similar, there can be no risk of discrimination on the grounds of race.

Disability discrimination   8.7

From October 2004 the current exemption from prosecution of small employers (ie those with less than 15 employees) will be withdrawn. This follows the implementation of the *Disability Discrimination Act 1995 (Amendment) Regulations 2003 (SI 2003/1673)*. All employers must ensure that they are compliant with the Regulations. They must therefore address when considering a disabled applicant whether there are reasonable adjustments to be made and if there are, make them. However, so as not to penalise the small employer, who generally will have less resources, the size and resources of the employer will be taken into account when considering the reasonableness of adjustments.

In addition, a number of occupations that were previously excluded from the Regulations will no longer be afforded this protection. They include but are not limited to:

- the Police; Fire Brigade; Prison Officers; British Transport Police;
- those employed on ships, aircraft or hovercraft; and
- the Armed Forces.

An important issue in regard to the Police Force, is that the Chief Officer will be liable for acts of unlawful discrimination or harassments against police officers in regard to their employment. This is a very important development. Currently, unlike general employers, the Chief Officer cannot be sued by reason of vicarious liability. This is all about to change and could result in a marked decrease in discrimination of black, Asian and female officers within the force as the Chief Officer will be personally liable for the actions of the members of the force.

Issues of direct discrimination and justification have also been changed. There is a new *subsection 5* of the *Disability Discrimination Act 1995 (DDA 1995)*, which brings the Act in line with the European Directive. This states that:

'A person directly discriminates against a disabled person if, on the ground of the disabled person's disability, he treats the disabled person less favourably than he treats or would treat a person not having that particular disability whose relevant circumstances, including their abilities, are the same as, or not materially different from, those of the disabled person.'

Therefore a person can no longer be discriminated against merely because they are disabled. However, less favourable treatment will be justified where it is required by legislation, for example health and safety issues.

The amendments also now make provision for indirect discrimination, thereby bridging the differences between the other two main pieces of discrimination legislation. The old wording of the *DDA 1995* did not deal with issues of harassment, unlike the *Race Relations (Amendment) Act 2000 (RRA 2000)* and the *Sex Discrimination Act 1975 (SDA 1975)*. However, this has now changed. An employee will not need to show that they have suffered a detriment because of their disability, but will be able to show that they have suffered unwanted conduct which has violated their dignity or created an intimidating, hostile or humiliating environment for them to work in. As with the *RRA 2000* and the *SDA 1975* the employee must show that the words and treatment were based on their disability and were therefore discriminatory, rather than just taunts and comments which the employee found offensive.

Section 4(A) of the *Disability Discrimination Act 1995 (Amendment) Regulations 2003* now makes allowances for this. Therefore where a criterion is applied to the workforce as a whole, but disabled employees are less likely to be able to comply with it, the employee will have the right to claim indirect discrimination. Therefore the regulations relating to reasonable adjustments are being expanded. This will result in employers having to consider even the most basic clauses in their contracts or handbooks and ensure that they do not discriminate against any employees whatever their disability. For example, where breaks are set at particularly times of the day in factories, allowances will need to be made for an insulin diabetic who needs to eat and take their medication at regular intervals.

There are changes in relation to post-termination discrimination, but these are dealt with as a whole below.

As discussed in **CHAPTER 4** in regard to recruitment, advertisements must be carefully worded. The amended Act makes further provision in regard to this. This will then correspond with the provisions of the *SDA 1975* and *RRA 2000.* An advertisement must not make reference to the fact that a person is more likely to be employed if they do not have a disability. However, a criterion can be put in to the advertisement where it is a fundamental part of the role that a particular disability could not be accepted. For example, a specific level of eyesight and mobility for a lifeguard may be required.

There is likely to be a significant impact from these changes. Therefore HR managers will need to ensure that their policies are in compliance with the amendments before the changes are brought into effect on 1 October 2004. Where the organisation was previously excluded under the regulations a whole new system of monitoring will also need to be put in place together with a comprehensive policy and period of training.

Dress codes   8.8

Although there is no future legislation relating to this area, it is impacted on by the Regulations, which were a result of the *Employment Act 2002* and will have a continuing effect in regard to the changes to the *DDA 1995* as set out above and the proposed implementation of age discrimination.

Many organisations have a form of dress code already, be it merely 'professional', or an actual uniform which must be worn at all times. The idea is to promote professionalism and corporate identity. In some cases it may only be for reasons of health and safety or food hygiene. However the changing demographics of society must be reflected within the dress codes of a company.

Where a man has long hair for religious reasons (as discussed in **CHAPTER 2**) some consideration must be made for this. As previously mentioned, if this is a health and hygiene risk, then not amending the code would not be discriminatory.

Where a dress code is particularly strict, it is important that such a policy is justifiable on the part of the employer. Whether it relates to hair length, facial piercing and tattoos or merely the length of a woman's skirt, the issues must be justifiable in regard to the business of the corporation.

Justification does not amount to one person's tastes against another's. The reasoning must be objective at all times and must not be unnecessarily restrictive. Proportionality throughout all of the organisation's policies is important.

Following the changes brought about by the Equality Regulations relating to sexual orientation and religion, employers must bear in mind these considerations when implementing or enforcing a particular dress code. Where as previously, religious groups did not have protection against discrimination, as they were not deemed to be a designated racial group, they will now be afforded protection in this area. However, dress codes for disabled employees within a small organisation should also be considered.

Dispute resolution   8.9

As discussed in **CHAPTER 4**, from October 2004 all employers must have a full and proper disciplinary and grievance procedure. They must also ensure that this is used properly.

ACAS have published a revised Code of Practice in relation to these changes. Any procedure should use the Code as a minimum procedure. The tribunal, should a claim be issued, will decide whether the employer's procedure was reasonable, based on the processes set out in the Code.

An employer's procedure can expand on the Code and be fuller or stricter, but this must be the minimum process that an employer follows when dealing with disciplinaries, dismissals and grievances.

The intention is that the employer and employee attempt as best they can to resolve the position in-house. If either fails to follow the procedure and the matter leads to litigation, conciliation will then take place. ACAS are to have a more hands on approach to conciliation and trying to ensure that employee and employer discuss the situation without the need to end in a tribunal hearing.

Should the matter not settle by mutual agreement and the tribunal decides that procedures were not correctly followed by one of the parties, or indeed, no policy existed, then the amount of damages awarded will be affected. There could be an increase or reduction in damages of up to 50 per cent depending on which party is at fault.

This in itself is a motivation for employers to ensure that they comply with their own policies and, where they currently do not have any in place, obtain them.

Post termination discrimination 8.10

Currently only discrimination under the *SDA 1975* and the *RRA 1976* can lead to claims for post-termination discrimination.

This occurs where an employee is treated less favourably after their employment has ended, due to their sex or race, and the discrimination or harassment they are suffering arises out of or is closely related to the previous employment relationship. Often the discrimination will be due to the employee having taken discrimination action against the employer in the past.

The most obvious act of discrimination would be the provision of a false reference. As mentioned in **CHAPTER 4**, it is unlawful for an employer to provide a false reference. This would include mentioning disciplinary action, where there was an investigation but no evidence found and defaming the character of the employee.

The amendments to the *DDA 1995* under *section 16(A)*, now allow for post termination discrimination in relation to disability.

Post-termination discrimination is not limited to references. It also applies to the appeal procedure. At all times the employer must act and be able to prove that they have acted reasonably.

In particular, consideration should be given to the joint decision in *Relaxation Group Plc v Rhys-Harper; D'Souza v Lambeth London Borough; Jones v 3M Healthcare Ltd [2003] IRLR 484* which confirmed that the conduct of an ex-employer following the termination of the employment contract, can amount to a detriment under the anti discrimination regulations.

Therefore when dealing with appeals and references, which are normally dealt with post termination, it is important to ensure impartiality and reasonableness at all times.

Many employers now revert to the basic reference, whereby only the reason for leaving (ie resigned or dismissed) is mentioned, together with the dates of employment and salary. Although in some industries it is important to be aware of issues of reliability and trust, these types of reference do tend to prevent claims, provided they are used as a standard and not as a way of further penalising an employee who has brought legal action against the company.

Where an employee does not have a discrimination element to their claim, they can still pursue an employer for a false reference in the County Court. The claim would be based on the losses suffered by the employee due to the poor reference. This would generally be the difference between the salary of the new position and their earnings (if any) following the reference.

Maternity and paternity   8.11

Although it is unlikely that the maternity leave periods will be extended further, there is a possibility that the additional period may involve some form of payment in the future. The main idea of the new regulations was to encourage women back to work once they have had children. It may therefore be a suitable suggestion for employers to offer their employees an enhanced rate of maternity pay to encourage them back to work. This would need to include a clause (much as in the way of training costs) that should an employee not return or leave within six months to a year of returning, the uplift or a proportion thereof, is to be repaid to the employer.

There is a possibility of paternity leave being extended to six months and the period being subject to a similar pay structure as maternity leave. Although, nothing further appears to be happening, it is an issue which employers need to address within their organisation's policies.

It is important to ensure that HR managers keep up to date on the change of benefits. As at 6 April 2004 the standard rate increased to £102.80 per week for maternity, paternity and adoption pay. For lower earners, the rate increased to £79 per week. These rates will be reviewed annually and will generally increase with inflation.

Age discrimination   8.12

Age discrimination is the biggest of all the likely changes to employment legislation. Currently once an employee reaches the age of 65 they no longer have any particular employment rights in relation to unfair dismissal. They are prohibited from bringing a claim in the employment tribunal under the *ERA 1996* in regard to anything other than breach of contract. As they are due to retire at the age of 65 they cannot claim loss of earnings or redundancy pay.

This was recently confirmed in the case of *Secretary of State for Trade and Industry v Rutherford & Others (EAT/1029/02)*. The claim related to the fact that current regulations discriminated against men who generally wish to work longer and later in life than women. However the Employment Appeal Tribunal (EAT) confirmed that on the whole few people work after the age of 65 and therefore the current regulations are not discriminatory.

However, the *Age Discrimination Act* is currently due to come into effect from October 2006, although implementation must take place by the end of December 2006 at the latest. This will then result in claims by employees aged over 65 for relief in relation to unfair dismissal and redundancy.

On the whole the Act is likely to be similar in scope to current anti-discrimination legislation. There will be issues of direct and indirect discrimination. However, an important issue will be that of justification. Where the amendments to the *DDA 1995* now prevent the fire brigade being exempt, it is likely that services such as these will amount to reasonable justification for dismissing or not employing members of staff over a particular age. Issues of health and safety will have to prevail.

The idea is not that every employer must have a token employee over the age of 65, neither will it be expected that an employer should employ someone over that age who is not competent or trained in the relevant role.

The high costs of training could also amount to a justifiable defence to age discrimination. There is after all no financial benefit to employ anyone, whatever their age, who is untrained over someone who can immediately undertake the role advertised. That is not to say, that in relation to redundancy, employees over 65 should not be offered alternative employment if it means that they must receive training. The current regulations on reasonable alternatives would still apply.

The Act is due to affect all workers and not the more restrictive group entitled 'employees'. As with other discrimination regulations, the Act will come into effect at the advertisement and recruitment stage, not just during employment.

The Act will have a large impact on employers throughout the whole workforce. It is important to try to ensure that internal policies are in force now, in relation to age discrimination. Many employers, for example supermarkets, do employ those members of the workforce who are over current retirement age however; others need to have clear business reasons in place as to why they should continue not to.

There are a number of issues which the government needs to address before implementation can be finalised, for example the effect on retirement ages. The regulations prevent a mandatory retirement age being enforced. However, this is often used by employers to regulate their work force and prevent unnecessary action being taken due to incompetence, which could be humiliating for older staff.

It is possible that the changes could affect the way redundancy is calculated. Currently the award is tapered depending on the employee's age. Starting at one half week's pay where the employee is under 22; increasing to one week until age 41; and finally one and one half weeks to age 64. It is possible that every employee will receive the same sum for each week of service, irrespective of their age, but subject of course to the amount of their weekly earnings. It is also possible that the criteria for selecting employees for redundancy may have to be changed. Currently one of the most common criteria is length of service. This could imply that older employees are more likely to have a greater length of service than the younger employees and could therefore be age bias. It is possible that this may have to be weighted differently, to show it is of less importance, or removed entirely. However, employers may feel that this is not in the best interests of the company as loyalty is an important issue, as is experience. If this is the concern, the criteria can be weighted in favour of skills. This should give the same result. The longer an employee has remained in an organisation, provided there is a proper training programme in place, the more likely they are to have the better skills to remain following a redundancy selection procedure.

As with all discrimination regulations, harassment and victimisation by reason of the employee's age will not be accepted. For an employee to prove harassment due to their age, they must follow the same procedures as set out above in regard to the *DDA 1995*.

So far we have only considered the issues relating to age discrimination for the over 65s. However, it is not just about retirement age. Age discrimination can occur at any age. Although *Perera v Civil Service Commission & another No. 2) (1982) ICR350* resulted in a claim for race discrimination the principle is the same. In *Perera v Civil Service Commission & another No. 2) (1982) ICR350* a 39-year-old Sri Lankan VAT officer wanted to apply to be an administrative trainee. The age limit was 32 for all applicants. It was found that the employee had been indirectly discriminated against as 22 of the 34 white officers were under 32, but none of the 13 ethnic officers were under 32.

Therefore it is important to consider whether any internal age limits are set reasonably and justifiably. If it is merely to prevent older people applying as once trained they will not have as many years left to work, this is not a fair reason.

Age discrimination can, like the other issues of discrimination, arise at any time, be it recruitment, retirement, promotion or even selection for training and redundancy. Therefore employers must ensure that none of their selection policies for any of the above (even retirement to an extent) is based on age. That is not just old age, but the young too. Advertising using wording such as 'lively and energetic' could discriminate against the older applicant; but so could 'experienced' discriminate against younger employees, as mentioned above regarding redundancy. It is fair to assume a young applicant will not have the experience of someone who is older.

As with the other regulations, age discrimination will affect all employers irrespective of size and access to resources. This Act will also apply to vocational training, thereby ensuring that 'workers' are included within the scope of the Act. However, unpaid voluntary workers are still not protected.

Direct discrimination 8.13

An employee cannot be discriminated against on the grounds of their actual or perceived age. The government is currently proposing a limited defence to direct discrimination, however this will only be in limited and exceptions circumstances. These include:

- health, welfare and safety;

- succession planning – for example, ensuring that there is someone available to take over a role when the senior employee in that area retires (especially due to early retirement wishes);

- specific training requirements for the role; and

- the need for a reasonable period between starting the employment and retiring, (this would only occur where the employer has justified a mandatory retirement age).

Indirect discrimination 8.14

This is one area where the proposed regulations do not conform with current practice for other areas of discrimination. Although an employee who is particularly at a detriment due to the fact it is difficult for them to comply with a particular criteria applied by their employer due to their age is indirectly discriminated against, there are more justifiable reasons in relation to age than any other area. The reasons must be objective and normally be for the reasons set out in direct discrimination above. There will need to be strong evidence on the part of the employer to prove that their argument is justifiable to a tribunal.

Therefore unless there are real reasons for the criteria, then it will not be justified. For example, insisting that all employees should have 20/20 vision could not be justified if there is no health and safety reason behind it. In these circumstances the older employee is more likely to be unable to comply with this criteria.

Mandatory retirement ages 8.15

Although in the first instance, mandatory retirement ages will be discriminatory, the Government is proposing that there can be a defence to this, although limited.

Again, those areas set out in direct discrimination will be the main focus of the defence. However, if should also be appropriate and necessary in regard to the employer's business.

It should be noted that the European Directive does allow employers to set age requirements in relation to access to pension schemes. However, caution should be taken to ensure that there is no prospect of sex discrimination. There is a possibility that employees will be able to draw their occupation pension whilst still remaining in employment with the employer who arranged the policy.

There is discussion of the possibility of a default statutory retirement age. Although nothing is yet certain, it has been suggested that this may be increased to 70. This will not prevent employers still employing employees over that age should they wish to do so.

Unfair dismissal   8.16

This issue will be greatly affected. Employers will be entitled to dismiss employees as of right should they reach the mandatory or the default statutory retirement age.

Normal procedures in regard to conduct and capability will still apply. Therefore the mere fact that an employee is older will not effect whether or not they can be dismissed, provided the process and final decision are fair.

Benefits   8.17

It is important to ensure that there can be no age limitation on the right to benefits, unless they are proposed by statute. For example, employees under the age of 18 may not be eligible for some benefits.

This does not affect the right to pay benefits or bonuses based on length of service. This is still encouraged as it promotes loyalty. Again there is an issue of justification, which the employer must establish in relation to the payment of benefits based on length of service or seniority.

Implementation   8.18

There are obviously practical implications with regard to these regulations. Not least ensuring that the company's policies comply with the change in regulations. However, the new regulations should not affect the choice of an employer to employ the candidate best suited for the role. As yet it is not fully clear exactly how the regulations will be implemented, therefore the following is merely a guide to ensuring the policies and procedures are in place so that the full framework can be put in place once the regulations are finalised.

Recruitment process   8.19

Implementation of course starts at the recruitment stage. The issue is not whether or not there is an obvious age specification within the recruitment process, which could cause an age bias. The issue of language as mentioned above and in **CHAPTER 4** is very important.

Although some matters can be justified, preference is not an issue. That would include wanting an older person to visit and care for the elderly, as the elderly would respond better to them.

Therefore it is important to ensure that there are no age limits on recruitment, whether upper or lower, unless they can be objectively and reasonably justified. There should not be any limitation on how an application can be made. For example applications, which can only be made by email, could be deemed to indirectly discriminate against the older applicant who is less likely to be computer literate. In the same vein, it is important to ensure that a variety of mediums are used for advertising to ensure that a wider spectrum of prospective applicants are reached.

Where age has been a deciding factor in recruitment in the past the whole recruitment process will need to be overhauled. The process will need to be based on ability, skill and competence. However a strict criteria in regard to qualifications could also discriminate on the grounds of age, for example insisting on a degree or A Levels, as many older applicants may not have had the opportunity to attend sixth form or university, whereas younger applicants may well have done. However, there is no reason not to specify basic skills such as numeracy and literacy, provided of course this does not discriminate against people with learning disabilities such as dyslexia.

Recruitment checklists must have each element within them considered and justified. Can the requirement for a specific level or amount of experienced be justified for the job in question? Full consideration needs to be given to the role being advertised. If necessary and justified, strict guidelines can be set for recruitment. However, such restrictions must be proportionate as those that might apply to the post of area manager would not apply to shop assistant.

Again, it is important to ensure that full and detailed records are kept of all decisions within the recruitment and selection process, including the reasoning behind the wording in the advertisement if it is thought that this could give rise to a possible claim. Again it is important to ensure that those people undertaking the selection and interview process do so with an open mind and in accordance with regulations as well as company policy.

In summary ensure:

- reference to age limits or restrictions are avoided;

- age or age related language is avoided;

- the selection criteria is clear and justified;

- the selection guidelines are strictly and consistently applied; and

- the recruiters are trained and fully aware of issues relating to equal opportunities.

Selection for training

Employers can be averse to agreeing to train older employees, unless the training is to be global throughout the organisation. Generally this is because it is felt it is not the best use of resources as the new skills are not put in to practice for as long as for younger members of staff.

It has been suggested that in recognition of this point, there may be a limited right to justify such behaviour in specific circumstances. These are likely to be exceptional and therefore should not be relied upon.

Selection procedures for training therefore may need to be overhauled. It is important to ensure that training possibilities are open to all employees and that they are encouraged to take them. Even if it is only to train to be a first aider, such opportunities should be encouraged.

Some organisations may assess training needs based on expenditure against the length of time the member of staff is likely to spend with them. In a firm, which has a high turn over of staff, it would not be justifiable to say an older employee could not give a very good return on the training investment as no members of staff stay with the organisation long term.

Where there is a large spectrum of ages within an organisation, it is important to also ensure that the style of training is suitable for everyone. This is not just in relation to age, but also learning abilities.

An issue, which will effect a number of large organisations, is the graduate training scheme. This is currently run in all the large Plc's. However, can it actually be justified? Does the graduate make a career with the company and stay long term or move on quickly once the training is complete? If the latter, it is unlikely that the scheme could be justified as the title implies young or relatively recent graduates. However, with the number of mature students increasing, such schemes may not be a problem in the future.

In summary:

- ensure that training is offered to all employees who could benefit from it;
- ensure that employees are encouraged to take up the training offered to them;
- ensure that the type of training is appropriate to those attending; and
- ensure that specialist training is offered on merit.

Promotion

Again it is important to consider whether the criteria used for selecting people for promotion has age as one of its factors. It could be suggested that the ethos behind the proposed regulations is to encourage people based solely on their ability and merit, therefore any movements in the workforce should not have age as a consideration.

Often this can be combated by the use of a regular feedback and review system. Thereby making it obvious whether an employee has sufficient skills and ability to be able to succeed if promoted. Therefore the decision can be seen to be based solely on merit and no other hidden agenda.

As promotions are normally based on the opinion of a supervisor, which is of course subjective, it is important then to ensure that there is a specific criterion for each role within the organisation, so that the procedure can be applied fairly across the board.

When assessing employees from this point of view, it is important to know that the assessors are working from the same criteria with the same way of 'scoring' an employee. This may involve training for both managers and general employees. The criteria for promotion should also be made available to employees so that they are aware of the way they are assessed.

When a vacancy occurs, it is important to ensure that all employees are made aware of it and how to apply for it. The internal selection procedure should also mirror the selection procedure used when dealing with recruitment.

In summary:

- ensure that all promotion possibilities are made available to all employees;
- ensure that the selection criteria is based on merit and ability;
- ensure that the selection panel are trained and are able to make objective choices; and
- ensure that the selection criteria mirrors the recruitment criteria.

Benefits 8.22

It is important to ensure that benefits are given fairly and that there is no age bias. Unless of course they can be justified on grounds of loyalty.

If an organisation does reward its employees in this way, ie long service awards etc, then the employer must be able to demonstrate that there is a good business reason for it. For example, it helps to ensure that the company does not have a high turn over of staff.

An employer will need to be able to show evidence that performance and service related pay and benefits are an asset to the company and work. Obviously performance related pay has been an incentive for many years. There is no reason why this should change, unless it is coupled with service.

Where employers provide non-monetary benefits such as health care and life assurance, failure to provide this to older employees will immediately be discriminatory. The fact that it will increase costs and affect profitability is not a good enough reason not to provide such benefits to older employees rather than younger members of staff. Policies need to be checked to ensure that such benefits are available throughout the term of employment and do not stop once a set age has been attained, particularly where a death in service benefit is provided.

Currently the national minimum wage is tiered on an age scale. It has not been confirmed whether this will continue once the regulations come into effect, although it is likely that it will. However, that will not necessarily justify other differences in wages within a company. Unless the difference is based on seniority, there should not be any inequality within an organisation.

In summary:

- check and review all benefits policies to ensure that they are age friendly;
- ensure that where long service is rewarded there is a sound reason for it; and
- ensure that there are no age restrictions which could result in a benefit being withdrawn from an employee.

Retirement arrangements   8.23

Bearing in mind that we live in an aging society, the changes to the retirement age may well result in a much older workforce, as employees are able to remain in their employment far longer should they wish to do so. This coupled with the fact that any employee currently 45 or under, is unlikely to receive a state pension on 'retirement', options need to be put in place for dealing with employees who, on the whole, are getting older.

There are currently no suggestions that encouraging early retirement through a good payment structure will be discriminatory. If this is dealt with by a carefully worded policy, ensuring that it is entirely the employee's choice as to whether or not to take the package, there can be some protection against claims for discrimination, whilst assisting organisations with succession planning. Obviously, the flaw here is that there is no guarantee that employees will take the option.

Where an employer has a comprehensive capability procedure, it is possible that retirement could be deemed to be one of the options. The choice would of course be voluntary, but does prevent the humiliation of dismissing an employee due to capability and performance issues when they have worked for the company for a long time, or are just merely senior in years.

Other options may be the opportunity to ask for flexible working hours, irrespective of whether the employee is responsible for the care of a child. This could involve a reduction in hours to assist the aging employee who is finding a 40 hour week taxing as they get older.

All in all, the issue is to ensure that those employees who wish to continue to work are able to do so. It is important to ensure that all employees are aware of any performance criteria and apply them consistently through the company. That way ensuring that both the young and new employees are treated in the same way as the older, long established employee.

It may be possible to arrange for pensions to be paid once the employee reaches a certain age irrespective of whether they continue to work. In this way no employees are prejudiced by wanting to retire or not.

It is of course important to remember, that whether or not an employee wishes to continue to work as they get older, they must comply with health and safety regulations. It would of course not be sensible to have a 70 year old fireman climbing ladders to rescue people.

In summary:

- offer alternative retirement packages which are flexible;

- review when pensions are paid out and who pays into them;

- ensure that whether or not an employee wishes to retire they suffer no detriment;

- ensure that performance criterias are in place and applied consistently; and

- ensure that health and safety risk assessments are undertaken regularly on all staff, thereby ensuring that older members of staff do not feel victimised by over attentive assessments.

All in all, the up coming changes can be dealt with now, by following the guidance in this book and making sure that policies already in existence are viewed and comply not only with the existing regulations but also with those that are proposed. Managers must be fully trained and policies applied consistently throughout the organisation. Ensure, as an HR manager, that you are up to date on the changes and you receive training regularly. As an organisation be proactive, not reactive. Ensure that the care of your employees is uppermost so that when problems arise they are dealt with promptly and properly with an effective documented paper trail.

Diversity is the future of the British workforce, soon it will also be the norm. Ensuring that the policies are up to date and correctly managed is ensuring that the time of the HR manager can be used productively rather than as a way to fight fires.

Index

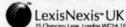

For Product Safety Concerns and Information please contact our EU
representative GPSR@taylorandfrancis.com
Taylor & Francis Verlag GmbH, Kaufingerstraße 24, 80331 München, Germany